TELEVISION
AND THE REMOTE CONTROL

THE GUILFORD COMMUNICATION SERIES

Editors
Theodore L. Glasser, *Stanford University*
Howard E. Sypher, *University of Kansas*

Advisory Board

Charles Berger   Peter Monge   Michael Schudson
James W. Carey   Barbara O'Keefe   Linda Steiner

Recent Volumes

TELEVISION AND THE REMOTE CONTROL:
GRAZING ON A VAST WASTELAND
Robert V. Bellamy, Jr., and James R. Walker

COMMUNICATION THEORY: EPISTEMOLOGICAL FOUNDATIONS
James A. Anderson

RELATING: DIALOGUES AND DIALECTICS
Leslie A. Baxter and Barbara M. Montgomery

DOING PUBLIC JOURNALISM
Arthur Charity

SOCIAL APPROACHES TO COMMUNICATION
Wendy Leeds-Hurwitz, *Editor*

PUBLIC OPINION AND THE COMMUNICATION OF CONSENT
Theodore L. Glasser and Charles T. Salmon, *Editors*

COMMUNICATION RESEARCH MEASURES: A SOURCEBOOK
Rebecca B. Rubin, Philip Palmgreen, and Howard E. Sypher, *Editors*

PERSUASIVE COMMUNICATION
James B. Stiff

REFORMING LIBEL LAW
John Soloski and Randall P. Bezanson, *Editors*

MESSAGE EFFECTS RESEARCH: PRINCIPLES OF DESIGN AND ANALYSIS
Sally Jackson

CRITICAL PERSPECTIVES ON MEDIA AND SOCIETY
Robert K. Avery and David Eason, *Editors*

MASS MEDIA AND POLITICAL TRANSITION:
THE HONG KONG PRESS IN CHINA'S ORBIT
Joseph Man Chan and Chin-Chuan Lee

THE JOURNALISM OF OUTRAGE: INVESTIGATIVE
REPORTING AND AGENDA BUILDING IN AMERICA
David L. Protess, Fay Lomax Cook, Jack C. Doppelt, James S. Ettema,
Margaret T. Gordon, Donna R. Leff, and Peter Miller

Television and the Remote Control

GRAZING ON A VAST WASTELAND

ROBERT V. BELLAMY, JR.
JAMES R. WALKER

THE GUILFORD PRESS
New York London

© 1996 The Guilford Press
A Division of Guilford Publications, Inc.
72 Spring Street, New York, NY 10012

Printed in the United States of America

This book is printed on acid-free paper.

Last digit is print number: 9 8 7 6 5 4 3 2 1

Library of Congress Cataloging-in-Publication Data

Bellamy, Robert V.
    Television and the remote control : grazing on a vast wasteland /
Robert V. Bellamy, Jr., James R. Walker.
      p. cm.
    Includes bibliographical references and index.
    ISBN 1-57230-085-X
    1. Grazing (Television) 2. Zapping (Television) 3. Zipping
(Video recordings) 4. Television—Channel selectors—Social
aspects.   I. Walker, James Robert. II. Title.
PN1992.55.B38 1996
302.23'45—dc20   96-14086
                                     CIP

Preface

When FCC Chairman Newton Minow delivered his "vast wasteland" speech to the National Association of Broadcasters in 1961, it was either one of the worst cases of audience analysis in the history of public speaking, or one of the boldest statements ever directed to a regulated industry. What is clear is that the phrase has been a rallying point ever since for critics of the television industry and its programming. Of course, Minow was speaking to a powerful industry whose basic technology had been through a period of unprecedented diffusion into U.S. homes, and had recently fended off calls for stronger government oversight in the wake of the quiz show scandals.

Minow's criticism came only after the economic structure of the television industry was solidified. Indeed, his statements were provoked by the rigidity and lack of diversity inherent in oligopolistic market structures. However, the operational assumptions of the broadcast system were well established and widely accepted by this time: broadcasting would be predominantly supported by advertising subsidy; the government's role included the protection of "free" radio and television; complex and expensive networking systems, combined with spectrum limitations, would limit distribution and access; and the production process would be based on the Hollywood system developed for the motion picture industry in the early 20th century. Despite Minow's memorable use of the wasteland metaphor, and his call for qualitative change in television programming, revision of the "comfortable" system would be limited to development of a single-channel public broadcast system. Public broadcasting would not only reduce the pressure on commercial broadcasters to meet the public interest "standard," but would itself, in reaction to the lack of consistent funding, increasingly become subject to political and corporate influence. With the addition of the public system, the players and their roles in the *first generation* of television were complete: studios produced, networks distributed, advertisers sponsored, and corporations bought access to an audience that chose from a limited number of "least objectionable programs."

Although still viewed as a wasteland by many, the topography of the television industry has changed. A combination of technological development and diffusion, and a decided shift to market-driven regulatory policy is the impetus for vast and continuing change in the industry. A major manifestation of the change is the increased level of control that individuals can exert over the output of television—a control that has called into question long-held assumptions about the structure of the industry, the nature of the audience, and relationship between the two.

The most commonly mentioned instruments of the change are cable television and the videocassette recorder. Both of these technologies have given viewers many more viewing options than were available when the commercial television industry consisted of network affiliates and a limited number of independent stations. However, the change is not just an increase in program availability; it is also about the use of television. The increase in channels available via cable strongly increases the likelihood that the viewer will switch channels. The VCR is both programming conduit and tool for the manipulation of time and viewing behavior. The time-shifting function allows for the development of personal television schedules. When watching a tape, the viewer often chooses to "zip" past objectionable content. In short, audience avoidance strategies are now easier to implement.

Often overlooked in discussions of the influence of cable and the VCR, however, are basic questions of how frequently audiences use such technologies. Clearly, mass diffusion of a technology is not equivalent to mass use. Each holiday shopping season gives birth to an new array of gadgets that will make the perfect gift for that hard-to-buy-for relative or friend. A year or so later, spring and summer garage sales are full of barely used hot-lather dispensers, individual hamburger makers, exercising gizmos, cordless power ratchets, and salad shooters. Examples in media include the failure of facsimile distribution in the 1930s and, more recently, the failure of videodiscs and teletext in the late 1970s and early 1980s.

The remote control device (RCD) is a significant media technology because its symbiotic relationship with both cable and VCRs makes these technologies more usable. RCDs give convenient and, in the hands of a skilled grazer, virtually instantaneous access to the myriad offerings of cable television and the VCR. For the more proficient users, RCD-controlled viewing sessions can average over a hundred channel changes per hour. The RCD makes VCR commercial avoidance on recorded tapes a reality by allowing viewers to zip by advertising spots at 10 times the normal speed (with no sound) from across the room. Television may still be a wasteland, but now it is even more vast. We can graze on it with far greater ease, and it offers a much wider variety of vegetation, if not necessarily improved nutrition.

Metaphors aside, there has been a qualitative change in the television industry and the way in which the audience uses the medium. We characterize this change as the *second generation* of television. None of the first generation of industry players have disappeared, but all have had to adjust to a new relationship of audience and medium. That relationship is a shift from the audience as predominantly passive *viewers* of content to active *users* of the television medium. Second generation viewers have redefined their relationship to television in a number of ways. They pay directly for both additional channels and specific programming through cable television subscriptions, videotape rentals, and pay-per-view. They sample a wider variety of program sources. They explicitly avoid certain content by zipping and zapping television commercials and other unpleasant stimuli (e.g., politicians, personalities, newscasters). They are more likely to select programs by first sampling many of the available options rather than reading a program guide. Once viewing begins, they are more likely to reevaluate the options at program breaks. Indeed, a substantial percentage of individuals do not watch a particular program; instead, they watch the medium, creating their own personalized programming mix. One of the two primary purposes of this book is to present a thorough and analytical review of these new usage patterns (see Chapters 2, 5, 6).

Clearly, the television industry is aware of these changes and, indeed, is adopting strategies to deal with the increased level of autonomy of the second generation viewer/user. Accordingly, this book (see Chapters 1, 3, 4) also provides an analysis of the tension between audience empowerment and industry desire to maintain and strengthen its control over its most precious commodity: the audience. By examining the ramifications of RCD diffusion for users and industry, we hope to provide insight into both the evolution of the television industry–audience relationship and its ongoing negotiation.

As a nonprogramming conduit, the RCD is not subject to the overt content manipulations of the television industry. Instead, it must be seen by the industry as a nearly universal technology of viewer control that must be factored into almost all conceptions of the audience. The industry's attempts to maintain (or reassert) control must then be accomplished indirectly through changes in industry structure and content. Our institutional analysis, therefore, devotes considerable attention to the ways that the advertising and television industries are countering the RCD-wielding viewer.

The historical patterns and the ongoing practices we discuss are highly relevant to the developing *third generation* of television use, in which interactivity and the "information superhighway" will likely be emphasized. We conclude (Chapter 7), then, by relating these patterns and practices to some speculation about the future of television's relationship with its audience.

Acknowledgments

───────────

I am indebted to John McDonald, the former Dean of the College and Graduate School of Arts and Sciences at Duquesne University, for approving a "nonteaching" semester that allowed me time to work on this project; Judith Hiltner for her deft copy editing; Charla Rylands Huber and Tom Perry for their general assistance; and, especially, my coauthor Jim Walker, who got me involved with RCD research several years ago and is the finest collaborator anyone could hope to have. As always, I thank my wife Cathy for her unwavering patience, understanding, and support for all my efforts. Finally, special thanks to Bob and Freda Bellamy. I wish everyone had such wonderful parents. My share of the book is dedicated to them with gratitude and love.

—RVB

I would like to thank Rob Bellamy for supplying the steady push that I needed to complete this project during a busy transitional year in my academic career. His insistence that we not co-manage a "fantasy" baseball team made this project happen. I also want to thank the many colleagues who have labored on the careful RCD research that formed the basis for much of what we are able to offer in this volume. I would like to recognize the library staff at Saint Xavier University, Chicago, for their efficient handling of my persistent interlibrary loan and copying requests. I want to acknowledge the unwavering support of Peter Wissoker, Editor at The Guilford Press, for this project. My thanks and love go to my wife Judith Hiltner, whose energy, intelligence, patience, and wit are my sustenance. Finally, I would like to dedicate my contributions to this book to my loving, wise, and supportive parents, Wynn C. Walker and the late Marie R. Walker.

—JRW

Contents

TELEVISION
AND THE REMOTE CONTROL

CHAPTER I

The Coming of a Second Generation
TELEVISION AND THE REMOTE
CONTROL DEVICE

The remote control device (RCD) is a subversive technology. By allowing the user to move rapidly between program offerings and avoid unpleasant or uninteresting material, the RCD works in opposition to the historic structure and operational parameters of the U.S. television industry. No longer can the viewer be conceptualized solely as a passive recipient of the messages of advertisers. Rather, she or he now has the means to construct an individualized media mix that may, or increasingly may not, contain advertising. In essence, the RCD allows the viewer to control some of the programming functions previously reserved for television and advertising executives.

The RCD user exerts this newfound control in a television landscape vastly different from that of 30, 20, or even 10 years ago. The diffusion of videocassette recorders (VCRs) to nearly four in five U.S. households and cable television to more than three in five, combined with the fact that substantially more than three in five households have more than one television set, has created a new television environment ("Buyer's Guide," 1993, p. 6).

Observers of the rapidly changing television environment have long been aware of the escalating acquisition of VCRs, cable, and multiple sets. However, only recently has the attention of the television industry and media scholars been directed toward the RCD, a device that is now in over

90% of U.S. households—a large increase from 29% in 1985 (Klopfenstein, 1993). Nearly 300 million RCDs were estimated to be in use with either broadcast television, VCRs, cable services, or audio CD players in 1995. This figure is expected to grow to nearly 400 million by 1997, as more consumer electronic devices are sold that have RCDs as standard equipment, and as more consumers purchase universal RCDs ("Buyer's Guide," 1993, p. 8). The RCD is so ubiquitous that we no longer need to compare RCD users to non-RCD users. The RCD has diffused even more rapidly and widely than VCRs or cable. The closest parallel is the diffusion of television in the 1950s, although the RCD entered U.S. households more rapidly than television itself. A media technology that has become close to universal in U.S. homes in such a short period of time demands serious critical attention.

An important aspect of the RCD's diffusion—and the primary reason the RCD has, until recently, received minimal attention—is its "invisibility." Because it is a tool used with other technological innovations (cable television, VCRs), the RCD is generally regarded as an extension of other technologies rather than as an independent innovation. The RCD's diffusion has made the ever more complex offerings of television easier to use and manipulate. Because of the RCD, contemporary viewing systems are more programmable, and any impact spatial distance between the user and receiver might have has been eliminated. The RCD has contributed to the successful diffusion of cable and VCRs into the majority of U.S. households by making these technologies user-friendly. It is likely that these technologies would not be used to the degree they are without the convenience of the RCD. As the humble RCD takes on more of the qualities of an "air mouse" (i.e., a move from push buttons to point and click icons as a means of operation) to allow the viewer/user control over myriad new options, its importance as the essential tool for the optimal use of television services becomes even more evident (Coates, 1994a). The RCD is similar to the computers that now contribute to the operation of automobiles, appliances, and other common devices, in that the "most profound technologies are those that disappear" (Coates, 1994b, pp. 10, 14).

A NEW GENERATION OF VIEWERS

The RCD has been recognized in previous research as one of the three major factors in programming choice (Heeter, 1988a), and as having exacerbated the grazing phenomenon more so than the proliferation of cable television channels (Heeter & Greenberg, 1988a). Ultimately, grazing behavior can change not only the manner in which we view/use television, but even how we function in society. In applying Meyerowitz's (1985) concept of "situational geography" (pp. 39–40) to the RCD, Lavery (1993) argued that "the electronic combination of many different styles of interaction" leads to "new behavior patterns with new expectations and emotions" (p. 231).

The ways in which the RCD is used have been the subject of recent analysis. Both scholarly research (Cronin & Menelly, 1992; Walker & Bellamy, 1993b; Wenner & Dennehy, 1993) and industry research (Kessler, 1985; Mermigas, 1984; Miller, 1989) have identified the most common RCD uses to be "zapping" (using the RCD to avoid advertising and other undesirable content), "zipping" (avoiding content by fast-forwarding through recorded programming), and "grazing" (combining disparate program elements into an individualized program mix that serves a wide range of gratification from amusement to information seeking). In an attempt to bring more specificity to these definitions, Eastman and Newton (1995) recently divided RCD use into "purposeful behaviors" (e.g. "arrowing," "jumping," "inserting"), and a more limited notion of grazing as "changing channels by using the up/down arrow slowly enough to take a look at sequential channels" (p. 83). Except when the differences in RCD use are particularly germane to the discussion, we will consider the combination of RCD activities to be general grazing behavior, encompassing both "tool" (purposive) and "toy" (nonpurposive) activity (Eastman & Newton, 1995; Wenner & Dennehy, 1993).

The study of RCDs is particularly suited to the uses and gratifications paradigm in mass communication research that posits the existence of an active audience as its foundation (Rubin & Bantz, 1987). One objective of RCD research is to identify the gratifications derived by television viewers from RCD use. For example, using data from a random sample of adult viewers, Walker, Bellamy, and Traudt (1993) identified six types of gratification. They were (1) the selective avoidance of unpleasant stimuli, (2) getting "more" from television, (3) annoying others, (4) controlling family viewing/accessing television news (these items were loaded together in a factor analysis), (5) accessing music videos, and (6) finding out what's on television (pp. 108–109). Wenner and Dennehy's transactional study (1993) of undergraduate students produced similar results.

INDUSTRY RESPONSES

The impact of RCD activity perhaps is most evident in television content. For example, certain television series and programming services (*Short*

Attention Span Theater, FX) are specifically designed to appeal to the zapper by consisting of short "pregrazed" segments that require only minimal attention on the part of the viewer. Advertising spots are often shorter and they are either edited in the rapid-fire pace popularized by Music Television (MTV) or they incorporate interactive and serialized narrative elements to catch viewers' attention and minimize grazing. IBM's "You Make the Call" spots on sports telecasts and the "Taster's Choice" spots featuring an ongoing romantic intrigue are examples. An increasing amount of advertising is also being integrated into program content. Primary examples at present include signs at sports venues and infomercials in which advertising is the sum total of program content. Ending credits for series have been enhanced (e.g., with outtakes) for the same reason. The beginnings of programs often immediately follow the credits of the preceding program in order to prevent or at least minimize zapping (see Eastman & Neal-Lunsford, 1993).

Beyond such obvious manifestations of the RCD's impact on television programming and advertising are the less visible but striking contributions it has made to the market structure of the U.S. television industry. Cable television has greatly expanded the choice of programming available to viewers. VCRs have done the same (through prerecorded tapes) and, at the same time, given the viewer an enhanced level of control over television.

Although not a programming conduit like cable and the VCR, the RCD gives the viewer/user instantaneous control over the many choices now available. As such, its diffusion must be seen as part of the "subtle revolution" that is affecting the ongoing structural changes in the television industry and the relationship between the industry and the viewer/user.

The RCD has been critical to the evolution of television's second generation, in which both choice and control have increased. Television's first generation was characterized by conceptualizations of a relatively passive audience with restricted viewing options primarily supplied by an oligopoly of the Big Three networks—television as a "passive, unknowing conduit" (Neuman, 1991, p. 52). The second generation audience has the power to participate actively in devising individualized media mixes from a relatively large number of video sources. This generational transition is manifest in the substantial changes in the televiewing experience that have converted many television viewers into television users, and in the struggle of traditional television entities to redefine themselves and devote more attention to the active viewer.

THE EVOLVING INDUSTRY–AUDIENCE
RELATIONSHIP

The focus of this book is the second generation of television viewership/use. Its purpose is to analyze the RCD's role in the quantitative and qualitative changes that have taken place in the televiewing experience over the last 15–20 years: changes resulting from the widespread diffusion of newer television and video technology as well as changes in the television industry in response to that diffusion. One of our central propositions is that the new level of content control being exercised by RCD users is closely monitored by the television and advertising industries, which naturally are interested in maintaining their power within the industry–viewer relationship. More fundamentally, we will argue that these industries have begun to counter the power of the active audience. In fact, the historical structure of the electronic media industries in the U.S. has been predicated on the ability to control, commodify, and sell the audience (Meehan, 1993). The diffusion of the RCD (and other television technologies) has intensified the industries' impetus to devise new ways to control its product (i.e., the audience).

Thus, any viewer empowerment arising from the diffusion of the RCD must be contextualized within the political–economic dimensions of the U.S. television industry. In doing so, we will demonstrate that RCD diffusion and reactions to that diffusion are products of such entwined historical forces as the economic structure of U.S. media industries, governmental oversight of media entities and management of technological diffusion, and conceptualizations of the nature of the audience.

POLITICAL–ECONOMIC
DIMENSIONS OF RCD DIFFUSION

The ability of RCD users to design new "texts" and engage in new "readings" is restricted by the raw material that the television industry distributes. As Morley stated in his critique of the cultural studies perspective's assumptions that viewers or readers have autonomy, "The power of viewers to reinterpret meanings is hardly equivalent to the discursive power of central media institutions to construct the texts that the viewer interprets" (1993, p. 16). The empowerment of the viewer is also disputed by Gerbner, who argues that grazers are basically "aimless" individuals who seek more of the same from the new video technologies (1993, p. 375). In fact, Will (1990) sees the RCD as a toy or diversion whose entertainment dimension distracts users from important issues of the day. In a similar vein, Neuman (1991) argues that the audience for television output basically is passive (p. 42), and that even in a time of channel proliferation the "economics of mass communications do not promote diversity" (p. 129).

Such analyses recognize that there has been a change in viewing behavior, and most recognize that economics have played an essential role in that change. However, they tend to understate both the actual and potential impact of the change (e.g., level of viewer empowerment) on the television industry.

Despite the well-known limitations of both qualitative and quantitative research, a substantial body of evidence demonstrating an increased level of television viewer activity has developed in the last few years (see Chapter 2). This evidence parallels trade press accounts that constantly report the means by which the television industry is attempting to understand and control this activity level (Gable, 1994; Graham, 1990). The previously mentioned changes in programming and advertising are the direct result of this desire. As Neuman (1991) stated, "the medium itself is cognizant of what messages are passing through and indeed is aware of how the user is responding" (p. 52).

The television industry is attempting to control the active audience in three ways. First, the recent mergers and consolidations in the media industries are concentrating media power in fewer and fewer hands. The Disney–ABC–ESPN–A&E, Fox–FX, and NBC–CNBC–America's Talking ventures exemplify how the television networks have extended their influence to cable television. In addition to these examples of economic integration, the Viacom–Paramount, Time–Warner–Turner, Sony–Columbia, and CBS–Westinghouse mergers of the last few years represent a continuing trend of vertical (i.e., hardware–software) integration on a multinational scale (Carveth, Owers, & Alexander, 1993). The mainstream media frequently represent these deals as cost-efficiency initiatives necessary to the development of the information superhighway. Promoters of the information superhighway promise that it will provide a nearly limitless number of channels and services, making it a touchstone for the rapidly developing global media business (Bagdikian, 1992; Gomery, 1993b; Schiller, 1987). As Schiller (1987) argues, "Concentrated private economic control over the entire information sector is now the dominant characteristic of the 'new' age of information" (p. 30).

The irony of such consolidation and globalization is that the vast increase in channels and television services available to U.S. households probably is leading to a smaller number of product suppliers, as major media firms join together to enhance their financial power and consequent control over a restless audience. As the structure of the media industries becomes increasingly consolidated, a large number of programs will be made available because of the need to differentiate the many channels from one another. However, the content or generic choices available to the audience probably will remain relatively conventional because of the high barriers to entry and limited innovation characteristics of oligopolistic market structures (Gomery, 1989; Picard, 1989). In short, a large number of video distribution systems does not ensure a diversity of content.

The case of magazines is instructive. Owen and Wildman (1992) argued that the "highly competitive, pluralistic" model under which magazines operate is coming to television, with the accompanying reduction of oligopolistic power and increase in content diversity (p. 1). However, Gomery (1993b) posited that rather than being in a "purely competive" market, magazines operate under a model of "monopolistic competition" (pp. 48–49). In this model, a large number of firms (sellers) divide into much smaller groups of sellers within a specific category or marketing niche where there are few competitors. This model already exists in cable television, with primary examples being the dominance of Cable News Network (and the co-owned Headline News) in the all-news, MTV (and the co-owned VH-1) in the popular music, and ESPN (and the co-owned ESPN2) in the national sports market segments.

The second reaction of the industry to audience empowerment is a change in traditional content and presentational structure. Programs and, more importantly, advertising messages are now designed to minimize the effect of RCD activity. As McAllister (1993) argued, advertisers want to "disempower the audience" by minimizing such "emancipatory technology" as RCDs and VCRs (p. 18). This containment is primarily accomplished through alterations of production techniques and scheduling conventions, a closer integration of program and advertising messages, more emphasis on place-based advertising, and the continuing refinement and application of integrated marketing techniques (see Chapters 3 and 4).

Finally, there is a continuing shift of the cost burden from program supplier and advertiser to user. Although the clearest extant example is the growing but still relatively small pay-per-view (PPV) business, of more importance are the various video-on-demand (VOD) services that will exact payment for access as part of the information superhighway. The integration of PPV–VOD is considered by the industry to be a fundamental element of the "choice" that television users will have in the "500-channel" television universe of the near future (Peppers & Rogers, 1994). The most troubling dimension of this cost shift is that as more and more of the supposed wonders of the information superhighway become technologically feasible, the costs associated with their access likely will disenfranchise many segments of the population (Schiller, 1993). As Bagdikian (1992) wrote, "Those who are not going to buy are not invited to read, hear, or watch" (p. 113).

Industrial Structure and Political Economy

The oligopolistic structure of the majority of media industries remains the most salient economic factor in considering these changing industries. Such a structure disguises, or at least obscures, a community of interest (i.e., the corporate interest in controlling and manipulating its output or product) under the guise of meaningful competition that allegedly is heavily regulated by governmental institutions. As defined by Gomery (1989, 1993a), an oligopoly is a market structure in which a limited number of large firms control a market with high barriers to entry for would-be competitors. Although the firms compete for resources and customers, they do so in a milieu where each entity knows much about what its competitors are doing and can react accordingly. In fact, the close relationship of these ostensible competitors fosters general agreement or consensus on how the industry is to operate. These agreements lead to minimal product differentiation or "numbing generic sameness" (Neuman, 1991, p. 194). Although models of monopolistic competition (for radio and magazines) and even monopoly (for most cable franchises) have relevance for analyses of media industries, the recent number of mergers, acquisitions, and coventures continue to make the oligopolistic market structure the primary locus for studies of media industries (Gomery, 1993a, 1993b).

The theory that market structure (oligopolistic or otherwise) is the primary determinant of market conduct (i.e., day-to-day operational parameters) and, consequently, market performance (e.g., profits, public service) developed primarily in industrial organizations literature (Bain, 1968; Caves, 1964; Scherer, 1970). More recently, the models and concepts of industrial organizations have been applied to studies of communication industries (Alexander, Owers, & Carveth, 1993; Gomery, 1989, 1993b; Picard, 1989). Such studies typically concentrate on how firms within an industry wield economic power and, more fundamentally, how they came into being in the first place. This can be seen as part of a general trend in U.S. mass communication research; it represents a reaction to more liberal–pluralist conceptions which posited that the behavior of media institutions is largely determined either by the development of consensus or by the temporary ascendancy of a position advanced from a more or less equal group of competing interests and influences such as the government, a citizens' group, or the courts (Cole & Oettinger, 1978; Krasnow, Longley, & Terry, 1982).

More recent approaches adopt a framework of analysis that posits the primary importance of economics in considerations of industrial structure and consequent conduct and performance (Curran, 1990; Murdoch & Golding, 1979). Often labeled "neo-Marxist" or "radical" perspectives, such approaches have become a major paradigm in the study of U.S. communications industries, through their recent combination with parts of the once-vilified "pluralist" perspective. As explained by Curran (1990, pp. 157–158):

> The most important and significant overall shift has been the steady advance of pluralist themes within the radical tradition; in particular, the repudiation of the totalizing, explanatory frameworks of Marxism, the reconceptualization of the audience as creative and active and the shift from the political to a popular aesthetic.

This level of analysis differs from traditional pluralism in that it assumes the inequality of resources and access, as well as the nonneutrality of the marketplace (Curran, 1990, p. 144). An industrial organizations perspective, with its emphasis on the predictive nature of industry structure, readily fits this approach.

The melding of two approaches that were recently considered to be diametrically opposed has led such observers as Neuman (1991, p. 42) to redefine political economics as a "combination of regulatory traditions and the economic dynamics of selling information and entertainment for profit." The synthesis has informed much recent work on mass communication industries (Horwitz, 1989; Schement & Lievrouw, 1987; Turow, 1992a, 1992b; Winston, 1986). Turow (1992b), for example, posited a "mass communication perspective" that stresses consideration of ownership and control as the essential first step in analyzing media messages and the application of media technology and their impact on individuals and society (pp. 107–108). Such a perspective is clearly tied to traditional political economic analyses. As recently defined by Meehan, Mosco, and Wasko (1993), political economic research "uncovers connections between ownership, corporate structure, finance capital, and market structure to show how economies affect technologies, politics, cultures, and information" (p. 105).

This synthesis of traditional pluralistic and radical approaches is the approach we use here. We argue that RCD diffusion, as an adjunct to such other technologies as cable and VCRs, is a consequence both of the consumer desire for television technologies that made the medium more user-friendly and of the deregulatory "ethos" that has been the primary touchstone of U.S. government–business relations for roughly the last 20 years (Horwitz, 1989; Polic & Gandy, 1993).

The Importance of the RCD

The RCD's role in the ongoing restructuring of the media industries must be placed in proper context. Basically, the RCD is important because it is synergistic with other technologies. For example, the RCD was never a major factor in the first generation of television primarily because of the lack of program choice available to viewers. The diffusion of cable television (primarily a product of regulatory decision making) led to an increase in channels, which in turn helped make grazing a mass phenomenon. The increase in grazing then became an inherent (if not always explicit) part of the ongoing argument that the traditional models of regulation and industry structure that separated broadcast, cable, and telecommunications services must be repealed or radically modified in order to allow competition for the attention of the restless viewer (Bellamy, 1993).

Winston (1986) posited "the 'law' of the suppression of radical potential," which holds that all technological advances must "conform to pre-existing social patterns" (pp. 23–24). The RCD as an "invisible" technology diffused rapidly while seemingly avoiding the application of this law. Regarded as a relatively trivial hardware accessory for other much more important new technologies (cable, VCRs), the RCD was not subject to the industrial and regulatory machinations of the programming-conduit technologies, although its influence on viewing behavior has been striking.

Even if the television industry had recognized earlier the impact that the RCD would have on the industry, there is little likelihood that it could have taken any action. There are two main reasons for this. First, the television industry has minimal influence over nonconduit hardware technology. General Electric's acquisition and breakup of RCA–NBC in the mid-1980s ended a major historical linkage of receiver sales and program services in the U.S. television industry (MacDonald, 1990). Much of the rapid diffusion of RCDs into U.S. households and the accompanying redefinition of RCDs from an add-on option to a standard feature occurred after this separation. Although such major integrated hardware–software providers as Sony–Columbia and Matsushita–MCA have developed in the last decade, their ability to enter the software end of the television industry derived significantly from their success in capturing a large segment of the receiver and VCR markets by incorporating such features as the RCD. The add-on nature of the RCD contributes to the technology's invisibility in that, with the exception of replacement and novelty RCDs (e.g., RCDs with sports logos or that look like handguns), there is no separate RCD industry. RCDs have been fully integrated as a replacement for tuning knobs in all but the least expensive sets for all major receiver manufacturers. Although the replacement market continues to grow at a rapid pace as consumers replace broken or lost RCDs or replace several older RCDs with a "universal" remote, it must be considered a relatively minor segment of the consumer electronics industry ("Buyer's Guide," 1993).

Second, the extremely rapid public acceptance of the RCD would have undermined any attempt to limit such diffusion. With the exception of some Federal Communications Commission (FCC) technical specifications and U.S. trade rules, no regulations affect RCDs (Aversa, 1994). This seemingly innocuous add-on clearly met a need in the marketplace which, combined with cost efficiencies of mass production, made it feasible and desirable for manufacturers to package RCDs with virtually all VCRs and television receivers. In applying the basic tenets of the diffusion of innovations perspective (Rogers, 1983; Rogers with Shoemaker, 1971) to the RCD, Klopfenstein (1993) argued that the RCD met the criteria of relative advantage over existing technology (the dial), trialability (due to its packaging with VCRs and receivers), lack of complexity, and low cost, which later became a nearly meaningless variable when RCDs were standard equipment (pp. 24, 37–38).

Any empowerment of the television viewer/user through access to RCDs must be seen as a crack in a tightly controlled political economic system. In this system, media institutions have long established themselves as an "elite power group" with enormous power to set the parameters of their relations with product suppliers (programmers), viewers, and governmental regulatory entities to favor their economic interests (Akhavan-Majid & Wolf, 1991, p. 149). Horwitz (1989) has categorized the growth of the cable industry and its challenge to the power of the traditional broadcast television industry as an "unintended consequence" of deregulation. Certainly, the diffusion of the RCD was an even more unintended consequence, in light of its increasing impact on the industry.

The crack in the system that allowed the widespread diffusion of the RCD and consequent empowerment of the active television viewer is now being "filled" by a television industry increasingly made up of combinations of once rival industries (i.e., broadcast, motion picture, cable, and telephone companies). However, the crack is neither small nor an illusion. Because it is impossible to disarm the RCD-wielding television user, the industry is both adopting practices that can limit the activity level of the user (i.e., content and stylistic changes in programming and advertising to make it "zap-proof") and accepting and pandering to the RCD user (i.e., new content forms, a move to PPV/VOD in which zapping is not as large a concern).

Although the diffusion of RCDs, VCRs, cable, and satellite transmission offers new challenges and opportunities to the viewer/user, policy makers, and the industry, the evolving relationship between the television industry and its viewer/users perpetuates the historical tensions over how the industry can best utilize its resources to control, manipulate, and sell the audience. A brief sketch of the industry–viewer relationship in the first generation of television (and its direct predecessor, radio) will make these impulses more explicit and demonstrate that (1) the audience for electronic media has never actually fit the model of passivity, and (2) the electronic media industries already have developed many of the skills necessary to cope with an active audience. This background makes explicit the related series of events that led to a transition from the first to the second generation of television. It also can help us understand present attempts to cope with the RCD's impact and give us glimpses of probable future actions in the industry.

HISTORICAL PATTERNS
OF MEDIUM–USER RELATIONSHIPS

The U.S. broadcasting industry developed, as did most other domestic industries, through the combined efforts of the private sector and the government. The shifting balance of these two forces informs the early history of radio, with government intervention critical to the privatization of the system. By the 1920s, earlier conceptions of broadcasting as a substitute for or supplement to point-to-point wired communications systems had been replaced by the realization that it was technologically and commercially more viable to employ the new system as the purveyor of advertising-supported and primarily entertainment-oriented programming (Barnouw, 1978). In order for such a system to operate with maximum cost efficiency, the private interests that were increasingly dominant in the industry sought government support to force small and noncommercial interests to either leave the air or move to less desirable frequencies. This was accomplished in large part by the Radio Act of 1927, which set up a licensing system that, while accomplishing the technically necessary goal of reducing spectrum interference, also institutionalized a privately operated and profit-oriented broadcasting system (McChesney, 1993). The economic depression of the 1930s and the refusal of the Federal Radio Commission (FRC) and its successor (the FCC) to reserve frequencies for noncommercial stations also was responsible for the decline of noncommercial stations. By the late 1930s, the vast majority of stations were actively selling advertising and most were linked to a national network (MacDonald, 1990; Sterling & Kittross, 1990).

Although the national radio industry would come to be dominated by an oligopoly consisting of the National Broadcasting Company and the Columbia Broadcasting System networks, two major interrelated factors delayed the full exercise of oligopolistic power by the networks. First, the model for the earliest radio entities was that of a common carrier. In this concept, the station or network was simply the "conduit for hire," with no control of the content. This telegraph–telephone method of operation was applied to radio, beginning with AT&T's "toll broadcasting" system on the New York station WEAF in 1922 (Barnouw, 1978). Although the Radio Act of 1927 explicitly rejected common carrier status for radio by making license renewal contingent on the licensee's ability to operate within the parameters, however ill-defined, of a public interest standard (Teeter & LeDuc, 1992), the then-unregulated network business had no such standard to follow. A primary effect of the common carrier model was the substantial control that the advertising industry had over program content and scheduling. With the exception of sustaining programs, in which no sponsor was available, networks had minimal centralized scheduling power. The lack of such control delayed the development of techniques designed to enhance the audience's flow from one program to another and prevent or hinder channel changing.

Second, many advertisers could afford to control entire programs, owing to the relatively low cost of radio production and advertising. Additionally, the low cost of radio sponsorship combined with the then-primitive nature of audience quantification and analysis of audience data to delay the implementation of alternate sponsorship techniques. The later discovery that there were major cost efficiencies in spreading advertising spots among several programs—which could reach either a varying audience or specialized demographics by using participating sponsorships and spots rather than maintaining control over individual programs—led to increased network scheduling power (Barnouw, 1978).

Of course, it would be ludicrous to argue that the later growth in network power, and particularly in television, weakened the overall power of the advertising industry in broadcasting. While networks did inherit almost all of the scheduling powers once held by advertisers, they did so with the support of, or even at the insistence of, advertisers.

The networks certainly were not devoid of oligopolistic tendencies in the early days of radio, as they sought to increase their value to advertisers and build barriers to entry for potential competitors in an increasingly lucrative business. CBS was particularly instrumental in developing network power, because of its aggressiveness in establishing relationships with major advertisers and its lack of historical ties to the common carrier era of radio. As befits the classic pattern of oligopolies, CBS's promotion of popular, expensive, and personality-driven programming and service to the advertising community, which allowed it to catch up to and surpass NBC as an advertising vehicle, was later adopted in large part by NBC (Barnouw, 1978; MacDonald, 1990).

As the economic power of NBC and CBS increased, certain joint rules of network conduct developed. These included creating coercive policies to force affiliate stations into surrendering much programming autonomy to the network, turning the programming schedule over to the advertising industry (although the networks would take on most of this function with the development of television and implementation of more sophisticated audience measurement methods), and developing audience analysis research that had as its raison d'être the discovery of audience motivations for commercial manipulation (Arens & Bovée, 1994).

A major by-product of the radio oligopoly was the nationalization and homogenization of programming, with the vast amount of it supplied by advertisers through time (i.e., access to audiences) purchased from the Big Three networks: NBC Red, CBS, and NBC Blue. The increasing power of the networks was recognized by the federal government, which lessened network control over affiliate schedules and mandated the sale of NBC Blue to Edward Nobel, where it became ABC (the American Broadcasting Company) in the mid-1940s (*National Broadcasting Co. et al. v. United States*, 319 U.S. 190 [1943]). Arguably, this action had the effect of further limiting audience choice, because NBC Blue had been a source of counter programming for the more economically successful NBC Red network. The new ABC network, however, immediately attempted to target the mass audience by scheduling the same types of programs available on CBS and NBC in order to prove its legitimacy to national advertisers (Sterling & Kittross, 1990).

Although World War II primarily was responsible for the delay in the authorization of a U.S. broadcast television service, the power of the broadcast industry to shape government regulatory policy was evident in the long delays in the approval of the technologically superior FM service, then a shift of FM frequencies that rendered all existing receivers obsolete, and the long delays and subsequent "freeze" that delayed the full implementation of the television system until the mid-1950s (MacDonald, 1990; Sterling & Kittross, 1990).

This power was such that the major radio entities had little difficulty becoming the dominant powers in the television industry. Although the refusal of the leading motion picture studios (which were involved at the time in a major antitrust action) to enter the fledgling industry was a factor, the key reason for the ease with which the same ownership interests came to dominate the radio and television industries was the tendency of governmental bodies to favor existing companies in a given industry over new entrants (MacDonald, 1990; Mosco, 1979). Obviously, existing firms were in a better position to devote considerable financial and political resources to self-promotion.

The technological challenges of implementing a U.S. television system were substantially greater than those of radio mainly because of the much greater demand for spectrum. However, RCA's early acquisition of VHF licenses was influential in the government's decision to implement a mixed VHF–UHF system of television broadcasting. While such a system was deemed necessary to the goals of "localism"—a large number of stations serving many different communities—the effect was that NBC and CBS—with their group of owned and operated stations in the major markets and their many affiliates, including many holdovers from radio—came to dominate the U.S. television industry. After its acquisition by United Paramount Theaters in 1953 and the demise of the underfunded DuMont network in 1955, ABC eventually was able to exert itself as a third member of the oligopoly. However, its lack of strong affiliates kept it in a relatively weak third place until the 1970s (Goldenson with Wolf, 1991).

The U.S. broadcasting industry, therefore, developed with a limited number of desirable distribution outlets. However, unlike many other nations that have used government as an instrument to encourage at least some level of content diversity, the United States has relied almost exclusively on the market system to accomplish the same task. And although the system surely fostered a degree of program diversification, this diversity always has been restrained by the perceived need of commercial enterprises to maximize profit. In a system with a limited number of suppliers and outlets, this generally means attracting the largest share of the audience possible. The emerging radio oligopoly and its direct television successor presented a relatively homogeneous product that was highly appealing to a mass audience. Nonetheless, the audience has long been receptive to and sought ways to exert its control over the broadcast medium.

Radio and RCDs

As Benjamin (1993) observes, the idea of a remote control device existed early in radio's development as a promotional tool. Although the early devices were cumbersome and not successful, some set manufacturers and entrepreneurs realized that the audience was interested in making the listening experience more convenient. By allowing the listener, without leaving his or her comfortable easy chair, to turn the set on and off, adjust the volume up or down, or tune from station to station, these devices had the inadvertent effect of giving the listener the power to design her or his own personal listening environment by combining the output of several stations into a coherent whole. However, the cost and awkwardness of the early radio RCD prevented it from ever being more than a novelty item (Benjamin, 1993).

Despite the failure of the RCD to become a major factor in radio, the potential impact of advertising avoidance apparently was noticed by the advertising industry, which mixed its appeals with programming content. This was done at first to a far greater extent than was possible after programming became network (or independent-supplier) controlled. Through the integration of programming and advertising, the advertising industry recognized the importance of placement in order to maintain the attention of an audience (Barnouw, 1978). One of the earliest demonstrations of the audience's willingness to switch stations to avoid undesirable content was the infamous *Mercury Theater of the Air*'s broadcast of Orson Welles's adaptation of *War of the Worlds*. One of the explanations for the ensuing audience panic was that a substantial number of listeners had tuned in after the program's disclaimer that the newscast format being employed was fictitious. They missed the disclaimer because they had been listening to the much more popular *Chase & Sanborn Hour* with Edgar Bergen and Charlie McCarthy until after the first skit (Cantril, 1947).

Although the advertising industry early on recognized the potential detrimental effects of audience grazing behavior, it would be erroneous to attribute that recognition to the presence of RCDs. Later technological and regulatory developments in radio were more important factors in grazing. The convenient push-button automobile radio, pioneered by such companies as Motorola and Zenith, made channel changing much more prevalent. The increasing availability of inexpensive table model radios, and the diffusion of portable transistor radio receivers in the post-World War II period, also encouraged channel changing. Such innovations, as well as the increasing number of radio stations (an effect of the long-delayed advent of FM service and an increasing number of radio licensees), the end of network radio as a full-time mass program provider, and the rise of music-dominated formats (Sterling & Kittross, 1990), combined to make radio increasingly subject to grazing.

As television replaced radio as the dominant national mass medium in the 1950s, radio went through a period of demassification, exemplified by the move from series to primarily music-based formats, with increasingly differentiated content designed to reach specific audience segments for the advertising industry. With the audience able to sample the increasingly demassified product of radio receivers at arm's length (e.g., on a nightstand, on a beach towel, or in the car), an RCD would have been superfluous.[1] Although personal viewing of television (rather than in a group) has been found to lead to more RCD activity (see Chapter 6), personal viewing or listening can also serve to limit the random grazing phenomenon. For example, the country music aficionado is unlikely to sample radio stations with a classical or rap format, just as the MTV devotee is unlikely to sample The Nashville Network. If a medium is providing specialized content, as is radio in urban areas, grazing behavior becomes more purposive and tied to a relatively limited repertoire of channels. So, the rise of format radio can be conceptualized in part as a reaction to the grazing brought about by the increasingly personal nature of the medium. And, even if portability and the development of niche programming eventually limits some types of grazing behavior, the effect on programming and on the industry in reaction to more random grazing has already occurred.

The radio audience's orienting search for desirable programming in a time of expanded outlets and more personal receivers has led to increased random grazing, which eventually evolved into personal station repertoires. However, radio's contemporary use as a background medium that sets a mood for other activities probably is a likely reason that the grazing phenomenon is primarily limited to television use. As a foreground medium that demands more attention on the part of the user, television occupies a major portion of the leisure-time activity of a substantial proportion of the population. Because the RCD facilitates user control over television content, the device became a highly desirable add-on product for receivers and a near necessity for VCRs and many cable systems.

RCDs and Television

Because radio and television jointly constitute the broadcast industry, it is commonplace to search for parallels in their development. For example, analyses of recent changes in television programming often equate them to the demassification process and era of specialization that radio programming entered in the wake of television's diffusion (Halonen, 1992b; Owen & Wildman, 1992). While such analyses are interesting and often instructive, they tend to gloss over some of the differences in the two media.

As noted, the RCD was never an important factor in radio grazing. As radio faced the television challenge, it essentially yielded the function of a national mass medium to television and became a specialized local service. Demassification in radio was a reaction both to television's diffusion and to the increased portability of radio receivers. In addition, the companies that controlled national radio made the decision to shift resources to the television industry. Although the networks maintained skeletal and highly targeted networks and continued to own stations in many major markets, the demassification of radio must be seen in part as a calculated move by the network oligopoly (Sterling & Kittross, 1990).

The most overt challengers to broadcast television to date generally have been niche media such as cable and VCRs rather than a medium that could replace the dominant outlet of electronic mass communication, as television replaced radio. Although clearly there has been some increased specialization of broadcast television content as its competitors have reached more households, the core concept of a mass medium remains alive and well in the television industry. There is strong evidence that the broadcast model will maintain a substantial audience indefinitely, because of its demonstrated ability to reach vast undifferentiated audiences without the need for physical connection to the intended receiver or any form of specialized receiving equipment. Such audiences remain appealing to mass market advertisers even as they shift some of their attention to niche video outlets (Jensen, 1994a; Leckey, 1994). This is why the traditional Big Three networks and the Fox Broadcasting Company are maintaining and strengthening their national broadcast services while at the same time entering other program distribution businesses. The radio model does not appear to be totally applicable to the evolving television environment.

The RCD is a key television technology because it allows the viewer to sample both the old (broadcast, mass appeal) and new (cable, VCR, niche appeal) content either at random or as part of a self-designed menu of content. Unlike radio, television has the capacity to offer both mass and specialized content simultaneously. Thus, the second generation of television is an evolution and incorporation of the first generation into a more diverse but still heavily controlled television economy.

The earliest television RCDs were cumbersome novelties. Zenith's "Space Command" and the other early RCDs were sold with more expensive models of color television receivers beginning in the late 1950s, primarily marketed as a luxury item rather than as a necessary accessory (Benjamin, 1993; Stern & Stern, 1992).

Zenith's longtime president, Eugene McDonald, saw the development of a user-friendly RCD as a key factor in the ultimate success of "quality" television. A well-known industry maverick, McDonald was an early champion of such innovations as automobile radio, FM radio, and pay television, and was a severe critic of advertiser-supported television and its advocates, RCA in particular. His advocacy of Zenith's "Phonevision" system of pay television was based on a belief that advertising revenue would not be sufficient to support quality television programming, such as recent motion pictures, that he thought the audience would demand. Phonevision was developed to deal with this perceived problem by allowing television stations to broadcast recent movies and special events via a scrambled signal, which would be unscrambled by a signal sent through the telephone line to those homes that had placed a call to order (and be billed for) a specific program. Phonevision was the precursor of the pay-per-view systems that are increasingly common today (Bellamy, 1988).

Robert Adler, the Zenith engineer often credited with the successful development of a practical wireless remote, has indicated that McDonald's belief that advertising would "ruin" television was the major factor in the push by Zenith to develop a practical RCD (Benjamin, 1993, p. 18). The idea was that the RCD would allow the audience to avoid advertising, which would cause the television industry to adopt a direct consumer payment mode of operation, such as Phonevision. Zenith's emphasis on devices (RCDs, Phonevision) that would allow for advertising avoidance can be regarded both as part of a strategy to gain customers for the company's television receivers and as a reflection of McDonald's distaste for advertising and the broadcast industry that opposed his positions (Bellamy, 1988). Although unsuccessful in his goal to stop the growth of advertiser-supported television, McDonald was perhaps the first major industry figure to realize the potential power and impact of the RCD.

Clearly, the ability of the increasingly powerful broadcast industry to hinder the development of alternative delivery systems such as pay television was a contributing factor in keeping the RCD a specialized rather than a mass consumer product for many years. Television could not become a serious grazer's medium as long as the number of channels and type of program offerings were limited, and as long as receivers were large, relatively nonportable, and so costly that few households owned more than one. It would require the diffusion of new video technologies to create the second generation of television viewers.

Diffusion of New Television Technology

In 1972 the FCC promulgated rules that would have direct and lasting impact on the television industry. First, the commission issued coherent guidelines for the diffusion of cable television service. Although the rules were highly protectionist for broadcasters, the FCC did, for the first time, lay out guidelines for the introduction of cable service to the nation's urban areas. In addition, the rules spelled out the manner in which cable services could and, in some cases, must operate as both distributors and originators of programming (Cable Television Report and Order, 1972).

As a result of these actions, cable soon became regarded as more than just a conduit for the delivery of existing broadcast programming. It was the critical element in the conversion of the community antenna television business into a distinct cable television industry that increasingly was able to compete with the broadcasting industry for resources and political influence. The 1972 rules were the first major government-sanctioned recognition of cable's ability to add quantity to the nation's television programming mix.

Another major FCC decision of 1972, the domestic satellite rules, ended the monopoly of the Communications Satellite Corporation in satellite distribution and for the first time allowed private interests to offer domestic satellite services (*Domestic Communication Satellite Facilities*, 1972). This decision enabled such companies as the Spanish International Network (now Univision) to link its broadcasting affiliates and, more importantly, to offer its signal to cable systems nationwide. The ability to interconnect distribution points without the prohibitive expense of AT&T-provided land lines was critical to the development of alternative video services. Several companies placed services on satellites in the mid-1970s. Major examples include Time, Incorporated's (now Time Warner) Home Box Office, Ted Turner's Atlanta independent WTCG (now WTBS), Pat Robertson's Christian Broadcasting Network (now The Family Channel), and Eastern Microwave's carriage of New York's WOR-TV (now WWOR-TV). These services became the foundation for a cable programming industry that would expand greatly in the late 1970s and early 1980s.

The increasing number of channels created more consumer demand for means of making sense of and controlling television's output. The cable industry provided one solution by offering both extended-length cables on converter boxes and, in some areas, wired or wireless RCDs. Of course, it was in the best interests of the cable industry to encourage grazing behavior as a means of getting the viewer to sample the new channels available for a fee. Another factor in the increase of grazing was the continuing cost reduction in portable television receivers, which allowed more and more people to watch television by themselves, a proximate factor in the amount of grazing one does. Of course, as in the case of radio, portability and personalization of the receiver is in some ways an inhibitor of random grazing. While vital, it is important to keep in perspective that none of these "environmental" factors was as important to the increase in grazing as the increasing amount of programming being made available to the viewer.

Another essential factor in the advent of television's second generation was the diffusion of the home VCR, led by a major consumer push from such Japanese electronics firms as Sony and Matsushita in the late 1970s and early 1980s. The VCR is unique because it is both a programming conduit like cable (when playing prerecorded tapes) and a means of control over the content of television (through time shifting). The time-shifting function is critical because it allows the user to develop new patterns of television usage (Levy, 1989). The VCR also offers the user the ability to avoid television advertising either by stopping the recording during advertising (a tedious activity probably not used by many) or, more commonly, by zipping past the advertising (and other undesirable content) at high speed during playback. By the mid-1980s, many in the advertising industry were expressing deep concern about zipping, which industry observers often called "VCR zapping" (Kessler, 1985; Kostyra, 1984; also see Chapter 2).

Despite the vast power of VCRs to alter television viewing/use patterns, they certainly would not be employed to the degree that they are without the RCD. The RCD allows the television viewer to take advantage of both the content diversity of cable and videotape, and the control features of the VCR. It is the tool that allows for the intricacies of the modern television viewing experience.

CONCLUSION

During the eras of almost total network dominance in the radio and television industries, the networks had little difficulty controlling the operational parameters of the broadcast industry and the impulses of the audience to exercise their own means of control over programming. The limitations of the broadcast spectrum and regulatory policies that typically allowed the broadcaster to set the regulatory agenda (Mosco, 1979) allowed a powerful oligopoly to exert its power to prevent meaningful competition. The relatively limited diversity of content produced by the network oligopoly and the advertising industry lessened the incentive of viewers to invest in RCDs, which, in any case, were not generally available as a receiver add-on. The broadcast and advertising industries also developed audience analysis and scheduling techniques that enabled them to exploit the listener/viewer inertia that was itself a product of the oligopoly (Eastman, 1993).

The combination of technological diffusion and regulatory policies ostensibly designed to encourage competition in the television industry created both serious problems and major opportunities for the industry. The proliferation of new video services and technologies that allowed the audience a means of control over these services seriously weakened the oligopolistic power once wielded by the networks. At the same time, governmental policy allowed more consolidation of economic power and the creation or refinement of new oligopolistic structures. There are clear parallels between present activity in the television industry and the reactions of the broadcast industry to previous challenges. Clearly, the increasing number of mergers and consolidations across the lines of broadcasting, cable, and telecommunications create barriers to entry for would-be competitors that are at least as prohibitive as the technical limitations of the past. Such activity is aided and abetted by the government under the guise of deregulation and competitiveness, which contributes to these barriers at least as much as, if not more so, than past regulatory activity (Polic & Gandy, 1993). And, as has been the case since the advent of the broadcast industry, the television industry of today is working closely with the advertising industry to develop the means to prevent or at least minimize the effect of user control over content. How this is being accomplished and the prospects for further audience control will be considered in later chapters.

Of course, the study of changes in industrial organizations and behaviors brought about by the advent of the RCD and related technology is but one part of the RCD's significance. Of equal, if not greater, importance is the issue of how RCDs are being used by the television audience. The measuring of and explication of the motivations for this usage is a critical first step in understanding the RCD phenomenon and its effect on both the viewing public and the television industry. We turn now to an analytical review and synthesis of studies that have attempted to identify the amount of RCD usage.

NOTE

1. Only in the last few years (and paralleling the diffusion of television remote controls) have RCDs become nearly universal as part of high-performance, component audio systems incorporating radios receivers, compact-disc players, tape recorders/players, and so forth. Such systems are often connected to video receivers and VCRs.

CHAPTER 2

How Often Is
the Clicker Clicked?

THE MEASUREMENT OF RCD USE

In this chapter, we address apparently straightforward questions about the extent of RCD use. Although these questions are obvious ones, their answers have been approached using a variety of methods that, not surprisingly, yielded inconsistent answers.

As with any research on human activity, the examination of television viewing behavior is shaped by the resources available to researchers and the motivations of the benefactors commissioning the research. Proprietary industrial research commissioned by advertising agencies, media corporations, or trade associations and executed by marketing and advertising research firms benefits from substantial resources (by academic standards) that allow for the collection of data from large, more diverse samples and for rapid turnaround, if needed. In contrast, university researchers often must rely on small samples, often of undergraduate students, and a publication process that can take years to complete. Industry researchers also profit from, and are limited by, the business imperative that requires standardized methods, so that competitors can battle on a stable, if not level, playing field. Thus, the limitations of long-accepted audience-ratings data collection methods (diaries, surveys, "audimeters") are frequently criticized but rarely changed (e.g., by introducing "people-meters"), and then only because of serious competition from outside

24

players (e.g., by AGB, the British firm that introduced peoplemeters). Because they are not as bound by the expectations of industry norms, academic researchers frequently have approached a new subject such as RCDs using a variety of old and new methods. This variety of approaches yields varying answers to even the simple question of how frequently the technology is used.

However, academic researchers do not face the same limitations that constrain marketing researchers. Since they are not profit motivated, academic researchers do not have as great a vested interest in preserving an existing data collection method. New methods, such as the conversion of audimeters to peoplemeters, or the transformation of local ratings from diary to metered data collection, can cost research companies market share and increase expenses considerably. In addition, changes in method invariably benefit one faction of the media industry at the expense of another. Peoplemeters initially reduced the ratings of children's programming, because children were less likely to record their viewing (Moshavi, 1992; Keefe, 1992; McClellan, 1991; "Cable Networks," 1988). Conversion from diary to meter-based local ratings helped cable networks and some independent stations, because participants do not need to write down the names of programs or networks, making it easier for less familiar program titles and station call letters to be included (Meyer, Eastman, & Wimmer, 1993).

Academic research also is not as clearly connected to the economic needs of the agencies commissioning the research. Profit-centered marketing companies produce research that can always be attacked as reflecting the needs of the corporations or trade associations that commission the research. A. C. Nielsen's meter-based research—which, until the development of peoplemeters, counted all time that the set was in use as viewing time, whether anyone was paying attention or even in the room—clearly benefited television networks and stations by inflating their inventory (program viewers). By the early 1970s, however, research supported by the National Institute of Mental Health (Bechtel, Achelpohl, & Akers, 1972) documented that a substantial component of the audience was paying little attention to the set. Just as Nielsen's meter-based research can inflate ratings, marketing companies also can modify the questions in their surveys in order to increase the levels of interest in new products or services developed by their corporate sponsors.

Both industry and academic research must be interpreted in light of their limitations and strengths. Reviews of industry research must consider results while taking into account the motivations of the sponsoring agency and needs for profit-motivated research firms to manufacture a marketable product. Interpretations of academic research should consider the impact of methodological choices forced by limited resources or dictated by the particular operational definitions of key variables. We will take this approach in this chapter while answering one paramount question:

HOW FREQUENTLY IS THE RCD USED?

Simple measurement of RCD use has turned out to be an elusive quest, with a multiplicity of explorers pursuing a multitude of paths. The most elemental question that can be asked about any technology—how much is it used?—has yielded a variety of answers and interpretations. The mean measured frequency of RCD use per hour has varied from 4.4 (Heeter, D'Alessio, Greenberg, & McVoy, 1988) to 107 (Ferguson, 1994). Interpretations of the significance of RCD activity have ranged from negligible to revolutionary. Part of the problem of measurement is that there has been no clearly agreed upon definition of what constitutes RCD use. Researchers employing survey methods (Ainslie, 1989; Walker & Bellamy, 1991a; Walker, Bellamy, & Traudt, 1993; Wenner & Dennehy, 1993) typically asked questions focused on viewer perceptions of the outcomes of the RCD activity: channel flipping or grazing, multiple-program viewing, channel changing, and, on occasion, muting. Researchers employing observational methods (Cornwell et al., 1993; Eastman & Newton, 1995; Krendl, Troiano, Dawson, & Clark, 1993) have identified particular RCD behaviors (patterns of button pushing) that viewers employ: punching a specific channel number, arrowing up and down to get to a particular channel, jumping to a previous channel, inserting a smaller picture within the larger one, scanning slowly enough to look at particular channels, and muting. Passive measurement techniques have been limited to recording channel changing at periodic intervals and inferring RCD use from that activity (Bryant & Rockwell, 1993; Ferguson, 1994; Heeter et al., 1988; Kaye & Sapolsky, 1995). Varying methods have led to varying definitions of RCD use.

In addition, the meaning of RCD use is, in part, technologically defined (Bryant & Rockwell, 1993; Heeter, Yoon, & Sampson, 1993; Molitor, 1992). The most modest RCD allows viewers to turn the set on or off, change channels progressively from lower to higher or higher to lower numbered channels, and to mute the sound. The next level of complexity adds random channel access by directly inserting the number of the desired channel. Many of these RCDs also allow the viewer to return to the last channel viewed by hitting a single recall or previous channel button. More complex RCDs allow the viewer to program several preferred channels while locking out all others, so that when the channel is advanced only one of the desired channels appears. Even more complex RCDs can be used to select picture-in-picture modes, which allow two channels to be viewed at once, or multiple, still-picture modes (Heeter et al., 1993) that provide still images from many channels simultaneously on the screen. Each of these options, and those that will be created in the future, expand the variety of possible RCD behaviors and lead to varying levels of RCD use (Bryant & Rockwell, 1993; Heeter et al., 1993).

The innocuous nature of RCD activity has also been a challenge to researchers. Pushing an RCD button is a momentary activity accomplished in less than one second. Since its duration is so short, its frequency can be very high (60 or more times a minute) or very low (two pushes per viewing session: one to turn the set on and the other to turn it off). Thus, during three hours of prime time viewing, RCD use can vary from 2 (turning the set on, turning it off) to 10,800 or more button pushes (although even the most aggressive channel surfer is not likely to push the upper limits). Coupled with this large degree of variation, the pressing of an RCD button is not a particularly memorable event. Ferguson (1994) compares RCD use to a variety of mundane activities such as checking a wristwatch for the correct time. Thus, as Ferguson and other researchers have noted (Eastman & Newton, 1995; Cornwell et al., 1993), it is nearly impossible to give exact estimates of the number of times the RCD is used. Indeed, most survey researchers have not asked for exact estimates of RCD behaviors (button pushes) but have requested perceptions of the relative frequency (never, seldom, often, very often) or percentage of time spent viewing that is occupied with a particular RCD activity, such as changing channels, flipping from channel to channel, or multiple-program viewing (Ainslie, 1989; Walker & Bellamy, 1991a; Walker et al., 1993; Wenner & Dennehy, 1993). Accurate measurement of a particular behavior is not necessarily the only desirable result. As Williams, Rice, and Rogers (1988, p. 94) note in their discussion of self-report and computer-monitored data, self-report items measure perceptions of behavior that can help us assess the importance of the behavior to the individual as well as its frequency, while electronically monitored systems typically only record the frequency of the behavior. Electronic devices may be a more effective way to record button pushing, but not to reveal the salience of the reasons for these pushes.

Finally, the number and variety of channels available to the viewers, as well as the types of respondents/subjects used in each study may also influence the frequency of RCD use. The case has been made (Ainslie,

1989; Ferguson, 1992; Walker & Bellamy, 1991a) that RCD use increases as the number and variety of cable channels increases. Greater variety in channels and content type should lead to increased sampling of that content and greater RCD use (Ferguson, 1992). As columnist Russell Baker has quipped, "What is cable TV for if you don't keep changing the channels?" (quoted in Ainslie, 1989, p. 10). As will be discussed more fully in Chapters 5 and 6, research has shown that males are more likely to use the RCD than females and that the young are more likely to channel surf than the old. Thus, the characteristics of both viewing options and viewers sampled must be considered when interpreting the results of individual studies.

As we review studies of RCD use, we examine how the goals of the research, method of observation, type of RCD technology employed, content viewed, and viewer characteristics may color the frequency of RCD use reported in the study. Our assumption is that no one study is without limitations, but thoughtful review of the multitude of studies of RCD use will yield a less clouded view of RCD activity.

INDUSTRY STUDIES OF RCD USE

As cable, VCR, and RCD penetration began to increase in the early 1980s, advertising agencies began to commission studies of RCD activity. As part of the coverage of conference sessions or opinion pieces, brief summaries of this proprietary research began to proliferate in the trade and national press by 1984. The central questions addressed in that research reflected the economic realities of the television industry in the United States. Although advertisers had long been aware that viewers avoid television commercials by leaving the room, talking, reading, or simply day dreaming during commercial breaks, the RCD posed a clear threat to television's captive audience. RCD users could avoid commercials by changing channels (zapping), by speeding through advertisements in recorded programs (zipping) at ten times the normal speed and with no sound, or by eliminating or greatly reducing sound levels (muting). (See Chapter 3 for an in-depth discussion of the impact of RCDs on the advertising industry.) Because of the RCD's affect on commercial viewing, most proprietary studies have focused on RCD use during commercial breaks with only occasional glimpses of its use during programming. Nonetheless, these industry studies present a detailed picture of RCD use frequently based on large national surveys and reanalyses of national ratings' data.

Industry studies have offered evidence of RCD activity using a variety of measures, including the percentage of the audience changing channels during an average viewing minute; the percentage of the total audience who are frequent channel changers, zappers, or zippers; and the percentage of commercials zapped or zipped. Because RCD use, particularly commercial avoidance, reduces the size of their inventory (of viewers), commercial television networks have tried to minimize the impact of RCDs on viewing by reporting the percentage of the audience who change channels during an average minute. Research sponsored by advertising agencies seeking compensation for the audience lost to zapping and zipping has focused on the percentage of viewers who say that they engage in particular RCD activities rather than on the specific amount of time spent using the RCD. None of the studies summarized here report the mean frequency of channel changes. First, we examine chronologically some studies of commercial avoidance (zipping and zapping), and then studies of channel changing during programs.

Zipping and Zapping

Early industry studies tended to focus on zipping: a new form of commercial avoidance made possible by the rapidly growing market for VCRs. Advertisers were particularly concerned with zipping at this time because A. C. Nielsen included VCR-recorded programming in estimates of viewing time without weighting for unviewed programs or making any adjustments for effects of zipping. Mermigas (1984, p. 83) revealed that industry studies showed that "64% of all VCR playbacks use fast-forward to skip over commercials." In the same article, James Spaeth, group manager of strategic planning and research at General Foods, speculated that by 1990 there would be "a 13% loss [of viewers] from electronic zapping (via such methods as using remote-control devices) and a 4% loss as a result of VCR playback of programs without commercials" (Mermigas, 1984, p. 83). According to Bronson (1984), A. C. Nielsen studies suggest that "about two-thirds of videocassette-recorder owners play back TV tapes to skip ads" (p. 66). Ainslie (1985) reported similar Nielsen estimates, suggesting 60% of commercials embedded in taped programs are zipped, while 20% of all recorded programs are never viewed at all. Offering only an estimate of the percentage of tapers that practice zipping but not the percentage of ads zipped, Miller (1989, p. 73) lamented that with zipping practiced by "anywhere from 50% to 70% of all VCR owners, it's easy to understand why advertisers are choking on their mid-afternoon sushi." As VCR penetration tripled between 1985 and 1990 (Klopfenstein & Albarran, 1991), Lublin (1991) reported that the most recent Nielsen study suggested that "VCR users currently ignore 40% of the commercials they record—either because they fail to play back programs or they fast-forward through ads on programs they play back" (p. B-3). Thus by 1991, the percentage of homes with VCRs had tripled, but the percentage of ads zipped, according to industry claims, had decreased by a third, from 60% to 40% of the commercials recorded.

Although VCR zipping received most of the attention in early industry reports of commercial avoidance, 1983–1984 studies by A. C. Nielsen and Information Resources, Inc. (IRI) ("How to Avoid Being Zapped," 1984) found that 5–6% of viewers were changing channels during the average commercial minute with more zapping occurring at the program breaks. In addition, zapping increased in RCD-equipped homes (fewer than 30% of households at this time) and between cable and pay-cable subscribers. Meanwhile, John Jacobs, a Grey Advertising executive, was suggesting that the "tune-out factor" was far larger than Nielsen and IRI's estimate: 40% of viewers (Kessler, 1985, p. 68). With RCD penetration at 25%, Fountas (1985) cited industry studies that documented three types of avoidance: physical zapping (leaving the room), zapping, and time-shift zapping (zipping). According to these studies, 30–40% of viewers physically zap a commercial and another 5.2% zap it. Zapping increased to 6.2% in pay cable households and 7.1% in RCD-equipped households: a 19% increase in pay-cable and a 37% increase in RCD households. Three years later, Lewin (1988, p. 118) noted that the advertising industry had learned the basic parameters of zapping: "that it is more likely to occur in spot breaks than in-program breaks; that not all dayparts [e.g., daytime, early fringe, prime time, late night] are affected equally, that not all programs are affected equally, and, most significant to us, that not all commercials are affected equally." At the same time, Miller (1989, p. 73) worried that VCR zipping and "various studies indicating remote-control users 'zap' away 10% to 20% of all advertising messages" are evidence of "a once captive audience now roaming freely across video-land." Using a different unit of measure, R. D. Percy & Co., a Seattle-based television viewing research company, found that households zap an average of once every 3 minutes, 42 seconds (16.2 zaps per hour) with men and the affluent being more active zappers. Studies also began to demonstrate what Lewin concluded: for advertising avoidance, as with most viewing behaviors, content makes a difference. According to Pahwa (1990), a study of ad zapping during the advertising spots of the 1988 Grammy Awards showed that high profile commercials with superstar Michael Jackson dramatically reduced the zapping audience from 10% to 1–2%.

As reports of zipping and zapping studies unfolded in the industry press between 1984 and the present, the percentage of audience members engaged in RCD-based advertising avoidance at any given time appears to have decreased, while the percentage of the audience with RCD, VCR, and cable technologies necessary for such dodging has substantially increased.

Channel Changing

Although primarily focused on commercial avoidance, industry studies also examined channel changing during programming. One early study suggested that the impact of cable and RCDs on channel changing would be limited. McSherry (1985, p. 146) reported that McCann-Erickson's proprietary study based on ratings company data found that "between 1978 and 1983, channel switching has not increased significantly despite many new alternate viewing options and the proliferation of remote control devices." In particular, the percentage of the audience switching channels during an average minute of prime time was 2.5 in 1978 and 3.3 in 1983, while the percentage of daytime viewers was 3.2 in 1978 and 3.8 in 1983. This represented a 32% increase in prime time and a 19% increase in daytime channel changing, although RCD penetration had reached only 24% by 1983 (Klopfenstein, 1993).[1] The low overall percentage of channel changing led to the conclusion that channel switching would be a minimal problem through 1990. Nonetheless, RCDs were increasingly seen as an important contributor to channel changing, with flipping levels increasing 75% when an RCD enters the home (Sylvester, 1990).

RCD penetration increased rapidly from 1984 to 1989 (Klopfenstein, 1993), and advertising industry distress intensified. In a *U.S. News & World Report* article, Sanoff and Kyle (1987) noted mounting concern among advertisers, citing a study by J. Walter Thompson that a third of viewers (58 million) "are perpetual 'flippers' who use remote-control devices not only to zap commercials but also to roam the airwaves in the midst of shows, sometimes watching two or more at once" (p. 56). Males and young viewers between the ages of 18 and 24 of both genders were the most likely flippers. Once again the significance of content as a mediating factor was noted: poorly rated programs were the most affected. Sanoff and Kyle (1987, p. 56) reported that "audiences for the bottom 20 in the Nielsen ratings during the past year fell 8 percent." At the same time, viewing levels for the 10 highest rated programs grew by 5%. Near the end of the decade, with RCD penetration at 72%, Marton (1989) reported dramatic growth in channel changing. Nine percent of the prime time audience (a 273% increase since 1983) was changing channels while 16% of the prime time and 23% of the weekend sports audiences were zapping commercials.

When researchers reported the percentage of viewers using their increasingly common RCDs, the figures became even more ominous. In 1988, *Channels*, the periodical most closely identified with the second generation of television, commissioned a survey by Frank N. Magid Associates of 650 U.S. adults over 18 (out of 2460 contacted) about their use of RCDs in the new viewing environment. The results of the study were reported in the magazine (Ainslie, 1988; Alfstad, 1991) and in more detail in a booklet (*How Americans Watch TV*, 1989). The *Channels* study examined five RCD activities: using the remote control, grazing (changing the channel during a program), multiple-program viewing (following two or more programs at the same time), orienting search (flipping through the channels when they begin to view), and changing the channel during commercials. Self-report measures with percentage breakdowns by category were used to operationalize each variable. The study also reported demographic breakdowns for each of these RCD activities and reasons for grazing that will be discussed in Chapter 5.[2]

The *Channels* study indicated that a considerable percentage of viewers were actively using their RCDs, with almost 68% of respondents reporting that they used them "frequently." Another 13.2% of respondents reported that they used the RCD "sometimes," and only about 16% of respondents said they used it "rarely." Nearly half (48.5%) of the respondents who used their RCDs "frequently" or "sometimes" said they changed channels during programs (grazed). Nearly 25% of this group said they were able to follow two programs at the same time, and another 13% were able to follow three or more programs. About 40% of the frequent–sometimes RCD users flipped through the channels at the start of half or more than half of their viewing sessions. When confronting commercials, 10.5% of the total sample said they changed channels, while an even larger percentage of respondents said they leave the room (13.7%), or ignore the commercials (22.3%).[3]

Results from the *Channels* survey indicated that a high percentage of U.S. adults were frequent RCD users, with nearly half of them changing channels during programs. However, reanalysis of 1990–1991 Arbitron and Nielsen data commissioned by the Network Television Association (NTA) (Mandese, 1992b) found much less channel changing, ranging from 3.3% to 5.0% of viewers in an average 30-second period of nonprogram, primarily commercial material. Percentage of viewers flipping by daypart were as follows: daytime, 3.3; prime time, 4.1; early morning, 4.1; network news, 4.5; late night, 4.5; and weekend sports, 5.0. Carter (1991) reported that the NTA concluded what academic researchers (Walker, 1988; Davis & Walker, 1990) had suspected: network audiences were less venturesome and thus network programs were less susceptible to zapping than programs on Fox, independent television stations, and cable networks. However, advertising industry critics questioned the comparisons with cable networks, noting that "the cable channels selected for comparison are among the most zapped by viewers. ESPN and TBS, for example, carry a lot of sports programs, by far the most zapped form of programming" (p. D-6).

Arrington (1992) outlined the confrontation between traditional broadcast networks and cable industry over the extent of zapping. While broadcasters, represented by the NTA, see zapping as a straightforward erosion of inventory, cable networks can actually benefit from increased channel changing because viewers are more likely to discover new and existing cable networks if they graze (Ainslie, 1988). Grazing also is a clear indication of dissatisfaction with more traditional forms of television. Since most cable networks draw from two streams of revenue (advertising and subscriber fees), commercial avoidance is a less severe problem for cable. Thus, unlike the NTA study, results from the Cable Television Administration and Marketing Society (CTAM) study of the "restless viewers" (RVs) paints a picture of vigorous RCD use among a sizable minority (23%) of cable viewers. According to CTAM, restless viewers are "young, recently wed, and affluent" (p. 11). Forty-three percent are between 18 and 29, while 71% are under 40 with a median income larger than any viewing group. In addition, 80% of restless viewers have two or more television sets and do not plan their viewing in advance. Most restless viewers (78%) say they watch television because there is nothing better to do.

Industry researchers have come to different conclusions about the impact of RCDs on the viewing experience. There is universal recognition that RCDs have increased zipping, zapping, and channel changing. However, there is considerable disagreement about the extent or importance of that increase. Broadcast networks have argued that commercial zapping and other forms of channel changing are being practiced by less than 5% of the audience during an average minute and this represents an increase of only 2% over viewing practices in the pre-RCD era. Survey researchers, representing cable and advertising interests, find that a large majority of viewers say they use their RCDs frequently, zap ads often, and nearly half report that they change channels during programs. CTAM, the research arm of the cable industry, reports that nearly a quarter of all viewers are restless viewers, young active RCD users, developing a new way to watch television. Although these results seem incompatible, both groups may be accurately representing different parts of a larger picture.

The inconsistency of these results may simply be the consequence of very different measures of RCD use. Network researchers have defined RCD use as a percentage of the total audience changing channels, using minute by minute analyses of metered ratings data. This method indicates what percentage of the audience changes, but does not indicate how many changes occur. In addition, we do not know if just a few viewers change channels constantly or many different viewers change channels intermittently. Survey researchers have relied either on items that determine only that the respondent performs an activity (yes/no items) or that measure respondent perceptions of the relative frequency (frequently, sometimes, rarely) of the activity. Neither approach actually documented the frequency of any RCD behavior. In addition, with the exception of the *Channels* study, all of these industry studies were proprietary, which thus makes it difficult to analyze the methodological limitations of these efforts. For specific studies of the frequency of RCD activities, we will turn to scholarly evaluations.

ACADEMIC STUDIES OF RCD USE

As noted earlier, academic researchers work under certain restrictions—having only limited samples in particular—but are free to experiment with new methods. Researchers have applied a variety of methods to the study of RCD use, including questionnaires (Ferguson, 1994; Ferguson, 1992; Ferguson & Perse, 1994; Greene, 1988; Walker & Bellamy, 1991a; Walker et al., 1993), direct observation (Eastman & Newton, 1995; Krendl et al., 1993), video or audio recording of viewing (Cornwell et al., 1993; Cronin & Menelly, 1992; Sapolsky & Forrest, 1989), and electronic recording of RCD use (Bryant & Rockwell, 1993; Heeter et al., 1993; Heeter et al., 1988; Ferguson, 1994; Kaye & Sapolsky, 1995).

Academic researchers have studied television commercial avoidance through zapping and zipping, the frequency of several types of specific RCD behaviors and, through a variety of methods, how often viewers change the channel. First, we will examine advertising avoidance, then the various approaches used to measure channel changing and related RCD behaviors.

Advertising Avoidance

In a survey of viewers in the United Kingdom with RCDs, VCRs, or both devices, York and Kitchen (1985) found that a substantial percentage of viewers reported both zipping and zapping commercials. Using a sample from four different neighborhoods, they found that only 9% "admitted to viewing commercial breaks when watching a recorded program from a commercial channel" (p. 23). Depending on the neighborhood, 53% to 80% claimed to zip recorded commercials, while 47% to 80% said they zipped the last time they had viewed a commercial break. RCD use was extensive as well; about 32% (the four groups' average) participated in orienting searches, 54% were highly likely or quite likely to zap commercials at programs breaks, and 23% were highly likely or quite likely to zap commercials at midprogram breaks.

Dividing their respondents into non-zappers (those who report no zapping at all) and zappers (those reporting some zapping), Heeter and Greenberg (1988b) summarized the results from their studies of adults and children. Although this two-category (zapper/nonzapper) system restricted the degree of variation among respondents, clear patterns of advertising avoidance still emerged. Men zapped more than women and the young zapped more than the old. In addition, zapping was clearly related to a pattern of viewing that involves less planning, less habitual viewing of programs, more background viewing, and more channel changing in general. Although there was no measurement of the amount of RCD use, just the ownership of an RCD had a modest affect on zapping: 34% of commercial zappers had RCDs, while 27% of nonzappers owned the device. Heeter and Greenberg predicted that zapping will be a growing problem for advertisers:

> More viewers will have some form of remote-control capability; more viewers will have VCRs and use them as a personal editor; child viewers will have matured with multichannel systems; and changing channels will be as natural to them as non-changing is to their grandparents. (p. 73)

In a study that compares noncable to cable viewers (30% and 70%, respectively), VCR to non-VCR viewers (50% and 50%), and RCD to non-RCD viewers (52% and 48%), Greene (1988) found that 10.8% of males and 6.1% of females said they channel switched during more than half the commercial interruptions, while 18.2% of males and 13.7% of females said they channel switched during at least some of the commercial breaks. In addition, 26% of males and 15% of females reported fast-for-warding (zipping) over commercials on programs recorded the previous evening. Respondents who channel switched (a combination of those that zapped during more than half the commercial interruptions and those that zapped during some interruptions) had commercial-recall scores that were 3% lower than those who did not (21.1% vs. 18.1%). However, commercial recall was higher in general in cable households, and there was almost no difference in the recall scores of those who owned RCDs and those who did not. Greene suggested that those without RCDs and/or cable were more likely to seek other distractions at commercial breaks (reading, leaving the room, talking, resting). Also, when a person switches the channel or zips, their attention is on the set, so they do actually attend to the commercials that they see.

In an observational study of VCR use, Sapolsky and Forrest (1989) examined the use of RCDs to zip through commercials. An episode of *The Cosby Show* with researcher-selected commercials inserted was viewed individually by 29 male and 57 female undergraduates, and 19 male and 16 female adults. The adults zipped an average 65.0% of the commercials embedded in the program, while the undergraduates zipped 20.2% of the ads. As in the study of commercial breaks during the 1988 Grammy Awards, there was considerable variation in the percentage of subjects zipping particular ads, ranging from 8 to 30.1% for the undergraduates and from 47.1 to 75.7% for the adults. Also, as in industry research ("How to Avoid," 1984), there was more zipping during commercial breaks placed later in the program.

In two later studies, Cronin and Menelly (1992) found that over 60% of commercials embedded in taped episodes of M*A*S*H were zipped. Nine out of 10 commercials were zipped as part of entire blocks of commercials. Thus, in most cases, viewers did not select specific commercials to avoid. The researchers videotaped the zipping behavior of 32 undergraduates in a laboratory setting and used an audiotape recorder to monitor zipping practice by 83 adult, nonstudent subjects while viewing in their own homes. The undergraduates watched only 25% of the commercials in their entirety, while the adults watched only 38.1% of the ads. Of the adult respondents, those under 40 were significantly more likely to zip ads than those 40 and over. As with earlier studies, the last commercial pod was zipped more frequently than earlier pods in the program.

Molitor's (1992) survey of 158 undergraduates found that self-reported avoidance of television commercials increases with the technological capacity of the viewing equipment. Ad avoidance increased in the following pattern of technological ownership:

TV only is less than
↓
TV with RCD which is less than
↓
TV/VCR which is less than
↓
TV/VCR with scan (viewing at rapid speed) which is less than
↓
TV with RCD/VCR with RCD which is less than
↓
TV with RCD/VCR with scan which is less than
↓
TV with RCD/VCR with RCD and scan.

Commercial avoidance and technological capacity were significantly and positively related; as capacity increased so did commercial avoidance. Molitor predicted that as VCR owners become more familiar with their technology they will use it more to avoid ads.

Although the generalizability of their study was limited by a small convenience sample, Moriarty and Everett (1994) found evidence of substantial channel changing, especially during commercial breaks, in an observational study of 55 individual and group viewing sessions of 45 minutes each. Trained graduate student observers recorded viewer responses to commercial and program breaks. The researchers found that the two most active categories of viewing, flipping (rapid changes lasting less than three seconds) and grazing (browsing through channels), were dominant in 57% of the viewing sessions. In addition, participants changed channels during 61% of the commercial breaks between programs and 46% of the blocks during programs.

To summarize, academic studies of advertising avoidance show a clear trend toward using RCD technology when available to zip and zap commercials. Both self-report studies (York & Kitchen, 1985; Greene, 1988) and observational studies (Sapolsky & Forrest, 1989) of zipping document substantial avoidance of recorded commercials, ranging from approximately 20% to 80% of ads zipped, with a 60% figure the most common estimate. Viewers were slightly less likely than that to use RCDs to zap commercials, but approximately a quarter of the respondents of one study said they zapped some ads (Greene, 1988), while subjects in an observational study (Moriarty & Everett, 1994) zapped 46% of the commercial blocks during programs and 61% of the blocks between programs. Ad avoidance also increased when an RCD was added to a viewer's technological arsenal (Heeter & Greenberg, 1988b; Molitor, 1992).

Channel Changing

Given the failure of industry research to document the exact frequency of RCD activity, we will concentrate on academic studies that report frequencies of channel changing. These studies are summarized in Table 2.1. Heeter, D'Alessio, Greenberg, and McVoy (1988) overcame the small sample sizes that characterize most observational studies by using a computer analysis of the viewing of 197 households, equipped with RCDs linked to a 34-channel cable system. The cable system's computer monitored the viewing time and channel selection at one-minute intervals for viewing reported over three weekdays. Changes occurring within one-minute frames were not counted. They found an average of 4.4 channel changes per-hour per household with great per hour variations among channel types (networks = 3.0, pay movie channels = 4.5, superstations = 5.3, independents = 4.8, general satellite = 6.7, automated = 10.0, PBS = 6.0, specialized satellite = 8.5, access = 4.5). The mean number of channel changes per hour was 5.5 for cable-only channels versus 3.1 for broadcast channels (nets and PBS). Channel changing peaked between 57 minutes after the hour and 7 minutes after the next hour, with other peaks at the half hour.

Ferguson (1992) employed a single-item measure of channel changing in a phone survey of 583 adults in a university town, asking respondents, "During a typical hour of TV viewing yesterday, how often did you change the channel?" The mean number of changes per hour was 4.92 (SD = 5.75, range = 0–50). As with Brown (1989), RCD use (used RCD in previous viewing day) was related to increased channel repertoire (M = 5.50 channels vs. 3.9 channels for non-RCD users). In more rigorous hierarchical regressions, Ferguson also found that RCD use was a significant predictor of increased channel repertoire. However, RCD motivations (reasons for using the RCD, such as avoiding boredom, avoiding ads or people you don't like, and seeing two or more shows at the same time) were an even stronger predictor. Indeed, motivations appeared to be more important in predicting repertoire than just having or using an RCD.

In a laboratory experiment, Bryant and Rockwell (1993) electronically recorded the channel changing of 80 subjects (40 males and 40 females) under four conditions: no RCD, an RCD with only an on/off

TABLE 2.1. Frequency of RCD Activity: Summary of Academic Studies

Study	Measurement method	Sample	Length of observation	RCD activity	RCD uses per hour
Heeter et al., 1988	Computer monitoring of behavior	197 house-holds with RCDS	3 days per household	Channel changes per 1-minute interval	M = 4.4
Ferguson, 1992	Self-report item	583 adults, 75% with RCDs	Typical hour of viewing	Channel changes	M = 4.92; SD = 5.75
Bryant & Rockwell, 1993	Electronic recording of behavior	40 adults with RCDs	30 minutes per subject	Channel changes	M = 6.75[*]
Cornwell et al., 1993	Observation of taped behavior	6 females; 9 males; 1 child with RCDs	122 hours total for all subjects	Channel changes, muting, turning set on or off	M = 13.7[*] with subjects in TV room
Ferguson, 1994	Electronic recording of behavior; self-report item	30 male and 19 female students with RCDs	60 minutes per subject	Channel changes per 1.6-second interval; hourly changes on the previous day	M = 107; SD = 82,5 for recorder. M = 38.5; SD = 53 for survey item.
Kaye, 1994; Kaye & Sapolsky, 1995	Electronic monitoring; questionnaire	44 partici-pants in 23 households	4 days	Channel changes	M = 36.6; SD = 41.3 for recorder. M = 4.8 for survey item.
Eastman & Newton, 1995	Observation of in-home behavior	44 group and 115 nongroup sessions with RCDs	3 hours of prime time per session	Punching, arrowing, jumping, scanning, inserting, muting	M = 6.83[*]

[*]Calculated from data in the authors' results.

switch and no channel-changing capacity, an RCD with on/off and ten-button random channel access, and an RCD with on/off, random access and volume control. Programming choices were limited to nine channels (three entertainment, e.g., sitcoms; three educational, e.g., science programs; and three informational, e.g., news programs). The 40 subjects with an RCD capable of channel changing averaged 6.75 changes per hour, a figure 78% higher than respondents with no RCD or one without channel-changing capacity.

Cornwell et al. (1993) videotaped and coded the RCD activities of 16 users in both individual and group viewing situations. The RCD was used (to change channels, mute, turn the set on/off) an average of once every 4.4 minutes (13.7 uses per hour) when RCD users were in the television viewing room. Males used the device once every 5.7 minutes (10.5 uses per hour) and females once every 5.2 minutes (11.5 uses per hour). The unexpected higher rate of RCD use by females was probably caused by the high level of activity observed in one particular woman who lived alone. Zapping, defined as switching from a commercial at any point prior to its final three seconds, occurred an average of once every 11.2 minutes of viewing commercials (5.4 times per hour of commercials). Cornwell et al. found that "on average, the RCD was used every 10.0 program minutes and every 8.7 commercial minutes" (p. 51).

Although others have criticized the reliability of self-report measures of RCD use (Cornwell et al., 1993; Eastman & Newton, 1995), Ferguson (1994) measured their reliability when compared to electronic recordings of RCD use and found that survey items seem to offer conservative estimates of channel changing. Measuring RCD use at intervals of 1.6 seconds, Ferguson's electronic counting device clocked a mean of 107 (SD = 85.5) changes per hour among 49 broadcast research students during hour-long individual viewings of a 40-channel cable television system. The mean for the self-reported exact estimate was 38.5 changes (SD = 53.0). Correlation with an exact (e.g., 15 times per hour) self-report estimate was .52. The correlation with a nine-point "never" to "always" item was .54, while it was .63 (40% of variance accounted for) with a nine-point "never" to "almost constantly" item. Although limited in both sample size and variety, this study provided the first direct correlation between self-reported and observed RCD use and suggests that self-report measures may underestimate RCD use.

Employing a similar approach over an extended period, Kaye and Sapolsky (1995) used microcontrollers connected to cable converter boxes in 23 cable-equipped households in order to monitor electronically the channel changing of 44 participants for over 374 hours of television viewing. Like Ferguson (1994), they also asked their participants to estimate their frequency of channel changing. The researchers' electronic assessment produced an average of 36.6 channel changes per hour, while self-report estimates yielded only 4.8 channel changes per hour. The electronic assessment also yielded great variation among viewers (SD = 41.3).

Using viewing style categories adapted from Heeter et al. (1988), the authors reported that 94.8% of the channel changes occurred during the 8.3% of viewing time that participants were scanning (watching for less than 4 minutes), while only 2.7% of changes occurred during the 12.7% of time involving extended sampling (watching between 4 and 15 minutes), and 2.5% of changes occurred during the 79% of time devoted to stretch viewing (watching for more than 15 minutes). Further analysis showed that 80.1% of all changes occurred after less than five seconds on a channel. This "rapid fire" viewing accounted for only 0.9% of overall viewing time.

Using a similar method over a greater period of viewing, Kaye and Sapolsky's (1995) study confirms Ferguson's (1994) results. When all channel changes are measured, the frequency is high, the differences among viewers is vast, and the viewers are likely to underestimate grossly the number of times they click the clicker. However, 80% of channel changes occur during rapid-fire viewing lasting less than five seconds. As did Heeter et al. (1988), the authors found that most viewing (79%) is in units of 15 minutes or longer, but over 20% of viewing time involved program segments of less than a quarter hour.

Finally, Eastman and Newton (1995) assigned 159 students to observe 115 nongroup and 44 group viewing situations (83% in homes/apartments, 15% in dorm or fraternity/sorority rooms) during three hours of prime time. Eighty-seven percent of respondents reported that the situation was unaffected by the observer's presence for more than the first few minutes of observation. The observers recorded six RCD behaviors: punching (channel changing by keying in a specific channel number), arrowing (channel changing by continuously pressing an up or down arrow to get to a predetermined channel), jumping (channel changing by using a "previous channel" button), inserting (placing more than one channel on the screen), scanning or grazing (changing channels by using the up/down arrow slowly enough to take a look at sequential channels), and muting (cutting off and later restoring sound).

During the 469 hours of observation, 3,204 RCD operations were recorded. Recalculation of the results shows that there was an average of 6.83 RCD uses per hour broken down by behavior as follows: punching,

1.87; arrowing, 1.83; jumping, 1.02; inserting, 0.12; scanning, 1.51; muting, 0.49. Males had higher levels of RCD activity: 47% of the men were high RCD users, as opposed to only 17% of the women. Older adults (45–64) used the RCD less than younger adults (18–44). In addition, 57% of the channel changes took place between the last five and first five minutes of the hour. Only sports (higher) and movies on pay-cable channels (lower) show different levels of total RCD activity.

Limitations of Academic Studies of Channel Changing

The variety of approaches taken in the seven academic studies discussed above provides some baseline measures of RCD activity. Of these studies, four (Cornwell et al., 1993; Eastman & Newton, 1995; Ferguson, 1994; Kaye & Sapolsky, 1995) had as primary missions the measurement of RCD activities. Studies that have reported specific frequencies, which can be calculated as uses per hour, have, with two exceptions (Ferguson, 1994, M = 107; Kaye & Sapolsky, 1995, M = 36.6), found frequencies between 4.4 and 13.7 per hour. However, each study had limitations that could have reduced or increased estimates of RCD use. We will examine each of these.

As Greenberg and Heeter (1988, p. 294) note, the estimate of 4.4 channel changes per hour reported in their electronic assessment study is almost certainly a conservative figure because only channel changes occurring at one-minute intervals were recorded by the cable system's computer. Many unreported channel changes may have occurred between one-minute sampling periods. Although the study is based on a relatively large sample of cable/RCD households monitored over three days, the computerized system used is best suited to providing comparisons of channel changing levels for various services or time periods (the focus of Heeter et al.'s study) rather than estimates of total RCD activity.

Ferguson (1992) benefited from the largest sample of any RCD use study, but relied on a single self-report item, raising concern about measurement reliability. His later study (Ferguson, 1994), correlating self-report estimates, suggests that the self-reported mean of 4.92 channel changes per hour may be lower than the actual figure. Also, only 75% of the respondents had RCDs, which should lower the mean level of channel changing.

Using a controlled laboratory experiment, Bryant and Rockwell's (1993) study more clearly documented the impact of RCDs. Subjects with RCDs capable of changing channels produced 78% higher levels of RCD use than subjects without that capacity. However, the 6.75 channel changes per hour (calculated from the authors' results) may be a low estimate, because of the small sample size, the artificiality of the viewing situation (a public waiting room, rather than a private home), and the limited variety of content (three major types on nine channels). Entertainment choices, in particular, were considerably less varied than in the typical cable viewing situation. This lack of choice may have reduced the frequency of channel changing. In addition, comparing the RCD to non-RCD groups in an experiment does not fully show the effect of the RCD. The non-RCD group in the experiment may have grown accustomed to making more channel changes because they regularly use an RCD at home in their natural viewing environment. Conversely, the absence of other viewers may have increased channel changing.

Cornwell et al. (1993) relied on careful observations of videotape viewing over a substantial (122) number of hours, but from a very limited number of respondents (16). Thus, the generalizability of their findings is clearly questionable.

Eastman and Newton (1995) benefited from a relatively large sample (159) that reported both group and individual three-hour viewing sessions. However, their data was gathered by 159 different undergraduate students with no interobserver reliability, raising concern about the accuracy of measurement across so many observers. They also reported a decrease in RCD use over the course of the viewing session, which may represent observer fatigue expressed in less frequent recording of RCD activity or actual decreases in RCD use. Although a self-report item indicated only 13% of the observed viewers believed it to be a problem, the observers were known by the respondents, and that familiarity, coupled with the typical problem of observer influence, may have reduced RCD use, an activity with some negative connotations (e.g., low attention span, "couch-potato" viewing).

Ferguson's (1994) observation of a mean of 107 channel changes per hour and Kaye and Sapolsky's mean of 36.6 channel changes per hour are the clear outlyers among these studies. Ferguson used a small number of students (49) from a broadcast research class, a potentially highly active and unrepresentative sample; although Kaye and Sapolsky's sample was more representative, it also was limited in size (44). However, the best explanation for the abundant RCD use found in these studies comes from the units of measure used. By either counting all channel changes or all changes that resulted in viewing of at least 1.6 seconds, these authors come closest to defining RCD activity as the number of button pushes per hour, which, (as we've argued earlier) could be as high as 3,600 per hour. Other studies have used longer measurement intervals (Heeter et al., 1988), respondent-defined definitions of channel changing (Ferguson, 1992), or defined RCD activities that may include many button changes in each activity (Cornwell et al., 1993; Eastman & Newton, 1995). Thus, part of the explanation for the sometimes extreme variations in RCD activity stem from the variations in what is being measured.[4]

CONCLUSION

Because of the limitations outlined above, we still do not have a single definitive evaluation of the frequency of RCD activity, although Ferguson's (1994) and Kaye and Sapolsky's (1995) electronic monitoring did yield the most accurate count of channel changes. Given the long measurement interval used by Heeter et al. (1988) and the likely underreporting of RCD use in the survey item used by Ferguson (1992) (the studies reporting the lowest mean channel changes per hour), it is likely that mean RCD use, as measured by sequences of RCD activities rather than each channel change, is at least at the levels of nearly seven consequential (perceived as a program shift by the viewer) changes per hour reported by Bryant and Rockwell (1993) and Eastman and Newton (1995). If all channel changes are used as the unit of measure the figure would be much higher, although probably closer to Kaye and Sapolsky's 36.6 per hour than Ferguson's 107 changes per hour (drawn from a unrepresentative sample and observed in an artificial environment).

Seven consequential RCD uses per hour is substantially more than would be needed to view television during its first generation. In an RCD-less world of three commercial networks and a handful of independent stations, channel changing could be limited to dial clicking at the conclusion of programs (although tuning inertia would prevent this from occurring at every program break). This might produce one or two sequences of channel changing per hour. A figure of even seven per hour suggests that RCDs in conjunction with cable and VCRs have substantially increased the mean frequency of channel changing. However, to adequately describe the nature of RCD activity it is necessary to examine more than just mean frequency.

Although reported in only three studies measuring exact frequency of RCD use (Ferguson, 1992; Ferguson, 1994; Kaye & Sapolsky, 1995) and in several studies measuring relative RCD use (Walker & Bellamy, 1991a; Wenner & Dennehy, 1993; Walker et al., 1993), the standard deviations for most forms of RCD use were particularly large (see Table 2.1). This suggests that many of the viewers who were studied varied greatly from the mean frequency of RCD use, a finding consistent with industry studies, which have concluded that RCD use is concentrated in an active minority of viewers, dubbed restless viewers by CTAM (Arrington, 1992). The majority of RCD users may employ the device more or less as it was intended: turn the set on and off, change channels at the conclusion of a program, adjust the sound to comfortable levels, and occasionally skip an ad or two. However, a substantial percentage of viewers deviate from the norm; they are the active zippers, zappers, and grazers. These restless viewers appear to be younger and more likely to be male, and their activity increases when they view in isolation.[5]

Restless viewers appear to account for the majority of RCD activity, but they are clearly a minority of viewers. Heeter et al. (1988) analyzed three types of viewing: string viewing (viewing a channel between 1 and 4 minutes), encompassing 8% of all viewing and 64% of all channel changes; ministretch viewing (viewing a channel between 4 and 15 minutes), equalling 9.9% of all viewing and 16% of all channel changes; and stretch viewing (viewing a channel for more than 15 minutes), occupying 82% of viewing and 20% of all channel changes. Although channel changes during intervals of less than one minute were not recorded, these figures show that only one-fifth of all channel changes occur during program-length viewing, while nearly two-thirds of all changes occur in viewing segments of less than four minutes. Subsequent research by Kaye and Sapolsky (1995) yielded very similar results. Grazers appear to account for much of the RCD activity, even if they are only a minority of viewers.

From this detailed examination of both industrial and academic studies of RCD use, we conclude the following:

1. Currently, RCD activity appears to average at least seven consequential uses per hour. If every channel change is measured, this figure grows dramatically, with the best estimate of over 35 changes per hour.
2. An active, substantial minority of RCD users, about one-fifth of viewers, account for the majority of RCD use.[6]
3. Viewers change channels substantially more often (an increase of 70% in one study and 75% in another) with an RCD than without one.
4. RCDs promote zapping, which affects between 5% and 20% of commercials (although some studies report much higher figures). At least 30% of males and 20% of females engage in some zapping.

5. RCDs promote the zipping of commercials in recorded programs, which, depending on the study, affects 20% to 80% of commercials taped.

6. For zapping, the content of advertising makes a difference. Some commercials are 5 to 10 times less likely to be zapped than others. However, zipping is more likely to take place in blocks with all commercials in a particular block avoided.

7. The impact of current RCD technology is likely to stabilize, since RCD penetration is approaching 100%. However, RCD use may increase gradually as viewers who were socialized during the first generation of television are replaced by viewers who have been raised in the second generation.

8. The levels of RCD use documented here are based on a technology limited to three basic actions: turning the set on or off, channel changing, and volume control. As newer technologies diffuse and as "smart" RCDs replace "dumb" ones (Heeter et al., 1993), RCD use may increase considerably.

Given the variety of approaches to measuring RCD use, it seems unlikely that the academic community will form a consensus in the near future about the best method for measuring both RCD behaviors and their significance to viewers. Perhaps this is just as well, as each new approach increases our understanding of RCD use and addresses some of the limitations of prior methods. What is clear from previous research is that the RCD is used by most viewers and is heavily used by a substantial minority of viewers to redefine the nature of television viewing. We now turn our attention to reactions of the media institutions most affected by these new restless viewers: the advertising and television industries (Chapters 3 and 4).

NOTES

1. In addition, many of the RCDs in use at this time were employed to control VCRs and, typically, not to tune televisions.

2. Since only relative categories (frequently, sometimes, rarely or yes/no) were used, the study did not provide specific measures of the frequency of any of the RCD activities. The low response rate also is a concern, because the results only reflect the activities of viewers most interested in discussing their viewing activities. However, the *Channels* study used a nationwide stratified sample and is the only industry-sponsored study to offer detailed reports on both method and results.

3. In addition to industry surveys, various public opinion polls have asked questions concerning zipping, zapping, and RCD use. From these polls, Mayer (1994) reports the following (the year of the study is in brackets):

   a. Percent that usually zip/zap VCR-recorded commercials: 48% [1984], 46% [1985], 37% [1987].

   b. Percent of RCD owners that use the remote to zap ads or turn the volume off during ads: 24% [1990].

   c. Percent that frequently turn down (mute) sound during commercials: 35% [1987].

   d. Percent of RCD owners that do the following fairly often: flip to other channels (37%), turn down the sound (18%), or flip to other channels from time to time during a program they are watching (19%) [1988].

   e. Percent of RCD owners that use the remote to switch back and forth between programs all of the time: 31% [1990].

4. We suggest an approach that could overcome the problems of sample size and representativeness, observer influence, artificiality of viewing situation, and reliability of measurement, and that would allow analysis/interpretation of the product of the RCD activity. We know that by 1992 VCRs had penetrated 77% of U.S. households (Klopfenstein, 1993) and that most VCRs today are equipped with RCDs that control the television as well as the VCR. With such devices we could record the viewing choices of a representative national or local sample of VCR owners simply by having them tape as they watch. Subjects would only need to be willing to tune their televisions through their VCR RCDs and to record their viewing for a representative period of time. Once their viewing had been recorded, content analysis could be used to determine not only the frequency of channel changes, but patterns of channel changing and the specific content that triggers and stops RCD activity. Differences in viewing activity during programming and nonprogramming, as well as during different time periods, could be identified. Because the VCR recordings would provide a permanent record of results of the RCD activities, they could be analyzed in a variety of ways and address different theoretical issues.

   A variant of this approach was used in a qualitative study with a limited sample. In a phenomenological study of RCD use, Traudt (1993) had a small convenience sample of RCD users tape two hours of their viewing. The respondents then reviewed and commented upon their RCD actions during a follow-up session with the researcher. These comments formed the basis of Traudt's analysis.

   Although considerable resources would be needed for videotapes, assistance in equipment set up, and coding, it would be possible to generate samples considerably larger and more representative than those used in most previous studies, and observations would be conducted with a less obtrusive apparatus. However, only RCD activities related to channel changing could be examined using this approach. Using the RCD to turn the set on or off or to adjust or mute sound could not be studied.

5. This pattern of heavy use by a small minority of viewers is common in studies of communication systems. As Rogers (1986, p. 125) notes "a common finding in research on new communication systems is that only 10 percent of the users represent 50 percent of all uses, with the other 90 percent of users making up the other 50 percent of uses."

6. Our survey research has also found similar percentages among adults who report they change channels very often. In a San Francisco phone survey of 209 adults (Walker, 1991), 17.7% of the viewers reported they changed channels very often and 26.1% claimed to be flipping from channel to channel at least half of their viewing time. The results from a phone survey of 315 Pittsburgh adults (Walker et al., 1993) were similiar: 13.3% reported changing channels very often and 16.7% flipped more than half the time.

CHAPTER 3

Zapped into Action
ADVERTISING INDUSTRY
RESPONSE TO RCD DIFFUSION

Despite the fact that there is no agreed upon measure of individual remote control use, there can be no doubt about the genuine alarm that the diffusion of the RCD has caused in the advertising industry and, by extension, the entire electronic media industry. This concern is likely to increase as more television channels become available to the audience, and as the children and youth of today replace the present adult viewers. As we show in Chapter 5, younger viewers have a higher propensity to graze and, even more problematic for the advertising industry, advertising avoidance is one of the more valued gratifications of grazing.

Consumer technologies that allow the user more control over the television viewing experience are becoming available. For example, programmable RCDs that will automatically seek specific program categories and avoid advertising are likely to be available in the near future (Heeter, Yoon, & Sampson, 1993). Already available is the "Commercial Brake," a device that marks commercials while they are being recorded on a VCR and then replaces them with a blue screen that automatically fast-forwards during playback. This consumer device is being marketed to VCR manufacturers as an add-on feature (Blankenhorn, 1994). Such advertising avoidance technologies seem likely to become common features of VCRs and RCDs, causing further concern in the advertising industry. Advertising avoidance has, in fact, long been a selling point for RCDs. As discussed in Chapter 1, it was a primary impetus for Zenith's development of the seminal Space Commander RCD-equipped television set. Advertising for this system stated that all it would take was "just a touch of the button to shut off the sound of long, annoying commercials" ("Viewers Add," 1992, p. 10).

The purpose of this chapter is to categorize and analyze the reaction of the advertising industry to the second generation of television viewers/users. We will concentrate on both the industry's evolving perceptions of the RCD-wielding viewer's power and how she or he affects the business of advertising, and on the specific strategies that have been implemented to combat or minimize the level of control available to the viewer. We will also examine arguments within the advertising industry over whether combatting the television viewer/user is even the appropriate strategy to adopt.

The issue of advertising avoidance is fundamental to the working of the U.S. mass media economy. Advertising has subsidized most U.S. media products for over 150 years. The relationship between advertiser and consumer traditionally has been one in which the advertiser picked up much of the overt cost of media content and its delivery in exchange for the consumer's assumed attention to the included advertising (Peppers & Rogers, 1994; Turow, 1992a, pp. 59–62). This advertising subsidy allowed publishers to price their newspapers and magazines below the actual costs of production and distribution and allowed radio and television broadcasting to be offered at no direct cost to the audience. The oligopolistic nature of most media markets and the general lack of other (e.g., public) funding models served to limit alternatives to this system. In return for their patronage, mass media advertisers received access to audiences that had access to a limited number of media outlets. They also gained vast influence and, in some cases, near control over the content of the editorial or programming matter that framed their advertisements (Barnouw, 1978; Sterling & Kittross, 1990). Therefore, the advertiser is both the client and customer of mass media distribution outlets and, quiet often, the major influence on the content that attracts (produces) the audience (see Chapter 1).

The symbiotic mass media–advertising relationship has withstood several periods of technological diffusion to reach its present status. A product itself of technological diffusion and the development of market economies, the relationship adjusted to the diffusion of television, for example, by reconfiguring radio as a local specialized medium (see Chapters 1 and 4) and magazines as a national specialized medium. Rather than leading to the demise of existing media as advertising vehicles, each round of technological diffusion increased the outlets for advertising and allowed it to take on more specialized forms.

Despite this history of adaptation, many observers today believe mass media advertising to be in decline, because the mass media audience has become so fragmented (Martinez, 1994; Rouvalis, 1994; Schrage, Peppers, Rogers, Shapiro, & Dix, 1994). Even those who are not willing to take such a radical position posit that the latest round of technological diffusion, which has encompassed the RCD, has forever changed the way advertising, and particularly television advertising, must be produced and disseminated (Mahler, 1991; McAllister, 1993). Both viewpoints see the increased number of media outlets, especially the increased power of the media consumer to avoid advertising content, as critical issues, because you can not persuade people to buy something if they do not attend to your message.

While the RCD has enabled many people to avoid advertising messages, such avoidance must be placed in perspective. The reality is that advertising avoidance is a problem of long standing for all commercial media. For example, print advertisers long have been honing their strategies for attracting reader attention and interest. These strategies concern both placement within a newspaper or magazine and placement of copy and pictorial matter within the advertisement. In magazines, such techniques usually are combined with specific demographic appeals to ensure that the advertising message reaches the intended recipients. Although direct response techniques (e.g., coupons) easily can be integrated into print advertising, the answers to most questions about whether or not such advertising reaches its intended audience are based on increases in sales, research studies of advertising recall, and, primarily, circulation figures (Arens & Bovée, 1994). As in the case of radio and later television, circulation was supposed to "prove" that the audience was exposed to the advertisement. The question left unanswered for much print advertising was whether or not the intended audience saw or paid attention to the advertisement. There are, in fact, no generally accepted ways of measuring the effectiveness of advertisements. The only exception is the direct-response advertisement, which can only supply information about those who actually respond, but not those who develop an impression of the advertised product or service and fail to respond immediately (Arens & Bovée, 1994; Stewart, 1992).

Although there has been some discussion of how new electronic forms of communication will impact print advertising, much more is being written about how the new forms will affect electronic and, especially, television advertising. One reason for this is that television has been regarded as the primary method of mass national advertising since the 1950s. The homogeneous nature of much television programming, compared to the demographically specific appeal or local appeal of other competing media, makes television's ability to cope with the "new age" more problematic (Halonen, 1992b; Mermigas, 1992c). However, of greater importance is the nature of the television medium itself and the biases that the advertising industry and the audience have long had about it.

From the time of radio's rapid diffusion into U.S. households, the inherent nature of electronic media advertising has been a controversial issue (Barnouw, 1978; McChesney, 1993). Print advertising has been regarded as relatively benign, except for the excesses of patent medicine and certain other forms of advertising that led to the Pure Food and Drug and Federal Trade Acts. But from the start, electronic advertising was regarded as too intrusive and too personal to be sent uninvited into listener's homes. Although the advertising and broadcast industries quickly overcame any qualms they had about radio advertising once it became clear that it allowed for new forms of effective advertising in a programming milieu that advertisers could dominate, public criticism of advertising grew as radio became more ubiquitous (Barnouw, 1978). The advent of the sound-and-motion medium of television, while proving to offer another winning outlet for mass advertising, came under even more criticism. As previously discussed, even electronics industry pioneer Eugene McDonald (of Zenith) was a primary opponent of the commercialization of television, although his longtime interest in the development of pay television partly explains his bias (Bellamy, 1988).

While national advertisers flocked to television to replace radio and magazines in reaching a mass national audience, they expressed qualms about the nature of the medium and its audience. In addition to the great expense of buying television time and producing television advertising, the medium was seen as one with lots of waste and clutter. From the outset, the advertising community believed that television reached too many viewers that were of little if any interest to many advertisers, and that the number of advertisements and other non-program material (i.e., promotions, credits, station breaks) was so great that advertisements could get lost in the clutter (Arens & Bovée, 1994). Another factor in the tensions between advertisers and television was that the control of programming, which is the framework for advertising, shifted to the television industry and away from the advertisers, a decided contrast to the model in radio (see Chapter 1).

As long as there were few, if any, alternatives to television advertising for the many products that needed to reach a mass and generally homogeneous audience, such commonly voiced concerns led to no action. Television's great appeal and its ability to promote the sale of products and services was undisputed. The system worked for the vast majority of advertisers. Although advertisers constantly griped about the cost and effectiveness of television advertising, it was too easy, too available, and too popular to give up, especially in the face of competitors who used the medium more and more. Advertisers developed techniques and conventions to increase the likelihood that viewers would notice and respond to their advertising, just as print advertisers had done. For example, advertisers carefully selected the dayparts and the programs in which they wished their advertisements to appear. They adopted certain modes of production and content to attract audience attention. For example, the Young & Rubicam agency taught its employees that the "one, inviolate rule" of television advertising was "AQRI" or "arouse quick related interest" (Norins, 1990, p. 99). The theory is that as television is a transient medium, with audience members constantly coming and going, the advertiser can waste no time in grabbing the interest of the audience with material that relates directly to the viewer's own life or experience (Norins, 1990, pp. 98–99). Although the AQRI approach was specific to Young & Rubicam, such conventions were generally accepted among all advertising agencies, and they became the conventional wisdom in television advertising. Thus, concern about audience inattentiveness existed in television even before the recent rapid diffusion of RCDs.

In fact, the zapping of commercials with the RCD has been mentioned as only one of the three types of zapping that affect television. Time-shifting through the use of a VCR, with the expectation that the taped commercials will be zipped on playback, has been categorized as another type of zapping (Fountas, 1985). However, the most prevalent and important form of zapping has been said to be physical zapping, whereby the viewer leaves the room or attends to something besides the television set when advertising comes on (Abernethy & Rotfield, 1991; Fountas, 1985). Fountas (1985), for example, reported that physical zapping was practiced by 30–40% of the television audience. The widespread acknowledgment of physical zapping among media buyers and sellers is reflected in such trade advertisements as that for the (Portland) *Oregonian* newspaper, which showed the toilet and the refrigerator along with the RCD as reasons that advertising on television is wasteful (Arens & Bovée, 1994, p. 554). The fact that some people do not attend to television, and especially television advertising, is the basis of long-standing criticisms of both television ratings and the effectiveness of television advertising.

Recent concern about television's effectiveness as an advertising medium, therefore, is partly a more intense manifestation of long-standing concerns in the advertising community. Since many of the changes in mass media are most evident in television, the brunt of the attacks on conventional media advertising have been directed toward television. The first realization that the RCD, the VCR, and cable were permanently changing television and its relationship to the viewer and advertiser occurred in the early to mid-1980s.

THE "PANIC" AND SUGGESTIONS FOR RELIEF

As detailed in Chapter 2, by 1984, the advertising and television industries were devoting considerable resources to measuring grazing behavior, as they began to recognize that RCD diffusion was a serious concern. As one would expect with an "invisible" technology like the RCD, the concern primarily revolved around the manner in which viewers were using RCDs with their VCRs. A statement from the J. Walter Thompson agency referred to zapping as the "topic of the year" (Kessler, 1985, p. 68).[1]

The Zapping Problem

While some industry figures claimed that zapping was a relatively minor problem and that VCR time shifting even produced a bonus audience, the general tone was one of considerable concern about the impact of zapping (Mermigas, 1984). Suggestions generated from a 1984 symposium included calls for more advertising-industry-supported research, the development of separate program and advertising ratings, the elimination of VCR viewing from ratings data that determine television pricing, a recognition on the part of sellers that the value of time had decreased due to zapping, the development of more creative programming and advertising, and experimentation with new forms of advertising (Lewin, 1988).

Vested interests such as the Television Bureau of Advertising (TBA) claimed that zapping was not a problem ("How to Avoid," 1984), and others claimed that further research was unnecessary because the movement of products was the ultimate determinant of zapping's impact ("Zappers," 1984). But the general view in the industry was expressed by Kostyra (1984) who claimed that zapping "looms as an uncontrollable and potentially commercially devastating force" (p. 94).

The chorus of concern continued with Martens's (1985) claim that "Madison Avenue faces the greatest threat since the inception of the FCC" (p. 30); Papazian's (1986) argument that the "growing emancipation of the viewer" was a problem that advertisers must not ignore (p. 103); Miller's (1989) articulation of the definition of grazing as "a once captive audience now roaming freely across video-land" (p. 73); and Alfstad's (1991) claim that "nothing is going to stop zapping" (p. 20). Such statements were based on a realization that zapping was "not simply a media buying problem, it's an advertising effectiveness problem" (Papazian, 1986, p. 104). By the early 1990s, it was proverbial in both the trade press and academic journals that the RCD "has forever revolutionized the way we watch TV" (Pahwa, 1990, p. 8), and that "advertising as a profession is very much in crisis" (Stewart, 1992, p. 3).

Reevaluation

As doomsday analyses received more attention, the inevitable counterarguments surfaced. These analyses typically were more sophisticated than the earlier assertion that zapping was simply not a problem, noted by organizations such as the TBA ("How to Avoid," 1984). As early as 1985, McSherry criticized the hype of some agencies and the trade press for confusing the issue of RCD and VCR usage by pointing out that programs with higher ratings were zapped less, that heavy zappers tended to be light viewers of television, and that program breaks contributed to most of the zapping—a problem that he implied was solvable. While recognizing that "zipping, zapping, [and] flipping" were problems, Wool (1985) called for historical context. He suggested that television was becoming less overstated as an advertising medium and more similar to magazines, radio, and billboards, which long had to deal with capturing audience attention in a crowded media milieu. Similarly, Stipp (1989) argued that grazing behavior was not new (i.e., it was a long-standing concern in print) and that the television advertising industry was simply in a period of "adaptation" (p. 30).

The reevaluation of grazing effects continued with Reiss's (1986) report on a study that found that zipping had little effect on recall scores and that the effectiveness of a television advertisement related more to its creative content than to whether or not it is zipped. Although the notion that zapping has little effect on commercial recall was disputed in Stout and Burda's research (1989), the latter authors did suggest that "brand dominant" advertising (a creative approach in which the brand name is seen early and often in the spot) did inhibit the negative effects of zipping and, in essence was, a form of "zip-proofing" (p. 31). In a similar vein, Greene's (1988) analysis of Gallup data found that while the RCD did contribute to reduced recall scores, cable viewers actually recalled more than broadcast viewers, and that the grazing phenomenon actually contributed to advertising exposure, because spots were seen that would have not been observed at all without grazing. McGann (1992) reminded his readers that while changes had occurred in the advertising industry be-cause of the diffusion of the RCD, the fact that television advertising expenditures continued to rise contradicted the prophets of doom. He also argued that practices such as increased demographic targeting offset the loss caused by clutter-induced grazing.

By 1990, the panic over the RCD-wielding audience, while not completely dissipated, was tempered more and more by evidence that the changing situation was manageable. A crisis seemed less imminent since the data on grazing effects was often contradictory. In addition, a consis-tent theme in almost all the studies was that the television advertising business was changing. Increasingly, it seemed that grazing was being tolerated "as a fact of television life" (Carter, 1991, p. D6) because there was little that could be done about it (Alfstad, 1991; Carter, 1991).

The negative implications of the "nothing can be done" explanation are contradicted by the third major reason for the reevaluation of grazing's impact on advertising; namely, that the industry was not only aware of the problem, but was taking corrective action. Marton (1989), for example, stated that now that advertisers and programmers recognized the RCD as a "predator of dull programming" (p. 30), both advertising and programming content was changing. Lewin (1988) echoed this argument with her claim that the impact of technological change simply added another advertising problem to the existing ones of inattentiveness and outright avoidance. The implication was that the problem could be addressed by modifying certain elements of the existing structure of television advertising and programming. According to another still-developing assessment, the problem of the restless audience can only be addressed by a near total revision of the structure of the advertising–television conduit relationship. In this scenario, the RCD, the VCR, and cable have forever altered the relation between medium and viewer, and the new relation can only be addressed through new methods and new systems. As Schrage et al. (1994) stated, "Advertising isn't dead, it's been reborn." While the authors base this conclusion on a dramatic and, arguably, futuristic conception of the "twin gospels of narrowcasting and interactivity," others have posited that the advertising industry, by combin-ing existing elements, already has the means to forge these new relationships and structures and, indeed, has started to do so. For example, Schultz (1990) wrote that with mass market consumer advertising no longer dominant, "advertising, public relations, sales promotion, direct marketing, packaging, personal selling, and even employee communications must be thought of as a single communications system" (p. xiv).

Thus, some observers claim that advertising is addressing the RCD "problem" by altering the existing system, while others argue that it is (or should be) creating new systems. Each of these responses requires closer scrutiny because of their crucial implications for the future of relationships among advertisers, television, and the viewer.

SYSTEM ALTERATIONS

It is misleading to polarize the above-mentioned views about the advertising industry and how it is evolving or *should* evolve. Although labeling the changes in the industry either adaptations or revolutions reflects the discussion that is occurring within the industry, the two positions can work together. There are those who take the view that the mass marketing "game is over" (Peppers & Rogers, 1994), and that new forms are necessary and, indeed, are being implemented. However, a more conventional point of view is that traditional media forms (e.g., broadcast television) are important components of the evolving media mix (Jensen, 1994b).

The fact that certain media forms cross boundaries between the old and the new also helps bridge the gap between these two interpretations. For example, infomercials are structured like traditional television series and, most often, are scheduled on traditional television stations. At the same time, their ability to integrate direct selling methods through interactivity, if only via the telephone, is a key element of the new media.

Ever since RCD and VCR diffusion first was identified as a problem, the advertising industry has been devising ways to blunt the power of the television viewer to avoid their product. The primary ways suggested and, at least in some manner, implemented relate primarily to targeting, spot length, the placement of advertising within the programming platform, advertiser control of programming, and content creativity.

Targeting

With the increased and successful emphasis on demographic targeting since the 1970s (Barnouw, 1978), many advertisers believed that better targeting would cancel out the threat of the now active audience (Martell, 1994; McGann, 1992). Miller (1989), for example, stated that the first rule in combatting grazers was to "know thy audience" and to abandon the lowest common denominator approach that had long been dominant in television advertising and programming (p. 74). Clearly, the advertising industry has become much more cognizant of the need for targeting in the last few years, an awareness reflected by the continuing and increasing support for many specialized cable services (Lippman, 1992a). In addition, there are continuing attempts to refine such methods as VALS (Values and Lifestyles research) that produce psychographic profiles of audience viewing and buying behavior (Arens & Bovée, 1994; Martell, 1994; Wilson, 1994).

Spot Length

One method for dealing with the RCD-armed viewer is to reduce the length of the television spot (Mandese, 1992b; Pahwa, 1990), based on the assumption that shorter commercials would not allow the viewer time to zap. Although the 30-second spot remains the most common type of television advertisement, the networks and other television distribution outlets commonly offer shorter spots of 15 seconds. Often these are sold in "split 30s," so that a company can separately advertise more than one of its products in the same 30 seconds (McDonald, 1986). The rise in RCD ownership parallels the increase in 15-second spots. Between 1981 and 1987, for example, the percentage of "15s" on the networks increased from 2% to 36% of all spots, while "30s" declined from 92% to 61% (Marton, 1989). One of the major problems with shorter spots is that they clutter, which has long been regarded as a major problem of television advertising and as an encouragement to grazers (Arens & Bovée, 1994; Marton, 1989). This has remained part of the conventional wisdom of advertising, although a Network Television Association study found that the network programs with the most clutter—daytime programs—were zapped less than programs in other dayparts (Mandese, 1992a).

Placement

Clutter is a major focus of concern when it comes to advertising placement within the television programming platform. An issue directly related to clutter involves identifying the most effective position within a commercial "pod" to place an advertisement, with the first pod position usually considered best (Cronin & Menelly, 1992; Lewin, 1988). Another issue is the placement of advertising within the program schedule. As early as 1984, the SSC&B agency was telling its clients to avoid buying spots at the beginning and ending of programs because of the amount of grazing that took place at those times ("How to Avoid," 1984).

As we show in the next chapter, network television programmers have worked diligently to address these concerns by delaying the first commercial break in programming until after the narrative has commenced, in order to hook the viewer. They have also increased the number of programs that immediately follow one another on the schedule with no intervening advertising or promotion. In fact, each of the Big Three networks increased the number of such programs in the 1994-95 season in order to combat the "epidemic of channel surfing." According to CBS executive David Poltrack, the 3–5% of the audience that grazes within-program advertising increases to 15–18% when the advertisements are between programs. However, the Fox network has been less aggressive in adopting this approach because of its concern about increasing within-program clutter (Goldman, 1994b).

Although he termed it "a modest proposal," Kostyra (1984, pp. 94–95) suggested that all broadcast and cable programmers should schedule commercials at the same time. Of course, this strategy would take considerable coordination and therefore will probably never be adopted. He saw this as the only way to "alleviate the future problem of zapping" (p. 95). Although nothing this radical has been implemented on a recurring basis, there have been some attempts at "roadblocks," in which one advertiser buys the same time spot on as many channels as possible (Bollier, 1989; Pahwa, 1990). Because of costs and logistical concerns, this technique seems best suited to such advertisers such as politicians, who often have the need and the financial resources to saturate the television medium for a limited period of time.

Programming Control

Another method of ensuring optimal position in the programming platform is to own the platform. Ownership also has the added benefit of lowering costs. For example, such major corporations and television advertisers as General Motors, Proctor & Gamble, AT&T, RJR Nabisco, K-Mart, and McDonalds are members of the Television Production Partners group. Established in 1993 to develop special programming for the Big Three, the partners predicted a 20–30% reduction in their normal network advertising costs as a result of pulling advertising spots from similar programs that they did not own (Mandese, 1993b). Clearly, the projected reduction in costs eases the sting of the grazing audience. Another example of advertiser ownership was the *Doritos Zaptime/In Living Color Super Halftime Party* program aired on Fox directly opposite halftime of the 1992 Super Bowl. This program appealed specifically to grazing viewers, by superimposing on the screen a clock that indicated the minutes until the game resumed. It also was a throwback to the past, and probably a preview of the future, with a single sponsor getting title credit and control of all advertising spots (Tyrer, 1992e). MTV used a similar clock superimposed over *Beavis and Butthead* during halftime of the 1996 Super Bowl.

Creative Changes

Those who maintain that the present system is still valid for advertising insist that the creative end of the business can temper the proliferation of grazing. Reiss's (1986) evaluation of the recall scores of zipped programming, for example, said that the effectiveness of an advertisement was related more to creative aspects than to whether or not it was zipped. Although Stout and Burda (1989) found that zipping did interfere with recall, they also argued that using a "brand dominant" approach could negate the interference. Although some observers have labeled creative approaches to grazing "hogwash" (Alfstad, 1991, p. 20), the emphasis on such approaches is increasingly evident in television.

By the mid-1980s, many advertisers and observers of the advertising industry were emphasizing creativity to develop "zap-proof" commercials (Kessler, 1985, p. 68). The changes in commercials that resulted from this emphasis fall into three overlapping types: (1) changes in pacing, (2) changes in internal structure, and (3) increased program–advertising integration. As the latter type is a key element in the new systems heralded by many advertising observers, we will include a discussion of it in the next section.

Minimovies

Apple Computer's "1984" advertising campaign for the MacIntosh is generally considered to be a breakthrough in advertising. First aired during the 1984 Super Bowl, the spot was seen as the prototype of the minimovie spot, which, supposedly, would both penetrate the clutter of television ads and neutralize the RCD-armed viewer (Kessler, 1985). Although the term "minimovie" has been applied loosely within the advertising industry, common characteristics include (1) a highly stylized visual approach; (2) an epic or blockbuster narrative quality, as in the Wrangler spots featuring a high action "Indiana Jones"–type series of images (Kessler, 1985); (3) a major prerelease publicity campaign in the trade and popular press that often takes the form of "news"; and (4) an expansion of a longtime advertising convention: the employment of superstar endorsers that emphasize performance aspects (Pahwa, 1990). Familiar examples of the latter, of course, include Michael Jackson's and Madonna's spots for Pepsi. Some research has suggested that this type of advertising can confuse viewers and consequently lower recall scores because the viewer cannot figure out what is being advertised (Tsiantar & Miller, 1989). Nonetheless, such formats have continued to proliferate.

A variant of the minimovie that may or may not incorporate an unusual visual focus is the advertisement that employs a continuing narrative. The requirements for such an ad were listed in *Marketing News* as (1) build interest slowly, (2) tell a story, and (3) "make it so cute that people want to watch" ("Viewers Add," 1989, p. 10). A prime example of this approach is the series of Taster's Choice instant coffee spots that featured the developing romantic relationship between a man and woman who have been brought together by their mutual love of Taster's Choice. Each spot ends with a cliff-hanger, whereby a new character is introduced or semimysterious dialogue is spoken by one of the lead characters. The coffee seller, of course, hopes that the audience will want to see each spot to keep up with the story line.

Pregrazed Spots

Psychological research conducted for the advertising industry has suggested that elements such as loud noises, sudden movement, and, in general, a more visual approach can attract attention (Allman, 1989; Arens & Bovée, 1994). The success of such cable programming services as MTV and CNN, which primarily consist of short and strongly visual segments, appears to validate such an approach in advertising ("Viewers Add," 1989). Indeed, fast-paced and visually dense spots have become common in the television advertising business (Carter, 1991; Marton, 1989; Pahwa, 1990). Examples range from the Michael Jackson Pepsi spots of the late 1980s, which featured a strong and fast-paced visual (Pahwa, 1990), to the series of "Energizer Bunny" spots that "made advertising history" through their carefully crafted spoofs of conventional television advertising and promotion (Arens & Bovée, 1994, p. 427), to the recent spots for Coors Light that feature very rapid cuts to the "programming" of a mythical "Coors Light Channel," on which all the "programs" are related to beer (Millman, 1994b).

The Coors Light campaign is a "Generation X"–type spot that was created by people in their 20s who incorporate rapid pace, contemporary structural conventions, and the grazing mentality into the spot—all things that they grew up with. The plentiful images and rapid editing replicate the grazing experience to the degree that we can label such advertising "pregrazed." Of course, the rationale for such spots is that the audience will not be as apt to zap them, since they simulate the pleasures of grazing.

In presenting such striking images in a humorous fashion, advertisers expect the spots to catch the attention of the heavy grazer, who is often similar in age to the creators of the advertising. Pregrazed spots are increasingly common. Another example is the Miller Lite beer campaign that mixes two sports in highly unconventional ways (e.g., baseball and bass fishing, football and golf). Beyond their essentially silly surface humor and eye-catching appeal, the spots also serve as parodies of the grazing behavior that is common among those who watch televised sports and consume beer.

Structural Alteration

The internal structure of certain television advertisements has been altered to encourage viewership. For example, IBM's "You Make the Call" spots, which debuted in the mid-1980s, were used on many sportscasts. The structure consisted of (1) a sports clip setting up a situation in which the umpire/referee had to make an important call, (2) a question to the viewer about what call she or he would have made, (3) a "break" that featured a traditional advertising spot for an IBM product, and (4) a resumption of the sports footage and the answer to how the call was decided (Martens, 1985). Miniprograms such as this and AT&T's "Great Moments in Sports" were designed to integrate the advertising message within ostensibly nonadvertising content (McDonald, 1986). Other examples of this approach are the various games, contests, and tie-ins to network promotional campaigns that are increasingly common in television advertising (Millman, 1994a; see Chapter 4 for an analysis of developing practices in television promotion). The obvious extension of miniprograms is the integration of advertising content into actual programming content.

While a variety of creative approaches have been employed to capture the attention of the restless viewer, the problem for the advertising industry is ascertaining which types of creative formats actually will arrest viewers. Although the techniques discussed above can work in certain circumstances, the qualitative nature of creative production makes it impossible to reduce it to a formula. Of course, if creative advertising was known to be the "solution" to the restless viewer, and everyone knew what "creative" meant, then everyone would employ that one specific strategy.

NEW SYSTEMS AND STRATEGIES

As we explained in Chapter 1, advertiser influence in electronic mass media once extended to nearly complete control of programming content and schedules. In the heyday of radio, for instance, the integration of programming and advertising was often explicit in the titles of programs and in the seamless segue from plot to advertising pitch (Barnouw, 1973; Sterling & Kittross, 1990). The clear advantage to such an approach is that the listener or viewer cannot zap the advertising without zapping the program. Although perhaps more subtle now than they were in radio and the early days of television, such approaches are again becoming popular.

Advertising–Program Integration

The integration of programming and advertising already is commonplace in such often-grazed program forms as sports, through both venue and electronic signage that appears consistently while the event is in progress (Bellamy & Walker, 1995). The continued integration of programming and advertising is considered a key strategy in the future of television and has long been advanced as a way to deal with the restless audience (Martens, 1985; Miller, 1989; Papazian, 1986). Although one suggested means of employing this strategy is to have a character in a series explicitly state a preference for a product (Martens, 1985), a more common approach appears to be "product related programs" in which a sponsor's product often is an integral component of the program. *Home Again with Bob Vila*, a home repair series sponsored in part by Sears (whose commercial spokesperson is Vila) and other sellers of home improvement products is a prototype. Other examples are auto repair and auto racing series that are sponsored by oil companies, and cooking shows that are sponsored by the makers of cooking oil (McDonald, 1986).

A related integrative form involves the payment of fees for placement of products within programming. This is a common practice in motion pictures, whereby advertisers pay or barter for their product to be prominently displayed or even favorably mentioned in a film (McAllister, 1993). Since almost all movies end up on television in various ways (e.g., home video, pay cable, broadcast), the value of the placement is multiplied. The success of this practice is likely to lead to an expansion of product placement in all forms of television.

Another developing form of advertising–program integration is the use of programming *within* advertising. A prime example of this is the recent Diet Coke campaign using the cast of the popular situation comedy *Friends*. In what has been labeled an "insidious" form of product placement (Marin, 1996, p. 77), the Coca Cola company paid an estimated $10 million to have the cast of *Friends*, in character, appear in a series of Diet Coke ads written by the program's writing staff. To make more explicit the linkage between program and advertiser, the campaign was tied to a contest that had as its major prize attendance at a taping of a *Friends* episode.

Advertising as Programming

Infomercials and home shopping channels are other types of program–advertising integration. Infomercials have been labeled a "zap-vaccine" because the program (as in the case of home shopping channels) is the advertisement (Pahwa, 1990). The growth in both infomercials and home shopping channels resulted from federal relaxation of television advertising limits as part of the deregulatory thrust in the early and mid-1980s (Zoglin, 1993c). The FCC's 1993 decision to extend cable must-carry protection to home shopping channels was another major stimulus to their continuing growth (Halonen, 1993).

The combination of convenient direct selling with a degree of interactivity and personal appeal is key to their success. As Stefanac (1994) claimed, the "feeling of intimacy they engender" is one of the reasons for their "phenomenal" growth (p. 47). Increasingly, observers are echoing Barlow's argument that "direct marketing is killing the advertiser-supported model" (1994, p. 86).

Place-Based Advertising

While the techniques of programming–advertising integration make electronic grazing less likely, they cannot eliminate it. In fact, integrated programming may lose the distribution outlet a considerable amount of viewership: everyone who is annoyed by advertising. In order to address this problem, more and more advertising dollars are flowing into place-based television services. Operating on the premise of a captive audience (Turow, 1992a), television advertising is now featured in airports, grocery stores, fast food restaurants and college cafeterias, video arcades, and schools, among other locales (Goldman, 1994a; Mahler, 1991; McAllister, 1993; McCarroll, 1993). Although some ventures have not been successful (e.g., Whittle Communications' "Medical Network" for physicians' offices), others have generated substantial revenue (Reilly, 1994). For example, Whittle's "Channel One" service for schools generates approximately $100 million a year in advertising revenues ("Media Empire," 1994). Such figures, along with the appeal of advertising that cannot be electronically zapped, is leading an increasing number of advertisers to use place-based media as a supplement to other forms of delivery.

Integrated Marketing

In addition to these specific examples of new systems and strategies of advertising, a more significant change in the advertising business is the increased emphasis on integrated marketing (IM) concepts. The term "integrated marketing" typically is used to describe the combination of once disparate elements of the marketing process, including corporate sponsorships, merchandising, promotion, and advertising (Duncan, 1993; Stewart, 1992). With consumers increasingly difficult to reach via conventional means, IM is seen as a way for both advertisers and the sellers of consumer access to shift their focus "from marketing oriented to market driven" (Arens & Bovée, 1994, p. 490). Thus, IM is a way for advertisers to reach more potential customers and access sellers in a time of industry flux. In addition, it is the way for program providers to further leverage their product. A key concept from the supply side is that a distribution or programming entity can provide one-stop shopping and value-added packages to potential advertising clients (Kiersh, 1992).

IM also encompasses the coordinated and, optimally, the ownership integration of distribution outlet and product. A prime example would be the joint ownership of the New York Knicks, New York Rangers, Madison Square Garden, and the MSG Cable Network. In addition to selling advertising time, MSG offers packages to advertisers that encompass game tickets, luxury boxes, venue signage, merchandise discounts, and catering services (Grimm, 1993). According to a major MSG official, the first step in the development of such a system "was establishing the network as a mouthpiece to the advertising community" (Grimm, 1993, p. 23). The Knicks and Rangers are thus components of an IM package. Another example of sports-related IM is the packages made available to sponsors of the 1994 Goodwill Games. Despite the generally low ratings of the games, advertisers were pleased with add-ons such as global advertising exposure, since the games were held in St. Petersburg, Russia. They also could exploit the various promotional activities tied to the games, which encompassed sponsor identification, hospitality suites, and the bonus advertising received from a *TV Guide* viewer's guide (Goldman, 1994c).

Although sports offer some of the best examples of IM plans, the term "integrated marketing" is fluid enough to accommodate many other arrangements. For example, the increasing amount of money spent on promotion as a supplement to conventional advertising falls under the IM rubric (Martinez, 1994). In fact, the shift from a 2:1 ratio of advertising to promotional expenditures to almost the reverse ratio in the 1980s can be seen as a sign of IM's growing popularity (Stewart, 1992, p. 2).

This popularity and such a major shift in the advertising–promotion ratio is further evidence of the effect of the advent of a second generation of television viewers/users. The RCD-wielding audience member, with access to an increasing number of video options, is a major factor in the decline of traditional advertising's value. In order to capture his or her attention, the advertising industry is devoting more and more resources to alternate methods of dissemination.

The increasing popularity of IM is also a function of the ever-tightening linkages of the television industry and advertisers, and the media industries and their primary program suppliers. Although changes resulting from technological diffusion and governmental action (or inaction) can create fissures in traditional relationships, they can also encourage closer relationships between traditional partners both to cope with uncertainty and, more importantly, to exploit new opportunities. IM schemes are the predictable products of the long-standing and symbiotic relationship of the television and advertising industries. Similarly, the partners in the relationship are interested in the potential of interactive technology as a means to regain or maintain audience loyalty.

Interactive Advertising

Despite the growth of the new methods, many are convinced that the future health of advertising and marketing is directly tied to interactive distribution. Some advertisers are funding the development of interactive television services (Arens & Bovée, 1994, p. 483). NBC is attempting to gain a toehold in interactivity through the integration of such existing technology as telephone information and print media to supplement its broadcasts (Mandese, 1993a). Indeed, most of the major media companies are involved in experiments of interactive systems.

Although we will reserve Chapter 7 for a full discussion of the various interactive systems under development—their likelihood of success, and their possible impacts on the television industry and the viewer/user—we need to make explicit here that advertisers will play a major role in any of the systems that will eventually win market acceptance. In fact, interactive television is likely to enhance the influence of advertisers.

The conventional wisdom about interactive television is that viewers will be able to exert much greater control over the content of what they allow to enter the home, perhaps even so much that they will not allow any conventional advertising into it. There are two drawbacks to such a posture. First, it will encourage advertisers to further integrate their message into program content through product placement, signage, and so forth. In fact, Schrage et al. (1994) in their almost giddy exposition on the wonders of interactivity, mention the possibility of advertisers developing "viruses" that could place their logo or any information they choose in specific content (e.g., Ivory Soap identification with bathing scenes) without any way for the viewers to rid themselves of the virus except for zapping, which means that the content being viewed/used must also be zapped.

The other drawback to blocking conventional advertising from the home is that the viewer/user will then have to pay directly for the use of the service. And with viruses and other methods available to advertisers, he or she will still be exposed to advertising. The pay-per-view or pay-per-use models of the future will not be advertising-free.

Because the viewer/user theoretically will have more control over content, advertisers probably will develop techniques to "bribe" the viewer into paying attention to advertising. As Nelson (1994) explains, Time Warner's "Full Service Network" employs "response-advertising bribery" whereby services or other products are offered if users will answer questions related to advertising and their consumer behavior (p. 41). As Peppers and Rogers (1994) subtitled a recent electronic article on this likely scenario, "If you pay attention, we'll pay your way."

Interactive television will allow advertisers to specifically target consumers through powerful direct-marketing techniques that are already the fastest growing type of advertising (Nelson, 1994). With some research indicating that the response rate for direct mail, presently the primary means of direct marketing, is 10 times that of newspaper advertisements and 100 times that of television advertisements (Smolowe, 1993), the prospects for the combination of direct marketing and interactive television are quite enticing to advertisers. This connection was made explicit by Peppers and Rogers (1994), who declared that "the right way to think of television advertising in the Interactive Age is to think of it as video mail." The analogy breaks down, however, in that ignoring direct mail advertising, a form of physical zapping, does not mean that one has to pay more for postal service than those who read or respond to the advertising. Unlike the publicly funded postal system that provides universal service, the television industry, regardless of its future form, will remain an advertising vehicle that inherently discriminates against less- or nonvalued segments of the population. The Interactive Age will not change this; it likely will exacerbate the discrimination.

CONCLUSION

Although perhaps not in a "crisis" (Stewart, 1992, p. 3), the advertising industry has and will continue to change its approach to reaching the television audience. The response to the advent of the second generation of television viewer/user is multifaceted and includes such alterations and enhancements of conventional means of reaching the audience as more (1) emphasis on specific audience targeting, (2) attention to spot placement and length, (3) control of programming, and (4) emphasis on the creative aspects of advertising content. In addition, new strategies, and in some cases extensions of existing strategies, are being implemented, including (1) advertising–program content integration, (2) place-based advertising, (3) integrated marketing and an increased emphasis on promotion, and (4) interactive advertising.

As in the case of the diffusion of previous media technologies, there is not likely to be a collapse of "old" media in favor of the "new." However, just as magazines and radio adapted to the diffusion of television, the traditional television industry is adapting to the diffusion of new technologies and services and the reality of an active RCD-armed audience. There is really no other way, of course, in a system wedded to and symbiotic with the advertising industry, whose only objective is to buy access to the best audience for the presentation of its wares. As the television industry changes, so does the advertising industry, through (1) consolidation of agencies; (2) more demands of accountability and "proof of performance" from their product suppliers (i.e., television program distribution systems); (3) more concentration on specific niche markets; and (4) forays into such new technologies as interactive television (Castro, 1993; Mandese, 1994; Martell, 1994; Pomper, 1993).

Nowhere is the concept of audience empowerment, resulting from the diffusion of RCDs and other video technologies, challenged more than in an analysis of the advertising industry. Even such strong proponents of the interactive age as Schrage et al. (1994) proclaim that the idea that the audience will have more power than the program suppliers in the new age is "fashionable, faux futurism." Instead, they see a renegotiation of the "power relationships between individuals and advertisers," with advertisers maintaining the upper hand. Similarly, McAllister's (1993) analysis of place-based advertising sees the form as a means to "disempower the audience: take away the emancipatory technology and return to the control advertisers had over behavior . . . [it] recaptures the glories of advertising past" (p. 18).

Analyses of advertising industry changes in reaction to the grazing viewer reveal further ironies related to the rise of an active audience. For example, Turow (1992a) noted that "a counterforce to fragmentation [of the mass audience] has developed, and it is conglomeration" (p. 252). As discussed in Chapter 1, large oligopolistic or monopolistic economic structures are not known for their innovation or product differentiation.

Commenting on the control that viewers now have over television's content, Stefanac (1994) made the point that "The more control viewers have over advertising they allow into their homes, the more information-packed and entertaining that advertising will have to become, blurring even further the line between programming and advertising" (p. 52). Thus, the commodification of the audience is almost certain to become an even more explicit goal of the advertising and television industries in the future.

Although the advertising of tomorrow is likely to be much more based on "bribing" the audience to participate with it in some fashion, the "bait" to get the audience to use a medium whereby they can be exposed to advertising will still be of the utmost importance. While there have long been forms of advertising (e.g., classifieds, yellow pages) in which advertising content *is* the content, and while such forms will likely become more widespread in the near future, most people will be exposed to advertising because of their willingness to be exposed to some ostensibly nonadvertising content. In order to ensure the value of the audience commodity that they sell to advertisers, product suppliers must work harder than ever to present an advertiser-friendly environment through value-added packages, integrated marketing plans, and the like. In addition to the "goodies" that the suppliers can offer advertisers, they must also attract (i.e., produce) a valuable audience by offering desirable content that will hold the attention of the RCD-wielding user of television.

This means, as it always has, that it will be necessary to acquire and schedule strong programming and to employ promotional techniques that will sell the programming to the viewer. We turn now to a discussion of how television programming and promotion has changed (and is changing) since the widespread diffusion of the RCD.

NOTE

1. The terminology used in the advertising industry in the mid-1980s differed from that which commonly is used today. At that time, all audience avoidance was characterized as zapping (Mermigas, 1984). Zapping was divided into physical zapping (i.e., leaving the room), electronic zapping (or channel changing), and time-shifting or VCR zapping, which is now usually referred to as zipping (Fountas, 1985).

CHAPTER 4

A Tool for a Second Generation
CHANGING PATTERNS OF TELEVISION PROGRAMMING AND PROMOTION

A nightmare vision of the 21st century home is one in which every member of the family occupies a different room with virtual reality headset intact or video on demand remote control in hand, imprisoned in his or her own narcissistic niche. ("Media Firms," 1993)

Former CBS President Howard Stringer's vision of a coming "electronic Yugoslavia" concludes with the audience retreating "to the distant past, when *Cheers* and M*A*S*H gave us the last great shared experience we remember but can no longer produce" ("Media Firms," 1993). Although exaggerated, Stringer's "nightmare" reflects some of the most important questions about programming in the second generation of television and beyond. As the advertising community continues to refine strategies to capture the restless viewer in a multichannel video environment, the programming "bait" must also be refined and redefined. With advertisers making increasing demands on television program providers and balking at paying ever higher rates for access to an increasingly fragmented audience, the programming segment of the television industry has no choice but to change.

One of the major purposes of this chapter is to detail the changes in programming content and scheduling strategies that have corresponded to the diffusion of the RCD and other video technologies. A second purpose is to analyze the growing emphasis on promotion and the establishment of brand identities for television program providers. Increasingly, promotion is regarded as a third leg of the television business, as important as programming and sales (Cowles & Klein, 1991). As an element of product differentiation, promotion's importance has increased with the establishment and success of alternative programming outlets (Bellamy, 1992). The third major purpose of this chapter is to detail the changing structure of the television industry, which is the determining factor in most of the ongoing changes in programming. Included will be considerations of ownership changes of traditional television entities (i.e., the networks), the creation of alternative programming outlets (e.g., Fox), and the impact of increasing economic integration on once disparate television entities.

The emphasis here primarily will be on national broadcast and cable services. There are two major reasons for this approach. First, and most importantly, local television and cable system operators, except for news and sports, function almost exclusively as distributors of national programming. This is even more true today with the advent of new broadcast networks (Fox, Warner Brothers, United Paramount Network), ad hoc syndicated networks (*Action Pack*, Spelling), myriad new cable services, and the ever increasing power of station representative firms and consultants to design local schedules. Second, the majority of local broadcast practitioners consider grazing to be a national or network problem, if they regard it as a problem at all (Eastman & Neal-Lunsford, 1993). The issue of coping with the restless viewer, therefore, is by default primarily a national concern. The emphasis on national television program providers also allows us to best illustrate the impact of the RCD on what traditionally have been among the most powerful entities in the television industry.

PRESENT STATUS OF TELEVISION PROGRAMMING ENTITIES

While the grazing audience often is discussed as a threat to the economic viability of traditional, commercial television programming providers (Mermigas, 1992c; Selnow, 1989), the enormous size and influence of the broadcast network segment of the television industry mitigates against a complete collapse of the industry's structure. The Big Three networks still maintain average cumulative shares of around 60% of all U.S. television households during prime time, a figure that increases to over 70% with the addition of Fox share data, as compared to 20% for basic cable, 4% for pay cable, and 3% for PBS ("In the," 1992; Mahler, 1993). Although this is a substantial decrease from the 90% plus Big Three prime time shares of 20 years ago, the broadcast networks continue to be the dominant force in television. The viability of broadcasting recently was reaffirmed by the establishment of the United Paramount Network (UPN) and Warner Brothers (The WB) networks and News Corp.'s investment in New World, which secured much stronger affiliates for its Fox network in several major markets (Mermigas, 1994c). Clearly, the access to audiences provided by broadcast networks and their affiliate stations remains of great strategic importance in the television and advertising industries.

The Audience for Broadcast Programming

In addition to still being the primary choice of most television viewers as measured by audience shares, the networks also fare better than their rivals in the way in which they are used by the audience. Heeter et al. (1988) found that 88% of network viewing is in "stretches" of 15 minutes or more (p. 58). Percentages for other program distribution outlets ranged from 65% for "satellite" networks (i.e., most basic cable) to 84% for pay cable (p. 58). Based on data from this study (pp. 56–57), we recalculated the authors' estimates of channel changes per hour in various program services. As reported in Chapter 2, we found that network viewers change channels less (3.0 times per hour) than the viewers of other types of television outlets. By contrast, the number of changes per hour for other services ranged from 4.5 for pay channels to 10.0 for automated (e.g., teletext) services.

A likely explanation for these results is that the audience for network television is older than that for most cable services (Lippman, 1992a). There is substantial evidence to suggest that the more active younger viewers already have curtailed their use of, or even abandoned, network television (Davis & Walker, 1990). This would help to explain both the audience attrition of network shares over the last two decades and the apparent stabilizing of "inheritance effects" (Walker, 1988).

While such data suggest that the network structure is not in immediate danger, the broadcast industry is unlikely ever to be as influential or as lucrative as it was before the rise of cable, VCRs, and an RCD-wielding audience. While the need of advertisers to reach the mass heterogeneous audience delivered by broadcasters is key to the maintenance of the industry, broadcasting has inherent weaknesses that have been carefully exploited by the other video providers.

Some analysts have predicted that the existing network structure is so economically inefficient and subject to the whims of a restless audience that its future prognosis is questionable. Lindheim, for example, argues that the networks will "die" without a more clearly defined marketing strategy and changes in the program development process (1992, p. 18). Reith (1991) states that traditional television will go the way of the "dinosaurs" without strategic planning to "minimize viewer control" (p. 34). He sees the diffusion of cable, VCRs, and RCDs as "the root cause of network viewership declines in the 1980s" (p. 34). Former NBC executive Tom Wolzien predicted the demise of the traditional networks as affiliates and viewers defect to alternate program distribution sources (Mermigas, 1992c).

Negative analyses of the network's prospects have also appeared from within the networks. In 1991, former NBC-TV President Peirson Mapes predicted that "a network could go bankrupt within the next five years" (Lieberman, 1991, p. 21). ABC Network President Robert Iger, who was then president of ABC Entertainment, specifically blamed RCDs for network problems and posited that the RCD-armed viewer is leading to a new environment in which there will be fewer hours of programming offered by the Big Three and ultimately fewer full-service networks (Bianco, 1991).

Such dire predictions are as hyperbolic as the current assessment that the broadcast business is *hot*. They must be tempered by the knowledge that network officials are unlikely to take a positive economic view of their business, except when they are talking to the investment community. Even so, the network business obviously is not the same business that it was a few years ago.

Cable Programming

While broadcast program providers have lost audience and advertisers, cable programming services have benefited greatly from the diffusion of RCDs, as have VCR manufacturers and the marketers of prerecorded videotapes. There is little doubt that without the RCD, many cable services would receive far less exposure, because of their weak dial positions and viewer inertia. The RCD is widely credited with having led to much sampling of cable programming (Dempsey, 1992; Eastman, 1993).

Cable viewers tend to be both younger and more affluent than broadcast viewers. As Telecommunication, Inc. (TCI) Chairman John Malone commented, "broadcasters are left with undisputed over-the-air access to the people who complain that the price of cable is too high"

(Donlan, 1992, p. 10). Clearly, the demography of the cable audience is highly desired by many advertisers. At the same time, the demography also makes cable more subject to grazing than broadcasting (Heeter et al., 1988).

The multichannel nature of cable television led that industry to devise an economic system based on infrequent use and grazing. The key element of the system is a dual revenue stream that relies on both advertising revenue and fees paid by cable systems, which are in turn collected from subscribers through increased fees. The dual revenue stream came into existence during the early days of the cable television program industry, when advertisers generally avoided the new services because of their minimal audiences. By combining system fees with what was then limited advertising revenue, the cable programming industry developed the model that was instrumental in making it the highly lucrative enterprise that it is today.

Because the audiences for cable programming services rarely come close to matching the size of network audiences, particularly in prime time, the cable industry has had to adapt its sales pitch to these realities. Essentially, basic cable has adopted a technique of the radio industry in stressing cumulative audiences (called "cumes"), total household reach, and demographic ratings rather than standard Nielsen household ratings and shares (Eastman, 1993). Such a system takes into account the whims of an active audience by stressing viewing over periods of time or from more than one showing of a given program, rather than targeting the audience for one point in time. Pay and pay-per-view (PPV) cable, which have been slow to accept direct advertising, have little reason to be concerned with such matters as long as the ratings translate into a low churn rate and high buy rate for their services.

While cable has benefited greatly from the sampling of RCD-wielding viewers, the industry clearly is no more immune than broadcasting to the restless viewer. There is considerable evidence, for example, that cable services are zapped more than broadcast channels (Carter, 1991; Heeter et al., 1988). As Dempsey (1992) reports, many cable networks are concerned about being shifted to pay tiers (especially if it entails a higher channel number) because "a large chunk of their viewers at any given time accidentally light on the channel while zipping through the dial with their remotes, stopping only because something on the screen catches their eye" (p. 38). Clearly the grazing viewer should be a concern for all television program providers. We turn now to an analysis of how these providers are using both traditional methods and implementing new strategies to cope with the second-generation viewer.

PROGRAMMING STRATEGIES

A cursory glance at the programming schedules of the broadcast networks, as well as the vast majority of basic cable services, reveals no obvious changes in the scheduling structure of 10 or 20 years ago. With the exception of sports and motion pictures, programs still are scheduled in either 30- or 60-minute time blocks that begin on the hour or half hour. This structure has its antecedents in radio, and has been reaffirmed by the concept of *flow* that has long been the modus operandi for programmers. Essentially, the concept of flow is based on viewer inertia: once the viewer is comfortable with a program, he or she is likely to stay tuned to that channel into the next program. In order to create a comfort level for the viewer, certain programming practices developed.[1] As detailed by Eastman (1993, pp. 135–138), the following are among the most prominent:

1. *Strong lead-in.* A successful (i.e., highly rated) program is placed at the beginning of a time block such as prime time. This practice is also called a *lead-off* strategy. The concept is that the program or programs that follow will inherit much of the audience.
2. *Hammock.* A new or less successful program is preceded and followed by successful series, thus enhancing flow-through and protecting the weaker series.
3. *Tent-pole.* This is the opposite of hammocking, in which a successful program is placed between two less successful or new programs. The concept is that the preceding series will benefit from the early tune-in for the tent-poled series, and that the program that follows the tent-poled series will inherit a substantial portion of the audience.
4. *Blocking or stacking.* Series of the same or similar genre, or that have similar demographic appeals, are scheduled back-to-back in order to avoid startling disruptions that might disturb the comfort level of the viewers and cause them to change channels. A very common and successful strategy used by all television programmers, this probably is the most basic of all programming strategies because of its facility of implementation, its success rate, and the ease with which it can be promoted.

Obviously, these strategies are not mutually exclusive. For example, the block programming strategy usually encompasses one or more of the other methods.

Strategies based on viewer inertia, of course, assume that the audience is passive. In fact, Klein's (1978) somewhat facetious "theory of the least objectionable program"—which maintains that the comfort level that will hold the attention of the viewer is the one generated by the program that offends her or him least—clearly is based on the concept of a passive viewer and provides the basis for the above practices (p. 186).

Even in a time of rising viewer activity, these conventional programming strategies continue to be relevant to television programmers (both broadcast and cable) because of their historic ability to enhance flow. Recently, the presidents of the entertainment divisions of both ABC and NBC used the concept of flow to explain why their respective fall schedules would succeed (Goldman, 1994c; Graham, 1994a). Television providers increasingly realize the necessity of maintaining the audience they currently have and, optimally, regaining some of the lost audience and attracting younger viewers whose viewing habits have not been established. In order to do this, the broadcast networks as well as many cable services are supplementing the tried and true scheduling methods with new strategies that encompass scheduling methods, promotion, and both the style and structure of programming (Eastman & Neal-Lunsford, 1993; Eastman, Neal-Lunsford, & Riggs, 1995).

Continuity Strategies

After attracting an audience to the program line-up through promotional strategies, the ultimate goal of programmers is to maintain that audience "forever," assuming it meets the salable criteria of size and demography. In order to reach this theoretical goal, the programming elements that have been shown to promote channel switching must be minimized. Chief among these are the breaks for advertising and other nonprogram clutter that occur between programs (see Chapter 3; "How to Avoid," 1984). The primary strategies employed to combat audience attrition at such times are as follows:

Reduction or Elimination of Between-Program Breaks

In some cases, the gaps between programs have been minimized or eliminated. Rather than a two to three minute break for advertising or promotion, the next program starts immediately after the end of the preceding program. This strategy, often referred to as "hot switching" (Eastman & Neal-Lunsford, 1993, p. 194), was employed successfully, as measured by the ratings, by NBC with the *Seinfeld–Frasier* tandem in the 1993–1994 season. Each of the Big Three networks increased the practice for the 1994–1995 and 1995–1996 seasons with NBC most prominently employing a seamless strategy between all prime time programs (Goldman, 1994c; Karlin, 1995).

Restructuring of End Credits

Another method to minimize channel switching between programs is the use of "living end" credits at the conclusion of series. In this strategy, the end credits are accompanied by outtakes or even an epilogue (Eastman & Neal-Lunsford, 1993, p. 194). ABC's *Roseanne* is an example of a successful series that employs this technique and whose audience has traditionally flowed in large part to the series that follows it on the schedule. One application of this approach is a split screen (i.e., picture within a picture) in which either program segments or, in most cases, promotional pieces that once would have followed the credits appear on the screen simultaneously. This technique has antecedents in the voice-over promotional announcements that both networks and local stations have employed for many years.

Elimination or Restructuring of Program Openings

Some series are dispensing with theme songs or separately constructed openings. For example, CBS's long-running *Murphy Brown* superimposes opening credits over the program's narrative opening. *Frasier* begins similarly, and this strategy combined with the hot switch from *Seinfeld* (in the 1993–1994 season), leads to the seamless transition (Eastman & Neal-Lunsford, 1993) desired by programmers. For the 1994–1995 season, ABC Entertainment President Ted Harbert called for the elimination of theme songs because he sees them as "invitations to graze" (Graham, 1994a).

Each of these continuity strategies clearly is designed to enhance flow and prevent channel switching. Eastman et al. (1995) called this "accelerated flow" (1994, p. 94). Of course, eliminating advertising breaks between programs, particularly high-rated ones, removes what were once considered prime locations for advertising (especially local advertising). The networks generally believe that the reduction in grazing that results from moves to more seamless program transitions—hopefully producing higher audience flow throughout a schedule—justifies the insertion of longer commercial breaks within programs. The theory is that once a viewer is hooked into a series, she or he will tolerate such a break. Fox executives, however, have expressed concern that the move to eliminate between-program breaks increases in-program breaks to levels that might encourage grazing (Goldman, 1994c).

Style and Genre Strategies

In addition to specific continuity strategies, the style and type of programming also has changed to reflect the new audience realities. The recent proliferation of network situation comedies is one way in which television programmers are dealing with changes in the audience and the television economy. Long a staple of prime time schedules (going back to the heyday of network radio), situation comedies are increasingly valued for their (1) short length and scheduling flexibility, (2) simple narrative structures that do not require much attention on the part of the audience, (3) cost efficiencies, (4) successful history in syndication, and (5) promotional opportunities whereby a block of sitcoms can be promoted as one entity (Eastman, 1993; Eastman & Klein, 1991).

The accompanying decline in network one-hour drama series has been attributed to an audience that is both restless and lacks a substantial attention span as a result of all the choices now available to it ("Cheers and Jeers," 1991; Tyrer, 1991). Network executives have explicitly blamed the proliferation of RCDs for the decline in drama series. ABC's Robert Iger stated that the RCD "has hurt dramas more that anything else" (Tyrer, 1991, p. 8).

Reality Series

Network executives now regard reality and news magazine programs as a substitute for dramas. ABC's Harbert has argued that such programs provide viewers a "drama fix" (Vaughn, 1993, p. 117). In addition, the proliferation of such programs serves other important functions for networks. First, the modular nature of such shows encourages short-duration tune-in, although with the hope on the part of programmers that the audience will stay with the program once they find it. As Harbert has argued, the dramatic structure of the stories on such series captures the attention of grazers (Vaughn, 1993). This generally is not true of more complex dramatic programs that demand a reasonable level of attention over time to be intelligible.

Second, and of arguably greater importance, such programs are much less expensive to produce than dramatic series. A one-hour news magazine, for example, costs from $500,000 to $700,000 per episode versus $1.25 million or more for a dramatic series. Reality programs (e.g., *Rescue 911*,

Unsolved Mysteries) range from $125,000 to $375,000 per hour, depending on whether or not recreations are used (Tyrer, 1993). Clearly, in a time of declining audiences, cost cutting is a major priority of corporate policy. Another benefit of news magazines is that networks have complete control over such programs, unlike entertainment programs which traditionally have been licensed from production studios. Also, many of the production resources for news magazines already exist within the networks. It is a shift of existing resources rather than the acquisition or creation of new ones. Such programs also serve as major promotional platforms for the other news programming of the network. The use of evening and morning news personalities in prime time, such as Dan Rather and Katie Couric, is a potent promotional vehicle for the non-prime time news and feature programs.

Dramas as Product Differentiation

While there is less emphasis on one-hour dramas on networks than was once the case, they have not disappeared from television. In addition to those on the Big Three and Fox, the syndication marketplace has increasingly provided such series to stations. This trend began with Paramount's successful syndication of *Star Trek: The Next Generation* and now encompasses over a dozen series, including *Star Trek: Deep Space Nine, Baywatch*, and *Highlander*. Such series are economically feasible because they attract high prices and barter advertising time for the producer (the *Star Treks*) from stations that wish to differentiate their programming from other providers by offering action-oriented programs with strong male appeal, an audience that is desirable to advertisers and often underserved by the networks (Hart, 1993). As a Warner executive explained, network strategies are "out the window" because there is "no more loyalty," which provides an opening for independent stations to prosper with such series (Hart, 1993, p. 2). Another factor in accounting for the popularity of such series is that they often are international co-ventures (e.g., *Baywatch*) which spread production costs among several entities. The relative popularity of dramatic programs in Europe and other international markets, compared to many other U.S. programming forms, increases the financial viability of such series (Walley, 1991b).

Producer Driven Series

Regardless of genre or the placement of programs within a schedule, there seems to be a revival of the long-held belief that hits beget hits. Although such strategies as developing spin-offs from existing successful series (Bellamy, McDonald, & Walker, 1990), and contracting with a producer for several programs that have a similar style (e.g., Warner Brothers for ABC in the 1950s and Norman Lear for CBS and Aaron Spelling for ABC in the 1970s) have been major programming strategies since the advent of television, there is an increased reliance on producer driven series (Tyrer, 1992d). The concept is that the producer of a hit series is more valuable than ever because she or he possesses the means to stop grazers in their tracks. As a result of this belief and the increasing difficulty of establishing a successful series (Zoglin, 1993d), several exclusive producer–network deals have been signed in the last few years. Examples include Stephen Bochco with ABC (*NYPD Blue*), Diane English and Joel Shukovsky with CBS (*Murphy Brown, Love & War*), and Linda Bloodworth Thomason and Harry Thomason with CBS (*Designing Women*).

The down side to such a strategy is that the considerable expense of these deals does not guarantee that the producer(s) can replicate previous successes. For example, Bochco, the primary creative talent behind such earlier NBC successes as *Hill Street Blues* and *L.A. Law*, had a string of unsuccessful and expensive programs at ABC (*Hooperman, Cop Rock, Civil Wars*, and *Capital Critters*) before establishing *NYPD Blue*. Neither English/Shukovsky or the Thomasons have been able to duplicate their earlier successes, although their programs are often given desirable time spots. Clearly, no producer has discovered the secret of stopping the grazers.

Content Standards

The proliferation and success of programs that reflect a "hip and often sick" aura straining traditional content standards (e.g., *Beavis and Butthead, Late Show with David Letterman, Ren and Stimpy*) is also seen as a reaction to the proliferation of channels. As explained by *Newsweek's* John Leland (1993, p. 50), "nothing stops a channel surfer like the word 'sucks.' " With the exception of *NYPD Blue,* which incorporated off-color language and partial nudity to a degree previously unknown in network prime time programming, series that deviate from traditional content standards are usually seen on cable or in fringe time spots rather than in network prime time.

Pregrazed Programming and Sports

Another trend in television has been the advent of *pregrazed* programs. Such programs consist of short "bits" that are collated into a coherent whole, and parallel the pregrazed advertising strategy discussed in Chapter 3. The concept is that the viewer has little motivation to zap because the program itself is constantly switching from one program element to another. Although "classic" series such as NBC's *Rowan and Martin's Laugh-In* might be considered the progenitor of pregrazed programs, new programming outlets such as cable and Fox have been most likely to schedule such innovative programs. Typical examples include Comedy Central's tongue-in-cheek *Short Attention Span Theater*, numerous MTV programs, and Fox's short-lived *The Edge* comedy program. Because these programs are explicitly designed to catch the attention of grazers, who tend to be young, there have been few attempts to schedule such programs on the Big Three networks, which continue to seek a more heterogeneous audience.

Sports telecasts constitute an increasingly important subgroup of pregrazed programs. Primarily because of their strong appeal to young males, sports programs are grazed more than other forms of programming (Eastman & Newton, 1995; Martens, 1985; Chapter 6). More specifically, sports are highly subject to multiple-program viewing, in which a viewer can follow the action of two or more sports events while also avoiding most commercial spots (Martens, 1985). Television has addressed these problems by carefully integrating advertising matter into the event (Chapter 3) and by moving to a presentational style that employs frequent switches to action, highlights, and updates within the structure of the telecast. Examples include coverage of the NCAA Men's Basketball Tournament (CBS), the *Baseball Night in America* telecasts (ABC and NBC), and, to a lesser degree, National Football League (NFL) telecasts (Fox and NBC). Each of these incorporate regional "splits" that allow the game of most local interest to be the primary telecast within a given region. However, within the telecast the action often shifts to other games that are being played simultaneously. At other times, graphic inserts keep viewers informed of the progress of other games and, in some limited instances, picture-in-picture technology is employed to allow for the following of more than one game at a time. In essence, such coverage manipulates and layers visual information in a way that replicates the hypothetical experience of a viewer equipped with an RCD and picture-in-picture technology.

Targeting Strategies

Another strategy adopted by television program providers in the multichannel environment is the specialization of content. This is employed by many cable services that can survive or even thrive on a relatively small but demographically valuable audience (CNN, ESPN, MTV) when combined with system fees. Nonetheless, several analysts have suggested that the broadcast networks also must specialize in order to survive. Former NBC executive Peirson Mapes claimed that a focused schedule was one of the 10 ways to "keep a network running" (Lieberman, 1991, p. 21). Lindheim (1992, p. 18) argued that a "clearly defined market segment" is key to network survival. Of course, the success of Fox, with its strong urban and youth appeal, also has been influential in such analyses.

Because oligopolistic media structures do not encourage product differentiation (Dominick & Pearce, 1976; Litman, 1979; Picard, 1989), typically there has been little to distinguish one network's programming from another; however, this has not always been the case. Before ABC's rise to economic parity with the other networks in the mid-1970s, it exploited its strength in urban areas and with young adults and children. Although not as pronounced, CBS, which was consistently the highest rated network in prime time before the mid-1970s, had a strong appeal to rural areas and older viewers (Bellamy, 1992). More recently, Fox's success among young viewers, African-Americans, and urbanites has seemed to support the notion that some level of product differentiation (i.e., the establishment of a specific brand identity) is necessary for success in a multichannel environment. NBC's Mapes, for example, argued that the Big Three should more tightly focus their existing brand images (i.e., ABC for the young urbanite, CBS for the older and more sophisticated, and NBC for the thinking person) in order to prosper (Lieberman, 1991, p. 21).

To date, network application of brand identification strategies has been sporadic, with the obvious exception of Fox. CBS, for example, redesigned its schedule to appeal to the over-50 crowd in 1992. As explained by then CBS Entertainment President Jeff Sagansky, "I don't think there's ever been a clearer time in broadcast history where there are clearly different strategies going on as far as who the networks are trying to appeal to" (Tyrer, 1992c, p. 5). In the same year, NBC cancelled high-rated series that had strong rural appeal (*In the Heat of the Night, Matlock*) in an attempt to attract a more urban and youthful audience. Outside prime time, NBC replaced its Saturday morning animated programming with live-action programs (e.g., *Saved by the Bell*) in an attempt to appeal specifically to the teenage audience.

For the most part, product differentiation strategies have not been fully implemented at the network television level because of the huge reach and audience of the Big Three, which makes such a strategy uneconomical except in certain non-prime time dayparts. The ending of the advertising slump and the failure of NBC's "rural purge" in 1992 have also served to prevent a fuller application of such a risky strategy. However, the next time that the market for broadcast advertising slumps, and as network shares continue to decrease, there undoubtedly will be another vogue for more specialized program brand identity.

Local Strategies

Although the emphasis of this chapter is on national television programming strategies, their implementation will have major implications for local affiliates. ABC's Iger, in lamenting the unprofitability of many network series, has predicted an increase in "local origination programs" as the traditional networks cut back on the amount of programming they will supply (Tyrer, 1991, p. 8). Other analysts predict that local television will become more like radio with a much greater emphasis on local programming (Halonen, 1992b). The problem with this prediction is that it glosses over some key realities. First, most radio stations became a local medium only to a degree. Although radio networks and syndicators no longer supply much series programming, the shift to a local disc jockey playing nationally available recorded music (often interspersed with national news, features, and advertising) would hardly constitute a substantial local medium.

Second, the basic economics of television work against localism. Local production is expensive compared to most acquired programming. As a result, one of the "solutions" to audience diversion adopted by many local stations has been a curtailing of local programming, except for news and in some cases sports. Another coping strategy is the increased number of markets in which one station controls or supplies the programming for another station in the same market (Walley, 1991a). While such moves limit localism, they do provide a laboratory for experiments that recognize the impact of grazing. For example, WCCO-TV in Minneapolis programmed a 10 P.M. newscast as well as one for KLGT-TV in the same market. The middle of the newscasts were different and the audience was encouraged to switch to the other channel for content they might find more appealing (Lafayette, 1994c).

News is so important to local stations that consultants are now factoring restless viewers into the data sold to such stations. For example, consultants are telling client stations to refashion their newscasts through shorter and more quickly paced stories, constant teases of upcoming stories, and differentiation of different newscasts (e.g., 5 P.M. news as a headline service, 6 P.M. news with prime time previews and lifestyle features, 11 P.M. news with headlines and lots of sports). Stations also are being advised to devote more time and resources to the promotion of their news product (Allen, 1993). In fact, the promotion of news demonstrates at least some recognition on the part of local stations that they must work harder to maintain their audience.

The retransmission consent provisions of the 1992 Cable Television Consumer Protection and Competition Act, which allow broadcasters to demand payment for the use of their signals on cable systems, has provided another means for local stations to cope with the changing television environment, by sharing in the dual revenue stream that has been critical to cable's economic success. The rules have led to the creation of several local channels (e.g., the Pittsburgh Cable News Channel) and national services (e.g., FX, ESPN2, America's Talking) that local broadcasters and networks demanded from cable in lieu of retransmission payments (Lafayette, 1993).

PROMOTIONAL STRATEGIES

As the need to maintain and gain audience is increasingly problematic in a multichannel television environment, promotion is seen as a key factor in accomplishing these goals (Bellamy, 1992; Eastman & Klein, 1991; Eastman & Neal-Lunsford, 1993; Walker, 1993). Promotion is vital to both the success of individual programs and to the development of brand image for the program provider. Although every program provider realizes the importance of programming, there is considerable disagreement on the utility of promotional strategies. It could be argued that at the network level the disagreement reflects a crumbling of the traditional oligopolistic market structure (Bellamy, 1992). However, it is more likely that the disagreement simply is a product of the uncertainty about how to cope with the second-generation viewer.

The Fall Season

A traditional application of generic promotion is the promotional push that surrounds the introduction of a new fall season (Eastman, 1991). The Big Three have differed in their assessment of the value of image-building strategies for fall promotional campaigns, such as slogans (e.g., CBS's "Get Ready"). While former CBS President Howard Stringer has argued that they are necessary to support the entire network schedule ("Promotion Executives," 1990), former NBC Entertainment President Brandon Tartikoff called such campaigns "just noise" that has little effect on the audience (Roush, 1990, pp. C3–C4). Fox is more vehement in its denunciation of such campaigns; Sandy Grushow, formerly in charge of Fox network programming, called them "a bunch of hogwash" ("NBC, ABC," 1990, p. 36). Some support for this perspective appeared in one of the few academic studies of the efficacy of network promotion. Walker (1993) found that the number of fall promotional spots is not positively related to program ratings.

In fact, Fox differs from the Big Three; it aligns itself with many basic cable services in opposition to the concept of a fall premiere week. Fox executive Preston Padden has categorized the fall promotional push as the "child abuse" of programming (Granger, 1991, p. 39). The rationale for this strong statement is the belief that starting the new season in a one- or two-week September window confuses the viewer and encourages grazing. This was the finding of Heeter's (1988c) study of channel changing over the course of a television season. She found that viewers do change channels more often earlier in the season; of course, such grazing may enhance a new program's chance for success, because that may be how viewers discover it. Although Fox has been more likely to schedule series debuts and season openers before the beginning of the traditional fall season, an approach increasingly being used by the other broadcast networks, it continues to join the Big Three in introducing most of its series in a fairly compact September framework.

Advertising Tie-Ins

There is also disagreement among the networks on the value of promotional tie-ins with major advertisers that include contests and promotional giveaways. As discussed in Chapter 3, such activities increasingly are valued by advertisers as components of integrated marketing. Recent examples of such schemes have included NBC–McDonalds, CBS–K-Mart, and NBC–Sears ("Network Lotto," 1990; Zoglin, 1993a). ABC has refused to enter into such deals because of the "hidden costs" related to the large amount of advertising inventory taken by the promotional partner ("CBS and NBC," 1990, p. 81). However, such campaigns are likely to continue because they appease major advertisers (Bellamy, 1992).

Promoting Grazing

Grazing has been a factor in recent network promotion, although the results have not been encouraging. In 1990, the networks were said to be "learning to make [grazing] work for them" (Graham, 1990, p. 3D) by appealing to grazers to switch from the competitors for specific programs. For example, CBS scheduled *The Flash* for Thursday at 8:30 P.M. and encouraged the viewers of the popular 8:00 P.M. programs on Fox (*The Simpsons*) and NBC (*The Cosby Show*) to switch over. This strategy failed, as did similar efforts to develop flow from the competition to Fox's *American Chronicles* and NBC's *Lifestories*. This discouraging record has arrested, at least temporarily, appeals to switch to regularly scheduled series from the competition. Of course, the fact that the network audience is older and less likely to graze (Davis & Walker, 1990) was no doubt a factor in the failure.

Although the promotion of grazing has not been successful with ongoing series, Fox was able to convince 21 million viewers to switch from halftime of the 1992 Super Bowl to its *Doritos Zaptime–In Living Color Super Halftime Party* program. The special finished second for the evening behind CBS's game telecast and was considered a success. Its popularity was attributed, in part, to the massive preshow publicity by Fox and the sponsor, publicity that was covered as a news event in many media outlets (Tyrer, 1992a).

Individual Program Promotion

Although there are serious disagreements in the industry over the best ways to implement image promotion, all television providers see the value of individual program promotion. A modified form of program promotion is block promotion, in which a group of similar series are promoted as a single entity. Examples include ABC's "TGIF" block of Friday night situation comedies and Nickelodeon's "SNIK" grouping of youth-appeal series on Saturdays. While this technique has been employed for many years, there is a much stronger emphasis on it today (Bellamy, 1992). For example, in a random sample of network promotional spots generated for a recent study, 55.2% of all spots promoted more than one series (Walker, 1993).

Another promotional technique that is finding widespread industry acceptance is the insertion of a small, nearly transparent logo in the corner of the picture during regular programming. The logos have the practical industry benefit of assisting viewers who are subjects in ratings surveys to identify the service they are watching when filling out their diaries (Eastman & Neal-Lunsford, 1993). The logos also build brand identity with the very valuable and increasingly desirable quality of being inte-grated into programming. Viewers cannot zap this type of promotion without also zapping the programming.

The changes in promotional strategies are a reflection and product of the vast changes occurring in the television industry. The rapidity of these changes works against industry agreement on what constitutes effective promotion. Nonetheless, there is agreement among all television providers that gaining the attention and, ideally, the loyalty of the restless viewer through promotion is one of their most vital tasks.

A CHANGING TELEVISION ECONOMY

The new strategies in programming and promotion are not the only changes occurring in the television industry. There have been changes as a reaction to the rise of the second-generation viewer/user and pressure from advertisers, and these can also be seen as resulting from a structural alteration in the television economy. As discussed in Chapter 1, changes in structure determine changes in conduct.

In the last two decades, and particularly in the 1980s, macroeconomic decisions were made at the national and international levels that have had far-reaching implications for the industry. Specifically, the ethos of deregulation led to a redefinition of the role of the broadcast and cable television industry from one in which public interest guidelines were seen as a counterweight to the commercial inclinations and desires of broadcast licensees and cable system operators to one in which the public interest was equated with the corporate interest (Polic & Gandy, 1993). The U.S. government adopted an economic philosophy which held that scaling back or even eliminating regulatory and legal boundaries would allow for more innovation and competition, which was equated with more public benefit. The implementation of this philosophy set in motion capitalist economic activity that led to the development of new economic structures in the television industry. These structures in turn have engendered new patterns of conduct and measurements of performance. Specifically, deregulation not only affected the way actual regulations were fashioned and promulgated, it also fostered a climate in which other branches of government, such as the courts and the U.S. Justice Department, adopted a relatively hands-off posture in reviewing regulations and enforcing antitrust law. These changes spurred the economic consolidation and convergence that is now the raison d'être of the television industry.

As discussed in Chapter 1, the linkage of the RCD to the changing television economy and to the recent vogue for deregulation, while critical to an understanding of the current status of the television industry, is both indirect and synergistic. The essential connection is that the RCD allowed the television audience to sample a variety of new program services, the number of which increased due to the newly active audience. The growth of these new services (e.g., cable) increased the power of the program providers, which led in turn to a series of reactions from both traditional industry powers and regulatory authorities.

Regulation and Deregulation

As the cable television industry grew and became increasingly dominated by major multiple systems operators in the years after 1972, it developed political clout similar to that long wielded by the National Association of Broadcasters. The cable industry began to lobby for relief from what it considered to be onerous restrictions on its program lineup, and, especially, on what it could charge for its service. The result was the Cable Communications Act of 1984, which essentially deregulated the cable industry. At least in part, products of the Act include the large expansion in the number of cable services, the increasing profitability of cable systems and services, the decline in network viewing shares, and the substantial increases in cable subscriber fees.

Another major result of the Act was the dilution of broadcasters' once special status with federal regulators. This status was the historical result of the licensing process, which, theoretically, forced broadcasters to operate in the public interest because of the limited amount of spectrum space. The rise of cable as a serious competitor to broadcast hegemony led to arguments from broadcasters that since they were no longer the only major television provider, regulations that impacted industry structure should be repealed in order for them to compete on "a level playing field" against cable and other future television providers (i.e., telephone companies). In response to these arguments, the FCC modified its ownership rules to allow broadcasters to own more stations and approved arrangements whereby a station could program a competing station. Under court order, the FCC scaled back the financial interest and syndication rules that had severely restricted network ownership and syndication of programming (Halonen & Mermigas, 1993). The FCC also loosened its rules to allow networks and affiliates to develop stronger economic ties. This deregulation has been partially responsible for the recent and unprecedented series of affiliation changes (Jensen, 1994a). Congress, in response to broadcast lobbying and perceived price gouging on the part of cable companies, reinstituted a limited amount of price regulation and instituted retransmission consent and must carry provisions in the Cable Act of 1992 (Halonen, 1992a).

A key thrust of the deregulatory ethos was to weaken oversight over media ownership. Deals that at one time probably would have received antitrust scrutiny are now approved routinely and even praised as necessary to the health of U.S. media companies in the international marketplace (McQuail, 1990).

Network Changes

The impact of deregulatory theory and practice can be seen in network television ownership. ABC's purchase by Capital Cities and investment in a variety of cable programming services (ESPN, A&E, Lifetime) has allowed the network to hedge its bets in terms of where the audience is likely to turn for its television viewing. Disney's recent acquisition of Capital Cities–ABC will further diversify the network's mix of programming outlets (Mermigas, 1995). Likewise, NBC's acquisition by General Electric and subsequent investment in a variety of domestic (CNBC) and international programming services (SuperChannel) allows it to do the same. Only CBS, after an early failure with CBS Cable, remained a traditional broadcasting company into the mid-1990s. The limits of this strategy were reached in 1995 when, after years of takeover rumors, a financially troubled CBS was acquired by Westinghouse (Graham, 1994b; Mermigas, 1995).

The success of Rupert Murdoch's Fox network is an object lesson in the vagaries of deregulation, technological diffusion, and the restless viewer. In order for Fox to be established, several things had to occur. First, Murdoch had to become a U.S. citizen to purchase the station group that gave the fledgling network a base of owned and operated stations. The fact that he was able to obtain citizenship, seemingly for this purpose, and receive FCC sanction to purchase the stations is compelling evidence of a new perspective on the part of the FCC. In an earlier era, it probably would have taken substantive action on the issue of licensee nationality. Second, cable had to be diffused widely enough for Murdoch's affiliated stations, many of which were on weak UHF signals, to have technological equivalence with the affiliated stations of the Big Three. Third, Fox was able to skirt the FCC definition of what constitutes a network and avoid regulations such as the now repealed prime time access rules, which would have prevented its affiliates from broadcasting off-network product (i.e., reruns), including product from Fox, in prime time. It also evaded the financial interest and syndication (FIN–SYN) rules that would have forced Fox to separate itself from the lucrative programming business represented by its Twentieth Television sibling company. Fourth, satellite technology had to be available for the distribution of the network feed (Sterling & Kittross, 1990; Thomas & Litman, 1991). Finally, there had to be an audience for the new service that was desirable to advertisers.

Fox's success in reaching a specific demographic audience (i.e., young, urban) rather than attempting to aim at an undifferentiated mass audience was evidence that a broadcast service no longer was compelled to seek out the largest audience (Turow, 1992a). Fox demonstrated that a desirable demographically defined niche audience could be very lucrative for a broadcast network. This lesson, which was demonstrated earlier by several basic cable services, has now become the modus operandi of an increasing number of program providers (including, to a limited degree, the traditional networks). Of course, the massive reach of the networks (including Fox) and dependence on advertising make it necessary for them to target a large niche or audience segment rather than the smaller niches that cable services can seek out.

Although Fox built its success as a limited service network (i.e., limited amounts of prime time programming, no news, no daytime programming except for a children's block), it is increasingly regarded as part of the "Big Four." Its acquisition of National Football League (NFL) rights in 1994 demonstrates Fox's willingness to spend substantial sums of money in order to become a "big" network (Zornow, 1994). In addition, the network entered into a deal with New World that gained it VHF affiliates in 12 major markets at the expense of the Big Three (CBS in particular). This "largest realignment in broadcast history" (Jensen, 1994a, p. 1) has set in motion a series of similar deals on the part of all networks (CBS–Group W, ABC–Scripps Howard) to secure new, or enhance existing, affiliation relationships (Halonen, 1994e).

Affiliate Relations

The network–affiliate relationship has always been the key to the network business. The large number of relatively low-power stations over a vast geographical area, and governmental restrictions on the number of stations that one entity could own, made the system of negotiation between networks and stations necessary to the establishment of nationwide program distribution systems.

After the most egregious network contractual policies with their affiliates (e.g., forced option time) were ruled a violation of the Communications Act in the 1940s (*National Broadcasting Co. et al. v. U.S.*, 1943), the relationship settled into a highly lucrative partnership pattern in television. An affiliation agreement was considered the most highly valued resource that a station could have beyond the broadcast license itself. At the same time, the network oligopoly was willing to share the revenue through station compensation in order to have the near universal access that a large group of affiliates could provide. The success of the partnership is evident in the long-term relations that the networks have with many affiliates. In fact, until the recent realignment set in motion by the Fox–New World deal, the only time in which there was a substantial shift in affiliate status was in the mid-1970s, when ABC achieved parity with CBS and NBC and was willing to cut favorable deals with certain strong stations (Hobson, 1978; Litman, 1979).

Although the network–affiliate relationship is extant, it is being altered by a series of industry changes. Among the most important of these are as follows:

1. The rise to prominence of Fox and the increasingly prolific syndication business gave stations an alternate to affiliation with the Big Three. This option gives more clout to affiliate stations in contract negotiations. The nascent United Paramount (UPN) and WB (Time Warner) networks will provide stations with more options to Big Three affiliation. In order to reach an active audience that has little loyalty to traditional program providers, stations are themselves less loyal to their network benefactors.

2. At the same time, networks no longer need affiliate stations to reach a mass audience. The 1970s switch to satellite distribution from physical long-line connections made it technologically feasible to distribute network programming directly to any user with cable or a satellite dish. Although the networks have yet to move to this operational model, owing to the benefits of access and of maintaining a local presence via affiliate stations, the possibility of their doing so further changes the dynamic of the network–affiliate relationship.

The results of these changes have included (1) cutbacks in compensation money for many time periods, as networks increasingly expect affiliates to share the cost of programming (Mermigas, 1992b); (2) special incentives to affiliates who clear certain amounts of programming (Mermigas, 1992a); (3) an increased likelihood of affiliate preemption of network programming in favor of more lucrative syndication fare (Mermigas, 1992b); (4) increased network pressure on affiliates to carry network programming, with penalties for those who do not (Halonen, 1994e); and (5) long-term network–affiliate contracts (e.g., the CBS–Group W contract was for 10 years) that make the parties partners in the acquisition of more television stations and the production of programming (Halonen, 1994e; Lafayette, 1994b). Combined with the soon-to-end FIN–SYN rules, such arrangements are likely to lead to increased vertical integration of networks and stations whereby the partnership produces programming, distributes it to markets where they do not own stations (including international markets) through syndication, and exhibits the programs on their jointly owned stations. The recently passed telecommunications legislation virtually ensures more network affiliate integration by allowing each broadcast network to own stations that reach up to 35% of the nation's television households ("A Telecom Act Primer," 1996).

Structural alterations have not been limited to the broadcast business. The reduction of boundaries between the once disparate broadcast and cable industries has led to a series of deals between onetime rivals in both the domestic and international television industry.

Consolidation and Convergence

The years of deregulation have been a time of increased vertical and horizontal economic integration. Such integration, traditionally considered socially detrimental because of the high barriers to entry set by such structures, is increasingly common and even celebrated as essential to the "synergy" necessary to compete in the new age of television. Two of the most prominent applications of this thinking are as follows:

1. The networks have been aggressive in entering into deals with their ostensible competitors in cable. Among the numerous examples are ABC's majority ownership of ESPN and ESPN2, NBC's ownership of the CNBC and Talk America services, and Fox's FX service (Bellamy, 1993; Walley, 1994a). Such deals are examples of the convergence of separate technologically bound programming distribution systems (e.g., network vs. syndication, broadcast vs. cable) into a "programming = software" model, wherein the distribution outlet is meaningful only in its ability to reach and hold the attention of the restless viewer (Halonen, 1994d; Mermigas, 1993; Tyrer, 1994).

2. An adjunct to the above is the increasing internationalization of the television programming industry. International co-ventures are funding more and more programming. Examples include *Baywatch* and CBS's *Scarlett* miniseries (Walley, 1991b). In addition, U.S.-based media companies are involved in a growing number of co-ventures with international companies and have acquired media assets in several nations. A few prominent examples are NBC's purchase of the U.K.-based SuperChan-

nel, the international availability of such cable program providers as TBS and MTV Networks, and Fox's investment in a large number of services in Europe, Australia, and Asia (Bellamy, 1993; Walley, 1993c).

As television program producers and distributors increasingly are removed from ties to traditional structures predicated on technology or public interest considerations, control of the means of distribution becomes more important. Of course, production and programming entities that control distribution and exhibition outlets have guaranteed access for programming. Although it usually would not make economic or legal sense for vertically integrated entities to deny access to other program producers, their ability to set the economic terms of entry for other providers can make it much more difficult for independent companies to afford such access.

The search for guaranteed access is now one of the most important components of media business restructuring (Maney, 1994; Mermigas, 1994a; "New Life," 1994; see Chapter 7). The present flux in the media industries has led to divergent opinions about whether control of outlet or control of content is most important, with many companies clearly hoping to do both. Although such "total control" scenarios are extremely problematic for those concerned about access, they clearly make a lot of economic sense, owing to their perceived efficiency and profitability. Control of the means of distribution allows for guaranteed access for the content created and owned by the outlet owner, and it provides a means of making enormous sums of money from the sale of access to other providers. In essence, control of distribution access means that the controlling entity profits regardless of what programming is being consumed or used by the audience. Although governmental regulators are on record as opposing excessive integration of outlet and content, federal acquiescence in the wake of recent corporate deals would seem to suggest that only the most egregious abuse of access power might lead to countervailing action (Davis & Davidson, 1993; Halonen, 1994a; "Merger Mania," 1994).

CONCLUSION

The evolving television industry structures and behaviors are the result of the synergistic interplay of regulatory action, technological diffusion, and the rise of an increasingly active audience. Although many of the traditional programming and promotional concepts are still regarded as valid, there remains general confusion over which methods are most effective in gaining the attention of the second-generation television viewer/user. This is due primarily to an industry structure that has yet to solidify. But it is also a product of a general lack of knowledge about the motivations of the restless viewer and the circumstances that affect his or her use of RCDs to graze and develop new television usage patterns. We now turn to these critical issues.

NOTE

1. As noted in Chapter 1, advertising influence on scheduling practices was so pronounced in radio and the early days of television that near-total network control of scheduling practices was not implemented until the cost of television advertising time became so expensive that it was no longer tenable for most major advertisers to sponsor entire programs.

CHAPTER 5

Using the RCD

WHO, WHY, AND
WITH WHAT EFFECT?

Because of the real and potential effects of RCDs, the advertising and television industries have responded to their proliferation with definitive actions. These industries are also increasingly concerned with the impact of RCDs on the demographic composition of their audiences. The television industry finds it especially sobering to learn that the male audience, already more difficult to attract, is also more likely to zap ads, and that the young, an audience for both the present and the future, are the most restless viewers. Thus, for economic reasons, these industries are interested in how groups differ in their RCD use and what unexpected benefits are gained by RCD use. In addition to their effects on the revenue streams of various television outlets, these distinctions have important theoretical consequences for the future study of mass communication. In this chapter, we first review recent research that identifies the groups most likely to use RCDs in ways that concern established industries. Next, we examine the motivations behind increased RCD activity and its links to the uses-and-gratifications tradition of media research. Finally, we comment on the implications of RCD use for some well-established theories of media impact.

WHO CLICKS THE CLICKER?

Although determining exactly how much RCD activity is taking place has been a question with an elusive answer (see Chapter 2), researchers have been more successful at identifying demographic and psychological variables that discriminate between high and low RCD users. One reason for this greater success is the nature of the question being asked. Frequency measures hope to produce precise measurements of the variable in question, but precision is not as necessary when one only wants to discriminate between groups. Imprecise categories like "rarely," "sometimes," and "frequently" do not yield exact frequencies of use, but are exact enough to show which groups are clicking the most. The measurement error that plagues memory-dependent measures, like survey items, is critical in precise measures of central tendency, but not in discriminations among groups (so long as the error is evenly distributed among the groups). In this section, we examine how effectively four demographic variables (age, education, income, ethnicity) and a range of psychological variables (novelty and sensation seeking, locus of control, desirability of control, psychoticism, extraversion, and neuroticism) discriminate RCD use, and we comment on the implications of these findings. Gender, the demographic variable most frequently discussed in popular press analyses of RCDs, will be discussed separately in the next chapter.

Age

RCD use has frequently been characterized as a "Generation X" obsession. Younger viewers are seen as part of the MTV generation: raised on a collage of rapidly shifting images, able to absorb visual information quickly, fascinated with new technology, and easily bored. Alfstad's (1991) observations are representative:

> Younger audiences—who were introduced to television by 3-minute segments of "Sesame Street" and grew up viewing the world in 1–2 minute bursts on the evening news and watching fast-cutting MTV music videos—have been "programmed" to switch their attention rapidly from topic to topic, image to image. (p. 20)

Conversely, older viewers socialized during the first generation of three-channel viewing are characterized as technophobic and uninterested in the new viewing environment. Comedian Jay Leno insists that his mother refused to use their first RCD because her misdirected zap might demolish a vase, or her husband (Lavery, 1993). Arrington (1992) summarized the results of a Cable Television Administration and Marketing Society study of restless viewers and reported that 43% of the most active RCD users are 18–23 and 71% are under 40. Likewise, results of eight academic and one industry study (summarized in Table 5.1) seem to support overwhelmingly a clear relationship between age and RCD use.

Three chapters in Heeter and Greenberg's *Cableviewing* (1988) reported solid evidence linking age to RCD activity. Greenberg, Heeter, and Sipes (1988) used electronic monitoring of 127 cable households over three days and a follow-up survey to analyze total channel changes and the amount of time viewing in intervals of less than 5 minutes, between 5 and 15 minutes, between 15 and 26 minutes, and more than 26 minutes. Age was not related to longer segment viewing, but predicted increased viewing in both shorter time frames. Younger viewers were more likely to spend time viewing short segments that require the frequent channel changing associated with grazing, multiple-program viewing, and orienting searches. In the same volume, Heeter and Greenberg (1988b) summarized surveys of 407 fifth-graders and their parents and 395 tenth-graders and their parents. Typically, children were twice as likely as their parents to report frequent zapping, multiple-program viewing, and channel changing. In addition, Heeter (1988a), in a door-to-door survey of 232 adults, found age was negatively correlated with reevaluation or channel changing and three types of orienting searches: exhaustive (checking all of the channels in the viewer's repertoire), automatic (searching channels in numeric order rather than jumping to specific channels), and elaborated (checking many channels).

The *Channels* study of RCD use (*How Americans Watch TV*, 1989) reported cross-tabulations between five age categories (18–24, 25–34, 35–49, 50–64, 65+) and six RCD variables (unspecified, grazing, zapping, orientation search, enjoyment of flipping, and multiple-program viewing). Younger viewers reported higher levels of RCD activity. The youngest viewers were about 20% more likely than the oldest viewers to change channels during a program (the definition of *grazing* used in this study) and to zap when ads come on. A third of the youngest viewers reported that they flipped through the channels when they began to view (orienting search) compared to only about 5% of viewers over 50. Younger viewers flipped more because they enjoyed flipping more. Nearly half of viewers aged 18–24 enjoyed television as much when they were flipping, while only about 17% of viewers 50 or older did. About two-thirds of the youngest viewers could follow more than one program, while only about 20% of viewers over 50 believed that they could. The conclusions from the study are clear: the young click more than the old.

TABLE 5.1. RCD Activity by Age: Summary of Studies

Study	Method	Sample	RCD variables	Results
Greenberg et al., 1988	Electronic measurement of cable viewing and follow-up survey	127 households	Channel changes; viewing in stretches of 5 min. or less, 5–15 min., 15–25 min., 26 min. or more	Younger adults change channels more and view more in shorter stretches: 5 min. or less and 5–15 min.
Heeter & Greenberg, 1988b	Surveys	407 5th-graders, 351 parents; 395 10th-graders, 180 parents	Zapping; multiple program viewing; channel changing during programs	5th- and 10th-graders zap, view multiple programs, and changing channels more during programs than their parents.
Heeter, 1988a	Door-to-door survey	232 respondents; 56% had remote selectors.	Orienting search; channel changing	Age negatively related to both orienting search and channel changing.
Sapolsky & Forrest, 1989	Video recording of VCR use	35 adults; 86 students	Zipping	Students zipped 20% and adults zipped 60% of ads.
How Americans Watch TV, 1989	Self-report items	650 adults	RCD use; grazing; zapping; orientation search; enjoyment of flipping; multiple program viewing	Younger adults graze and zap more often, can follow multiple programs better; use orienting searches more often; enjoy flipping more.
Walker, 1991	Phone survey	209 adults	Total RCD use	Viewers 18–25 and 26–35 use RCDs more than older viewers.
Cronin & Menelly, 1992	Audio recording of commercial zipping	83 adults	Percent of commercials zipped	Subjects under 40 significantly more likely to zip ads than those 40 or older.
Perse & Ferguson, 1993	Written survey; phone survey	566 adults; 615 adults	Channel changing; RCD motivations	Age inversely related to two types of channel changing and most RCD motivations.

(cont.)

TABLE 5.1 *(cont.)*

Study	Method	Sample	RCD variables	Results
Walker et al., 1993	Phone survey	315 adults	RCD use; seven RCD gratifications	Age not significantly related to RCD use but trend in expected direction; age positively related to getting more from TV and controlling family viewing and accessing news, but negatively related to accessing music videos and annoying others.
Eastman & Newton, 1995	Observation of in-home behavior	44 group and 115 nongroup sessions	RCD use	Older adults use RCD less; largest differences between those 45–65 and those 18–44.

Although primarily concerned with gender differences, Perse and Ferguson (1993a) reported differences between older (age 30 and older) and younger (under 30) respondents in two large studies of channel changing and RCD gratifications. In a written survey of 566 adults, they found that those under 30 had a greater propensity for changing in the middle of programs and for using RCDs to avoid commercials, watch more than one program at a time, check what else is on, see if something better is on, seek variety, see what is on other channels, and see what they are missing. In a phone survey of 615 adults, they found viewers under thirty more likely to change channels, watch two or more programs, avoid commercials, and use the RCD to relieve boredom, annoy others, and satisfy their curiosity about other programs. They also found RCDs a useful tool in accessing music videos and as a substitute for print program listings. Age was significantly related to 16 of the 24 RCD-related variables analyzed in the study.

Other researchers have reported similar results. In a phone survey of 315 adults, Walker, Bellamy, and Traudt (1993) found age positively related to some RCD gratifications while negatively related to others.

Older respondents were more likely to use the RCD to get more from television and to control family viewing or accessing television news. Younger respondents were more likely to use the RCD to access music videos or annoy others. The results of an unpublished telephone survey of 209 San Francisco residents (Walker, 1991) found viewers 18–25 (52.3%) and 26–35 (63.9%) were significantly ($\chi^2(3) = 11.73, p < .01$) more likely to be high RCD users than viewers 36–50 (42.6%) and older than 50 (29.4%). Finally, Eastman and Newton's (1995) observational study of 253 adults and children reported that "the big differences in age were between the oldest group (45–65) and the others; the 25–44-year-olds looked much like the 18–24-year-olds in RCD activity" (p. 11).

Sapolsky and Forrest (1989) provide the single exception to the pattern of greater RCD use by the young. In their observational study of commercial zipping, their adult subjects zipped a higher percentage of ads than their younger subjects. However, they used a convenience sample that could easily produce unrepresentative results. Conversely, Cronin and Menelly (1992) found in their convenience sample that adults under forty zipped a significantly higher percentage of commercials than those forty or older.

To summarize, 9 of the 10 studies reported in Table 5.1 offer confirmation of greater RCD activity by younger adults. Younger viewers appear to exceed their elders in most forms of RCD activity, including total RCD use, channel changing, grazing or ministretch viewing, multiple-program viewing, zapping, orienting searches, enjoyment of flipping, and many RCD gratifications. It is clear that the young are on the forefront of redefining the relationship between viewer and television content.

Although it is possible that this youthful fascination with flipping will dwindle as this cohort ages, we believe that outcome is unlikely. Viewing styles, like most media habits, are acquired early in life and typically change only gradually, if at all, with age. With 80% of children having access to an RCD by the early 1980s (McCready, 1992), the next generation will have had plenty of opportunity to practice zapping, grazing, and multiple-program viewing. As we noted in Chapter 4, television networks are already operating under the assumption that a substantial portion of the audience is RCD active, often using programming and promotion strategies that complement (and reinforce) RCD use. In addition, the overwhelming acceptance of video games by the young has trained a new generation to expect more from their televisions than a one-way reception. The concept of interacting with television using a wired or wireless controller is second nature to most children, laying the groundwork for a more interactive relationship with television (see Chapter 7).

Education and Income

Income and education are important in consumer research and are frequently included in academic studies of media use. Differences among various income and education groups in RCD use have been assessed in several studies. Generally, these variables have not been significantly related to RCD activities or gratifications. Heeter (1988a) found education weakly (r = .13) related to automatic orienting searches, but not to exhaustive or elaborated orienting searches or to channel changing (labeled reevaluation in her study). Income was correlated (r = .18) with channel changing, but the relationship was not strong enough to emerge in a subsequent multiple regression analysis. Income was not related to any type of orienting search. Likewise, in their regression analyses, Greenberg et al. (1988) found income was not a significant predictor of channel changing or any of the four types of stretch viewing they analyzed. Education was unrelated to channel changing and three types of stretch viewing, but was negatively associated with time viewing in maxistretches (at least 26 minutes). In short, more-educated viewers watched for longer time periods. Similarly, Heeter and Greenberg (1988b) report no relationship between either income or education and commercial avoidance in their profile of zappers.

The nationwide study of grazing sponsored by *Channels* (*How Americans Watch TV,* 1989) compared viewers earning less than $30,000 to those earning more than $30,000 on four RCD variables. There was little difference between income groups in RCD use, whether it was changing channels during a program or choosing to flip through all channels or just channels of interest. In addition, the two age groups differed little in the percentage of respondents who believed they could follow only one or two programs at the same time. However, a greater percentage of higher-income viewers (16.8%) than lower-income viewers (9.9%) believed that they could follow three or more programs.

Finally, reanalyzing data from Pittsburgh (Walker et al., 1993) and San Francisco (Walker, 1991), studies of adult RCD use produced no indication of a relationship between total RCD use and income. For both data sets, income was not significantly related to RCD use. Likewise, education was not related to total RCD use in the Pittsburgh study. However, in the San Francisco survey of 209 adults, only about one-third of the respondents with at least a college education were frequent RCD users, compared with about 54% of those with less than a college education. This difference was significant ($\chi^2(2)$ = 6.0, p < .05).

Income and education have received only modest attention in RCD research and the results summarized here suggest that this is all they merit. The general pattern is for small nonsignificant differences in RCD activity among different income and education groups. Those with higher incomes are more likely to report that they can follow three or more programs, but income is not consistently related to any other RCD variable. The pattern of relationship for education is contradictory. Education was positively but weakly related to automatic orienting searches and negatively related to viewing in longer stretches—findings that are consistent with more RCD use. However, in one study, those with college degrees were less likely to use their RCDs. The relationships between education and RCD activity may also be confounded by the positive relationship between age (a significant discriminator of RCD activity) and education. Since today both undergraduate and graduate degrees are increasingly completed later in life, younger, more RCD-active viewers are likely to have lower levels of education.

Ethnicity/Race

Ethnic differences have been examined in only a few studies and as a central issue in only one. In a study of RCD gratifications (Walker & Bellamy, 1991a), race was significantly related to two gratifications. White viewers were more likely than nonwhite viewers to use an RCD to find out what is on and to avoid commercials. Analysis of Pittsburgh survey data (Walker et al., 1993) produced no differences between white and nonwhite respondents in total RCD use, but nonwhite viewers were more likely than white viewers to use an RCD to access music videos and to control family viewing and access to television news. In a San Francisco survey in which about 35% of the sample was nonwhite, Walker (1991) found significant ($\chi^2(3) = 15.99$, $p < .01$) ethnic differences. About 40% of the white sample were high RCD users, but approximately 48% of the African-American, 71% of the Hispanic, and 77% of the Asian viewers were in the high RCD group. Of the seven RCD activities analyzed by Wenner and Dennehy (1993), ethnicity was a significant predictor only of entry scanning, with white viewers slightly more likely to "run through the channels to see what is on" (p. 119).

Umphrey and Albarran's (1993) study of RCD use is the only one to focus completely on ethnicity, surveying 1241 respondents (37% Hispanic, 28% African-American, and 34% white) from Dallas. They found that whites (84%) were significantly more likely to have RCDs than African-Americans (72%) or Hispanics (67%). After controlling for age, education, and income, Hispanics had higher gratification scores than whites on 6 of the 10 motivations examined: two commercial avoidance items (can avoid commercials and can watch fewer commercials), news and weather accessing items, one ease-of-viewing item, and one multiple-program viewing item. Whites had higher scores than Hispanics for one gratification: changing channels without getting up. Hispanics had higher scores than African-Americans on six motivations: both commercial avoidance items, separate accessing news and weather items, one ease-of-viewing item, and one multiple-program viewing item. African-Americans also had a higher multiple-program viewing gratification score than whites. Although 17% fewer of the Hispanic respondents had RCDs, Umphrey and Albarran's results show that they derived more gratification from their use. Umphrey and Albarran concluded that the increased gratifications derived from RCD use by Hispanics may be the result of their greater dissatisfaction with television, which has been noted in other studies (Wilkes & Valencia, 1989; Faber, O'Guinn, & Meyer, 1987). In this instance, RCD gratifications may be symptomatic of the limited value of any one channel and the desire to get more out of the medium by exploiting its diversity.

Conclusions concerning ethnicity should be cautiously drawn from these few studies. In a survey of San Francisco adults (Walker, 1991), nonwhites had higher levels of RCD use than whites; and in Umphrey and Albarran's survey of Dallas adults (1993), Hispanics appeared to derive more gratification from their use. These results may be related to the relative importance of the medium of television for minorities documented in some studies (Bower, 1985; Gerson, 1966; Greenberg & Dervin, 1972). If television is a significant source of gratification, then the device that helps one access it is also a source of considerable gratification. However, the lack of significant findings in other studies of ethnic differences in RCD use suggests this conclusion is, at best, tentative.

Psychological Variables

Four RCD–channel changing studies have included a variety of psychological variables that generally have been related to RCD uses and gratifications (these are outlined in Table 5.2). Heeter (1988a) examined the relationship between three types of orienting searches and channel changing, and two types of novelty seeking from Pearson's (1970) scale: external–sensate (e.g., rafting, riding a roller coaster) and external–cognitive (e.g., reading the *World Almanac*, figuring out how a light meter works). Both forms of novelty seeking were significantly and positively correlated with channel changing and exhaustive orienting searches. Sensate novelty

TABLE 5.2. RCD Activity by Psychological Variables: Summary of Studies

Study	Method	Sample	Psychological variable(s)	Results
Heeter, 1988a	Door-to-door survey	232 adult respondents; 56% had remote selectors	Novelty seeking: sensate and cognitive	Sensate novelty seeking correlated with three types of orienting searchers and channel changing; cognitive novelty seeking correlated with exhaustive-orienting searches and channel changing.
Bryant & Rockwell, 1993	Electronic recording of behavior	80 adults	Locus of control	Viewers high in internal control changed channels more than those high in external control.
Wenner & Dennehy, 1993	Written survey	A priori list of reasons for channel changing	Desirability of control, sensation seeking, novelty seeking	Desirability of control negatively related to muting and total RCD use; sensation seeking positively related to RCD dominance, entry scanning, and commercial avoidance; novelty seeking positively related to entry scanning, muting, and total RCD activity.
Weaver et al., in press	Written survey	635 undergraduates	Psychoticism, extraversion, neuroticism	Viewers high on psychoticism used RCDs to control viewers; those high on neuroticism used RCDs for content avoidance.

seeking was also significantly and positively correlated with automatic orienting searches and to elaborated orienting searches. The correlations were weak (one at .34; the rest under .19) and none of these relationships continued in more rigorous multiple-regression analyses of channel changing and the three orienting searches. Thus, the study provides only a weak indication that novelty seeking is related to RCD activity.

In their laboratory experimental study of RCD channel changing, Bryant and Rockwell (1993) reported a substantial relationship between locus of control (within the individual or external to the individual) and channel changing. Using Rotter's (1982) 23-item internal–external locus of control scale, the researchers divided 80 subjects into 40 high external (controlled by external events) and 40 high internal (in control of their own behaviors and fate) groups. Each group watched television for 30 minutes. Half of each group had RCDs capable of changing channels. Respondents in the high internal control group changed channels 128 times, significantly more than those in the high external control group, who changed channels 83 times. Thus, the sense of control over one's fate that is characteristic of those high in internal locus of control was transferred to their control of television viewing.

In a hierarchical regression study of seven RCD activities (RCD dominance [proportion of RCD changes made in the presence of other viewers], entry scanning [orienting search], commercial avoidance, muting, multiple-program viewing, grazing, and total RCD activity), Wenner and Dennehy (1993) found support for Heeter's (1988a) earlier finding that sensation seeking is related to certain types of RCD–channel changing activities. Wenner and Dennehy found that novelty seeking, as measured by Lawrence's (1990) seven-point version of Pearson's (1970) scale, was a modest predictor of entry scanning (similar to Heeter's orienting search), muting, and total RCD activity (similar to Heeter's reevaluation). These relationships were all positive. Desirability of control, measured by Burger and Cooper's (1979) scale, was also a significant predictor of both muting and total RCD use, but was negatively related to these criterion variables. Thus, respondents with a high desire to control used the RCD less, but, according to Bryant and Rockwell (1993), viewers who believe that they are in control (high internal locus of control) use the RCD more. Finally, sensation seeking that was measured by Zuckerman's (1974) scale was not a significant predictor of any of the seven RCD activities examined in the study. Entered as the second of six blocks of variables in their seven hierarchical regression analyses, the three psychological variables were significant predictors of entry scanning, muting, and total RCD activity.

Finally, using the Eysenck Personality Questionnaire (Eysenck, Eysenck, & Barrett, 1985) to assess psychoticism, extraversion, and neuroticism, Weaver, Walker, McCord, and Bellamy (in press) surveyed 635 undergraduates concerning the relationship between these three personality traits and three RCD gratifications (content avoidance, viewing satisfaction, and control of others). Respondents with high psychoticism scores were higher in RCD gratification that was derived from controlling coviewers. Those high on neuroticism derived the most gratification from content avoidance.

Each of the four studies examining psychological variables has found some evidence to support a relationship between these variables and certain RCD activities. The support seems particularly strong for a relationship between novelty seeking and channel changing, including orienting searches of various types. Respondents looking for what's new and different seem to employ the RCD in that quest. The issue of control is more complex. Desire for control and locus of control are very different things. Respondents who believe that they are in control of their behaviors and fates seem to exercise more control over the viewing environment by changing channels more frequently. However, those who desire control, but do not necessarily believe that they have it, appear to use the RCD less. Perhaps their desire for control is partially the result of their perceived lack of real control. Those who desire control may be more likely to be high in external locus of control. Finally, viewers who score highly on a measure of neuroticism also appear to enjoy controlling content, while those high in psychoticism are more interested in using the RCD to control coviewers.

The strength and consistency of these results suggest that RCD activity and gratification have psychological precursors that should be explored in future research. In addition, uses and gratifications models that include psychological variables (McGuire, 1974; Palmgreen, Wenner, & Rosengren, 1985; Wenner, 1985) should provide especially useful guidance in understanding RCD gratifications. These models will help researchers do more than identify motivations for RCD use; they will help them explain what motivates viewers to seek particular gratifications.

Summary of Group Differences in RCD Use

Although RCDs are rapidly becoming universal in U.S. households, clear differences in RCD activity exist among various demographic groups and personality types. Based on our review of recent studies, we conclude the following:

1. Remote control use and the gratifications obtained from it are greater for younger viewers than for older viewers.
2. Income and education are poor predictors of differences in RCD uses and gratifications.
3. Although studies are limited, ethnicity may be related to RCD uses and gratifications, with minorities using the RCD more frequently, and ethnic group differences in gratifications varying by RCD gratifications.
4. Psychological variables have been found to be related to RCD uses and gratifications in three studies and show great promise for enriching our understanding of RCD behaviors.

WHY CLICK THE CLICKER?:
GRATIFICATIONS OF RCD USE

Some reasons for using the RCD are manifest. Remote controls make it easier to turn the set on or off, change channels, and adjust sound. These functions are basic to any radio or television receiver. But beyond these self-evident purposes, studies grounded in the uses and gratifications tradition of media research have identified gratifications derived from RCD use and channel changing. Uses and gratifications researchers seek to identify the gratifications sought and obtained from various forms of media consumption, asking not what using a device such as an RCD does to viewers or media industries, but what people do with the device (Katz, Blumler, & Gurevitch, 1974; Palmgreen, Wenner, & Rosengren, 1985). The approach assumes an active audience that seeks to gratify particular needs by consuming mediated messages and using media technology (Rubin & Bantz, 1987; Williams, Phillips, & Lum, 1985), and that this gratification contributes to continued use. As a technology that facilitates audience activity, the RCD has been theoretically linked to the uses and gratifications tradition (Walker & Bellamy, 1991a; Walker et al., 1993; Wenner & Dennehy, 1993; Ferguson, 1992; Perse & Ferguson, 1993b; Umphrey & Albarran, 1993). As we noted in an earlier study (Walker et al., 1993):

> The intrinsic nature of remote control devices (RCDs) suggests that the uses and gratifications approach is particularly well suited to studies of RCD use. RCDs require active participation from their users if the viewer is to derive full benefit from the television receiver and cable system and/or VCR connected to it. Uncovering the motivations for viewer involvement is an important issue in uses and gratifications research. (p. 103)

The first job for researchers is to identify the unique gratifications obtained from RCD use. As Rice (1984) notes in his general analysis of new technologies, "Research aimed at understanding human benefits from new media should focus on the unique strengths of each medium; rather than only on how they compensate or substitute for more natural media linkages" (p. 80). Encouraged by new technology, scholars such as Rice (1984) and Williams, Phillips, and Lum (1985), along with survey researchers (Walker & Bellamy, 1991a; Walker et al., 1993; Wenner & Dennehy, 1993), have identified six to seven specific motivations for RCD use. The gratifications in these studies have centered around the RCD's ability to increase the value of cable television, to enable audiences to avoid unpleasant aspects of viewing, and to control the viewing of others. These gratifications have, in turn, been related to background attributes, including demographic, personality, and media use variables.

As a communication technology, RCDs are subject to considerable "re-invention" (Rogers, 1986, p. 121) by the consumer, leading to gratifications of RCD use never intended by the manufacturer of the technology. As the new applications for the device are discovered by manufacturers, they may be incorporated into newer RCD designs. For example, more recent RCDs allow viewers to return to a previous channel or limit the number of channels to a few. This advancement facilitates multiple-program viewing. RCD-controlled picture-in-picture television receivers also allow viewers to view two channels at once.

Eight studies have sought to identify or evaluate motivations for, or gratifications from, RCD use or channel changing. The eight studies identifying gratifications are summarized in Table 5.3. Five studies (Ferguson, 1992; Heeter & Greenberg, 1988a; Heeter, 1988b; *How Americans Watch TV*, 1989; Umphrey & Albarran, 1993) have evaluated a priori lists of reasons for general channel changing or changing during a program. The motivations evaluated were supplied by the researchers or derived from other research. Three other studies (Walker & Bellamy, 1991a; Walker et al., 1993; Wenner & Dennehy, 1993) have been based on factor analyses of items drawn from open-ended questions that were answered by 75 undergraduates in a pilot study. Table 5.3 presents the mean response to each gratification identified in these studies. Except for the percentages reported for each channel-changing reason in the *Channels* study, means have been adjusted to reflect a 1 (lowest) to 10 (highest) scale, facilitating a direct comparison of gratifications means across studies.

Upon examination, certain patterns emerge in the eight studies. Seven of the eight studies include gratifications that highlight the RCD's ability to enhance the viewing experience by allowing viewers to get more out of television or relieve boredom while watching it. The means for this gratification ranged from the middle to the high end of the gratification means, from 4.65 to 8.30. The highest mean in four studies and the next highest in four others was the desire to see what else is on. These gratifications are logically connected. The desire to relieve boredom or get more out of television motivates viewers to change channels in their search for a better program. Changing channels to see what else is on is the only way (other than using a viewing guide) to find that better program. The gratification that comes from commercial avoidance is near the top of the gratifications list in five studies and in the middle in three

TABLE 5.3. Identification of RCD–Channel Changing Gratifications: Summary of Studies

Study	Method	Sample	Procedure	Gratifications' means (1 to 10 scale)[*]
Heeter & Greenberg, 1988b	Not reported	Not reported	A priori list of reasons for channel changing	6.8 to see what else is on 6.2 to avoid commercials 5.6 because they are bored 5.0 for variety 3.8 to watch multiple programs
Heeter, 1988a	Phone survey	254 adults	A priori list of reasons for channel changing	6.48 turn to a specific channel[**] 5.45 see what else is on 4.65 because of boredom 4.25 to avoid commercials 2.98 watch multiple programs
How Americans Watch TV, 1989	Self-report items	650 adults	A priori list of reasons for channel changing during a program	% *responding* 29.4 bored with program 28.4 make sure not missing a better program 22.7 avoid commercials 10.8 keep track of more than one program 4.1 want all the information can get
Walker & Bellamy, 1991a	Written survey	455 under-graduates	Factor analysis of gratifications generated from open-ended responses	7.60 finding out what's on 7.26 avoiding commercials 6.02 accessing music videos 5.92 getting more from TV 5.54 selective avoidance 5.30 accessing TV news 3.97 annoying others
Ferguson, 1992	Phone survey	412 adults	A priori list of 6 motivations	7.15 escape boredom 6.83 check out other programs 6.18 avoid commercials 5.98 avoid missing a better program 5.23 selective avoidance 4.40 multiple-program viewing

(cont.)

TABLE 5.3 *(cont.)*

Study	Method	Sample	Procedure	Gratifications' means (1 to 10 scale)[*]
Walker et al., 1993	Phone survey	315 adults	Factor analysis of items from Walker & Bellamy, 1991a, and open-ended items	8.00 finding out what's on 6.62 avoiding commercials 6.12 control family viewing and accessing TV news 6.04 selective avoidance 5.80 getting more from TV 5.62 accessing music videos 3.94 annoying others
Umphrey & Albarran, 1993	Phone survey	1241 adults	Ten items derived from Walker & Bellamy, 1991a	8.68 change channels without getting up 8.34 check out other channels 8.30 change channels if bored 8.10 makes it easier to watch 7.76 avoid commercials 7.72 in control of my TV viewing 7.38 watch fewer commercials 6.84 watch more news 6.70 watch several channels 6.58 watch weather anytime
Wenner & Dennehy, 1993	Written survey	219 undergraduates	Factor analysis of items from Walker & Bellamy, 1991a	7.28 environmental convenience 6.88 commercial avoidance 5.96 music scanning 5.19 news scanning 4.55 selective avoidance 3.40 aggressive play

[*]To facilitate comparison, all means from studies using ordinal or interval scales (Heeter, 1988a; Heeter & Greenberg, 1988b; Umphrey & Albarran, 1993; Walker & Bellamy, 1991a; Walker et al., 1993; Wenner & Dennehy, 1993) were converted to a 1 (lowest) to 10 (highest) scale.

[**]Separate male and female means were averaged.

others. Across the eight studies, it is the second strongest gratification, next to finding out what is on, which suggests that the concerns of advertisers about commercial avoidance are justified.

The studies are also split on three issues. The a priori studies included multiple-program viewing as a gratification/reason for channel changing rather than examining it as a type of RCD use. In each of these studies, the mean gratification level for multiple-program viewing is substantially lower than for other motivations. In addition to commercial avoidance, the factor-analytic studies all identified three content-related gratifications: accessing music videos, accessing news, and (the more general gratification) selective avoidance of unpleasant stimuli. Means for selective avoidance were generally in the middle of gratifications' means, while music video and news gratifications varied depending on the sample. Student samples received more gratification from accessing music videos,[1] while the adult sample received more from accessing news. Finally, the three factor-analytic studies all identified an annoyance–aggressive play factor with a low gratification score.

To summarize, for most viewers RCDs are especially useful because they allow viewers to find out what is on other channels, to change channels conveniently, and to avoid commercials. They are also valued for their capacity to help relieve boredom and get more from the medium. Gratifications derived from accessing particular content (music videos, news) or selective avoidance are of importance but are a less significant source of gratification. On the average, viewers derive less gratification from using the RCD for multiple-program viewing or to annoy others.

RCD Gratifications and RCD Use

Because viewers who derive more gratification from RCD use are more likely to repeat the gratifying activity, it is not surprising that several studies have found RCD use a good predictor of RCD gratifications and vice versa. In stepwise regression analyses, Walker and Bellamy (1991a) revealed that RCD use was the strongest predictor of six of the seven RCD gratifications and the second strongest predictor (after age) of the other gratification (annoying others). In their adult sample replication of this earlier RCD gratifications study, Walker et al. (1993) confirmed that RCD use was, once again, the strongest predictor of six of the seven gratifications. RCD gratifications have also been used to predict RCD use. In a hierarchical regression analysis, Wenner and Dennehy (1993) found that their block of RCD gratifications significantly predicted total RCD use, even when it was entered last, after all other predictors had accounted for variation in RCD use. Finally, in a correlational study of 583 adults, Ferguson (1992) reported that flipping frequency was significantly, although weakly, related to six RCD motivations: avoid boredom ($r = .11$), curiosity ($r = .17$), avoid ads ($r = .26$), see better shows ($r = .26$), avoid people you don't like ($r = .19$), and seeing two or more shows ($r = .25$). Clearly, viewers who receive greater gratification from the RCD are likely to use it more frequently.

Television Gratifications and RCD Use

Critics who analyze the impact of RCDs are split on the issue of whether RCD use is related to mental passivity or activity. Some critics argue that the clicker can be a tool for expression verging on the artistic. Umberto Eco (Stokes, 1990, pp. 39–40) asserts that the clicker gives him the capacity to "make television into a Picasso" by assembling fragments of programming into a video collage. Lavery (1993) reports that active RCD use enabled him to construct a richer, more complete view of the 1989 San Francisco earthquake than would have been possible without the humble RCD.[2] However, more conservative critics (Will, 1990) see RCDs as expanding not the mind but the amount of time wasted watching television, allowing viewers to graze "in private in a vast field of frivolous choices, actively choosing which pictorial stimuli passively to absorb" (p. 4).

Increasingly, scholars have distinguished between active or instrumental gratifications of television and passive or ritualistic (Perse, 1990; Rubin, 1984; Walker, 1990; Windahl, Höjerback, & Hedinsson, 1986) gratifications of the medium. In particular, RCD gratifications have also been found to be related to passive gratifications/benefits of television viewing. Walker and Bellamy (1991b) found that, after controlling for sex, race, age, household income, television exposure, and television affinity, total RCD use was significantly related to the use of television for diversion/escape, but not to the use of television for cognitive or personal identity reasons. Thus, RCD use was related to the more passive use of the medium (escape/diversion) than to more active gratifications (cognitive learning and personal identity). Subsequent research seems to confirm this finding. In a phone survey of 615 adults in a midwestern university town, Perse and Ferguson (1993b) examined the relationship between newer media technology (VCR ownership, cable subscription, channel changing) and both television satisfaction and seven benefits of television. Although it was entered last in their hierarchical regression, channel changing was still significantly related to two passive benefits of television: "helps me pass the time" and "keeps me company." Perse and Ferguson concluded "The results of our study suggest that the remote control's greatest benefits may not be associated with selecting specific programs. Channel changing instead may enhance television exposure that is unplanned or when there is nothing specific to watch" (pp. 849–850). The relatively high levels of RCD gratification for relieving boredom and finding out what is on television that have been reported in other gratifications studies (see Table 5.3) certainly supports their conclusion.

Perhaps the association between RCD use and more passive gratifications should be anticipated. Watching television is, by and large, a passive activity and RCDs make it possible for viewers to spend more time with that medium. Analyses of audience ratings over time (Barwise & Ehrenberg, 1988) show that the majority of a weekly television series' audience is composed of viewers who did not see the previous episode. This limited loyalty is symptomatic of the minimal importance of most programs to most viewers. Scheduling techniques that are based on audience flow between programs assume that the audience will not exert the minimal mental and physical energy necessary to change channels if the program that follows the one they just viewed is not too unappealing (see Chapter 4). As Kubey and Csikszentmihalyi (1990) concluded from their study of self-reports collected randomly from respondents during television viewing, "Television viewing is a passive and relaxing, low concentration activity" (p. 171). Since most television viewing is passive and RCDs can be used to extend viewing time by allowing viewers to graze and view multiple programs when there is not one program of interest available, it is not surprising that RCD use is linked to more passive gratifications of the medium.

RCD Gratifications and Channel Repertoire

Obtaining gratifications from the RCD appears to predict having a greater repertoire of channels better than simply using the device does. In a study based on a phone survey of 583 adults, Ferguson (1992) reported that RCD use (based on a yes/no response to the question "Do you use your RCD?") explained 2% of the variation in channel repertoire after cable subscription and VCR ownership were entered in a hierarchical regression. However, six RCD motivations (see Table 5.3 for the list) entered as a block added 6% to the variance explained. Channel flipping (measured using one self-report estimate of channel changing during a typical hour of previous day viewing) was not related to channel repertoire. Increased levels of motivation were more important in predicting an increased repertoire than just using an RCD. Since this is a correlation-based study, it is not clear if those who find the RCD a source of gratification develop an interest in a greater variety of channels, or if those who are already attuned to the greater variety offered by cable television become more enthusiastic RCD users.

RCD Deprivation

If many viewers are deriving considerable gratification from RCD use, what is their reaction when the RCD is lost or broken? Based on the strong market for replacement remote controls (Gill, 1993), a quick trip to the K-Mart may be in order for many. One way of assessing the importance of a medium or a communication technology is to analyze what happens when users must do without it. Studies of media deprivation due to strikes have a long history in mass communication research (Berelson, 1949; Cohen, 1981; de Bock, 1980; Kimball, 1959; Walker, 1990; Windahl, Höjerback, & Hedinsson, 1986), and one attempt has been made to systematically examine RCD deprivation. Ferguson and Perse (1994) convinced a convenience sample of students ($n = 47$) to give up their RCD for one week. Although the mean deprivation score was moderate (5.65 on a one, "not at all deprived," to eight, "extremely deprived," scale), cheating was common; 31 out of 46 subjects said that they cheated by using their RCDs during the week. Interestingly, perceived deprivation was higher for females than males. These RCD-deprived subjects were less motivated to watch television, received fewer gratifications, and spent less time viewing broadcast channels. They found television viewing less informational, relaxing and entertaining, and received fewer companionship gratifications. The authors concluded, "We found strong evidence that the RCD changes the way that people watch television. After only a week without the RCD, we found significant differences in our subject's television viewing styles" (p. 15).

Summary of Motivations for RCD Use

Just as RCD use varies among different demographic groups, motivations for RCD use vary among individuals. Gratifications studies have described the gratifications obtained from RCD activity, showing how these gratifications relate to RCD use as well as to the more general gratifications gained from television viewing. In particular:

1. Researchers have identified seven gratifications derived from RCD use: finding out what is on television, avoiding boredom or getting more out of television, avoiding commercials, selective

avoidance of unpleasant stimuli, accessing music videos, accessing news, and annoying others.

2. Higher levels of most RCD gratifications are positively related to higher levels of RCD use.
3. Although research is limited, frequent RCD users are more likely to use television for passive gratifications.
4. Subjects who are denied the use of their RCDs often cheat and use them anyway. They report moderate levels of feeling deprived.

THEORETICAL IMPLICATIONS OF RCD USE

One of the major gratifications obtained from remote control use is the power to switch off what is not wanted. Viewers can quickly quiet the politicians, commentators, celebrities, and "realities" they abhor. Has the remote control robbed television of its power to change society by reducing its ability to reach the disaffected or the uninterested? The capacity of RCDs to increase the degree of selectivity exercised by second-generation television audiences has implications for several long-standing theoretical issues in mass communication; some of these include selective exposure and avoidance theory, play theory, and theories based on limited content choice such as cultivation theory, demassification, and agenda setting. As RCDs grow in sophistication and capacity, these mass communication theories may require modification.

Selective Exposure and Avoidance

Selective exposure and avoidance theory is well established in mass communication research (Katz & Lazarsfeld, 1955; Klapper, 1960; Zillmann & Bryant, 1985). From this perspective, viewers are seen as active choosers of what messages they consume, with a particular tendency to select messages that reinforce their attitudes, values, and beliefs and to reject conflicting points of view. This selectivity reduces the power of the media's influence, because conflicting messages are rarely encountered. However, selectivity can be enhanced or retarded by the medium delivering the message. Disinterested voters can easily ignore a campaign ad in a newspaper, but may find it difficult to ignore a similar ad placed on a large billboard that they pass on the way to work each weekday. Similarly, television has long been seen as a medium that allows candidates to reach the less interested or even the adversarial potential voter because the political message has been sandwiched between program segments and other commercials. Hsia (1989) notes what was true in the first generation of television:

> A glaring drawback of the broadcast media is that no broadcast program allows random access, because they must be sequentially presented in accordance with schedules. With newspapers, readers can read the last page first and they can also skip, stop, and restart reading at their own will. (p. xx)

While cable has increased the diversity of television content, VCRs and RCDs have increased our accessibility to that content; RCD-toting viewers are more likely to randomly access the increasing number of cable channels they encounter (Bryant & Rockwell, 1993; Ferguson, 1992; *How Americans Watch TV*, 1989; Wenner & Dennehy, 1993), while VCRs allow viewers to time-shift programs. These recorded programs can be played back at any time and in any order and viewed with an RCD at one's side, making it easy to zip by commercials or undesirable program segments. The synergy among RCDs, VCRs, and cable television is manifest: cable provides more specialized programming worth taping on VCRs, while RCDs make both the selection and VCR programming processes more convenient. In short, the RCD, the VCR, and cable are, each in their own way, tools of selective avoidance and in combination their impact is even greater.

As noted earlier in this chapter, several studies of RCD gratifications (Walker & Bellamy, 1991a; Walker, Bellamy, & Traudt, 1993; Wenner & Dennehy, 1993) have found that the selective avoidance of unpleasant stimuli, including politicians, political ads, news reporters, and others is an RCD motivation of moderate strength and is significantly related to RCD use. In our study of undergraduates (Walker & Bellamy, 1991a) and adults (Walker et al., 1993), we found that the percentages shown in Table 5.4 of students and adults agreed with these selective avoidance items.[3] In both studies, a substantial minority (and in some cases the majority) of our respondents agreed with the avoidance items, which would suggest that for many viewers the RCD is perceived as a useful tool in the rejection of unwanted stimuli. Perse (1990) has also noted this potential for RCD control over television content. In a gratifications study of channel changing, she observed that channel changing may strengthen audience immunity to persuasion. She stated that "increased channel changing coupled with lower attention may weaken media impact. It may be that the higher levels of channel changing may be a sign of an obstinate audience not likely to be affected by media content" (p. 693). In short, obstinance may increase with each click of the clicker.

TABLE 5.4. Percentage of Respondents Agreeing with Selective Avoidance Items

Students	Adults	Selective avoidance items
		I like to use the remote control because . . .
58.3	43.2	I can change channels when some politician that I don't like comes on.
45.2	43.8	I can avoid people on TV that I don't agree with.
55.4	36.5	I can change channels when some news reporter that I don't like comes on.
47.0	40.6	I can change channels when political ads that I don't agree with come on.
58.7	59.4	I can change channels when some news story that I don't like comes on.

The effect of this rapid growth in selectivity suggests an increase in individualized television use and less sharing of information, opinions, and concerns within the general population. The self-serving grazer is less likely to listen to the arguments of groups that oppose his or her point of view, in effect, withdrawing from democratic debate. Possible outcomes of this isolation are a hardening of attitudes and an increasing intolerance of others and their beliefs. Even more unsettling, with a quick button push, the uncomfortable realities of modern life (e.g., crime, poverty, social injustice) can be marginalized. In an era when most of the population receives their news from television, social problems become hidden problems. Thus, although it may be personally desirable, an increased capacity for selective television viewing may not be socially beneficial.

Play Theory

Although selective exposure and avoidance appears to stimulate some RCD activity, grazers also graze just for the fun of it. In *The Play Theory of Mass Communication*, William Stephenson (1967) argues that most media scholars have overlooked the delight that viewers derive simply from using a medium: what he terms "communication pleasure." Stephenson contends that the typical reaction to a new medium or communication technology is to analyze its potential harm, rather than discover its capacity to facilitate our enjoyment. Given this point of view, it is not surprising that the disruptions to domestic tranquility traceable to selfish grazing and the problems zapping presents to advertising, rather than the benefits of the technology to the individual, are emphasized in early RCD research. But Stephenson encourages us to examine the pleasures consumers gain from the manipulation of media messages. Although grazing from channel to channel has only recently concerned scholars, audiences have always "played" with a medium, consuming it in unintended ways. At a time when RCDs were only luxury extras for the few, Stephenson (1967, p. 151) wrote of grazing in the print media, noting that readers derive enjoyment from simply milling about: skimming some articles and skipping others, only later to return for more thorough reading. Confirming Stephenson's observations, Ruotolo (1988) uncovered an active group of "scanners," who derive considerable pleasure from this "hop, skip, and jump" style of reading.

Of course, RCDs allow grazers to flip through video images even more rapidly than they turn the pages of a newspaper or magazine. As Ferguson (1994) discovered, this playful approach to television can lead to an average of 100 or more channel changes per hour among restless viewers. Although essentially an audio–video experience, Lavery (1993) offers a detailed verbal rendering of one grazing escapade that was recorded in Memphis, Tenn. on June 25, 1992. Here is a portion of his description:

> A small boy at Saint Jude's Hospital is fed intravenously during chemotherapy; on *A Different World*, college women talk of "reappropriating the symbols of our oppressors." On a cable access channel, local experts talk about home insurance; on *Drexell's Class*, two teachers meet at a drinking fountain; whale watchers track killer whales; students remodel a house; a spokesman for Sears makes a full disclosure about recent charges of fraud in automotive repair; Lloyd Bridges narrates an unidentifiable documentary in which a man plays Santa Claus; a posse tracks some outlaws; the name of a QVC winner is selected from a clear plastic barrel. (p. 227)

Play theory implies that chaotic collages like the one above are an important element in the grazer's delight: a joy that comes not just from the images encountered but from the control they have over those images (Wenner & Dennehy, 1993). This "communication pleasure" has been associated with print by Stephenson and others (Ettema, 1989; Stipp, 1989) and by one estimate it consumes about 25% of the time spent using teletext (televised print and graphics) (Greenberg & Lin, 1988). Now, as we concluded in Chapter 2, at any one time about one-fifth of all viewers may be restless grazers, drawing communication pleasure from one of the viewing styles of the 1990s (Walker, 1992).[4]

As television viewing evolves into television grazing, with its associated communication pleasures, the next generation of television users is learning to use the medium in ways never intended by program creators. Their playful flipping establishes patterns of behavior and attention that are more akin to those associated with video game playing than traditional television viewing. Television becomes an activity that demands physical as well as mental response to disjointed visual stimuli. Viewers are encouraged to seek immediate gratification from particular images and sounds, regardless of their connections to an ongoing plot or developing characters. Graphic violence and intense sexual activity are enjoyed for their own titillations, rather than as an integrated component of a developing narrative. Since violent acts are no longer tied to mitigating antecedents or painful consequences, they may stimulate more antisocial behavior than televised violence that is conceptually justified or properly punished. If the grazer routinely flips away from the negative consequences of sexual activity, such as sexually transmitted disease, unwanted pregnancies, or broken relationships, televised sex could be more readily imitated. Finally, as we shall argue in the next section, the communications pleasure derived from RCD grazing also increases the variety of television channels viewed, lessening the impact of any particular program source, and reducing the medium's ability to impart a shared cultural experience.

Limited Choice Theories: Cultivation, Demassification, and Agenda Setting

If cable and VCRs increase choice and RCDs make that choice easier to access, mass communication theories that rely on notions of a limited symbolic environment should be revised (Bryant, 1986; Webster, 1989a; Webster, 1989b). Both experimental and survey research suggest that RCDs increase channel repertoire and exposure to a variety of content (Bryant & Rockwell, 1993; Ferguson, 1992). This greater exposure to the variety available on cable television and in video rental outlets has the potential to weaken the cultivation and agenda-setting effects of television, while strengthening arguments that predict the gradual demassification of the media.

Cultivation Theory

Cultivation theorists (Gerbner & Gross, 1976; Signorielli & Morgan, 1990; Gerbner, Gross, Morgan, & Signorielli, 1994) contend that television is a major socializing force and is especially effective in influencing our perceptions of reality. Stereotypical and limited depictions on television are the major source of information about the world that we do not directly experience. Evidence of television's considerable influence on perceptions comes from comparisons of heavy and light viewers. Heavy viewers have perceptions of reality similar to those documented in quantitative analyses of television programming, while light viewers have perceptions that more closely resemble data found in the real world.

Television is important because it bridges the gap between our generally limited experience and the larger world. Gerbner and Gross (1976) note that most viewers have limited personal contact with contexts that are common in the world of television (hospitals, courtrooms, police stations, prisons, corporate board rooms, etc.). Much of our collective knowledge of these unfamiliar locations and the actions of those who occupy them is supplied by television: our most pervasive medium of mass communication.

The importance of television in the cultivation process is based on an assumption of a homogeneous symbolic environment. If cable and VCRs make more choice available and RCDs make it easier to access that choice, then the power of television as a unifying cultivation force may be waning. Cultivation critics (Bryant, 1986; Webster, 1989) have contended just this. Networks still dominate prime time viewing in the United States, but an increasing portion of the audience is viewing more specialized video sources. With over 61 million ("Cable Subscribers," 1994) of the over 94 million U.S. television households ("Demographics Estimates," 1994) wired for cable and over 77% of television households in possession of VCRs (Klopfenstein, 1993), it appears that most viewers want more variety than the first generation of television offered. RCDs make it easier for viewers to encounter these new distribution channels and to return to them if they prove gratifying. As we argued earlier (Walker & Bellamy, 1993a), viewers can draw from several sources in developing their perceptions of reality.

> The active grazer may learn about the courtroom from Court TV as well as *Matlock*, about the operating room from medical programming on Lifetime as well as reruns of *St. Elsewhere*, and about jail from *Cops*, an HBO behind-the-scenes documentary, and *In the Heat of the Night*. Cable television brought choice, but the RCD made it easier for viewers to be choosy. (p. 11)

Cultivation advocates counter that increases in distribution alternatives (cable, VCRs) and ease of selection has not led to a "substantially greater diversity of content" (Gerbner et al., 1994, p. 19). Most cable and video fare presents the same stereotypes common to network television. Indeed, the rapid pace of vertical integration in media industries (see Chapter 4) has led to a concentration of program decision making that may lead to less, not more, diversity of content.

Despite the theoretical contentions, little research has been conducted on the relationship between RCD use and the cultivation process. Only one study has examined the possible impact of RCDs on cultivation theory. Perse, Ferguson, and McLeod (1994) found RCD ownership and channel changing were negatively related to cultivation effects, but these relationships were not statistically significant.

Demassification

While cultivation researchers are usually concerned about the misleading and potentially destructive information that homogeneous media content offers to viewers, critics who are concerned with demassification lament the loss of the media's effectiveness as a consensus builder.[5] The expanding choice that is integral to the popularity of cable and VCRs, and greatly assisted by the omnipresent RCD, has raised concerns about the consequences of a demassified media. As more and more channels of distribution compete for approximately the same number of viewers, the tendency may be for the audiences of the most popular channel to decrease while the audiences for newer program sources increase only slightly. Just as the magazine industry demassified in the 1950s and 1960s, the television industry will demassify in the 1990s and beyond. Many argue this process is well underway, as prime time shares for the three largest networks (ABC, CBS, NBC) have declined from 97% in 1972 to 80% in 1984 (Webster, 1989b, p. 204) to 53% for the first half of the 1995–1996 television season ("Weekly Averages," 1996, p. 24).

Some scholars and critics see a clear trend toward demassification. Webster (1989b) identified three characteristics of cable, satellites, and VCRs (programming is diverse, programming is correlated with channels, channels are differentially available) that lead to audience fragmentation and polarization. Similarly, Rogers (1986) claims that audience segmentation in the mass media is one of seven social impacts of the newer communications media. Industry critic William J. Donnelly (1986) sees new communications technology as splintering the United States, embarking the country on the "Confetti Era, when all events, ideas, and values are the same size and weight . . . when ideas and experiences float down like cheap confetti" (p. 182). As newer channels gain strength and can compete more vigorously for original, high quality programming, the trend may accelerate.[6] A possible consequence of demassification is a decline in the agenda-setting effect of the mass media.

Agenda Setting

Since RCDs facilitate the use of cable and VCRs, thus contributing to the demassification of the television medium, they may also contribute a reduction in the agenda setting effect of television. Although considerably qualified by later research and criticism (Iyengar & Kinder, 1987), the central proposition of agenda-setting was attributed by McCombs and Shaw (1972) to Cohen (1963). Cohen argued that the press "may not be successful much of the time in telling people what to think, but it is stunningly successful in telling its readers what to think *about*" (p. 120).

If television content continues to diversify and audiences continue to segment, the agenda-setting capacity of the news media may erode simply because fewer people are watching news and the news they are watching is more tailored to their particular interests (see Chapter 4). The much touted 500-channel cable systems of the near future, and television receivers equipped with "smart" remotes (Heeter, Yoon, & Sampson, 1993) make that possibility a compelling one.

A reduction in the agenda-setting effect of television during political campaigns could lead to greater fragmentation among the electorate, as voters selectively focus on only the issues that directly affect them rather than those that impact the larger society. Because of the medium's weaker role in prioritizing issues for voters, politicians are encouraged to avoid issues completely, focusing on personal attacks and ideological labeling. These conditions nurture a less informed and more cynical electorate, reenforcing the trend toward lower voter turnout. Thus, what it takes to be elected becomes more painfully detached from what it takes to govern a nation.

CONCLUSION

In this chapter, we have reviewed the research literature concerning group and demographic differences in RCD use, the gratifications obtained from RCD use and their relationship to other television research variables, and theoretical implications of this research. As we have seen, RCD use varies considerably among groups and produces a unique set of gratifications that are associated with more passive uses of television. Although studies are limited, RCD use potentially modifies theories of selective avoidance, play theory, cultivation theory, demassification, and agenda setting. However, considerably more research needs to be conducted to specify the nature of these theoretical modifications. In our next chapter, we examine the group distinction that is most frequently associated with RCD use: the contrast between women and men, and their battle over who will control the clicker.

NOTES

1. Heeter, D'Alessio, Greenberg, and McVoy (1988) found substantial evidence that many viewers use RCDs to access music videos on MTV for only brief episodes. In their minute-by-minute analysis of channel changing, only 9% of channel changes to MTV led to watching it for 15 minutes or more.

2. More recent special opportunities for RCD active viewers include the 1991 Gulf War and the flight of O.J. Simpson from the California Highway Patrol. In all of these events, different news organizations had different sources of information about and different visual accounts of a breaking news story before the facts of the story have been fully assembled. The RCD allows viewers to switch between news sources, obtaining a richer, more complete account of the events as they happen.

3. The student and adult percentages are not directly comparable because the students responded on a six-point scale (strongly disagree, disagree, mildly disagree, mildly agree, agree, strongly agree), while the adults responded to a five-point scale (strongly disagree, disagree, neither agree nor disagree, agree, strongly agree).

4. Using data from a survey of San Francisco adults, Walker (1991) examined whether the propensity toward flipping was common to several mass media or just television. Respondents were asked two types of questions about their use of four mass media (television, newspapers, magazines, books). The first set of four questions asked whether respondents always finish a text once they start using it. These variables were called television, newspaper, magazine, and book closure. The second set of four items asked if they liked to flip through the medium looking for an interesting television program to watch, newspaper article to read, magazine article to read, or section of a book to read. These variables were labeled television, newspaper, magazine, and book flipping. Television closure was positively and moderately related to both newspaper closure ($r = .36$, $p < .01$) and magazine closure ($r = .35$, $p < .01$), and less strongly related to book closure ($r = .21$, $p < .01$). Television flipping was positively and moderately related to newspaper flipping ($r = .29, p < .01$) and less strongly related to magazine flipping ($r = .20, p < .01$). Television flipping

was not significantly related to book flipping ($r = -.08$). This one study suggests that there is some tendency for RCD grazers to exhibit similar behavior when they are reading newspapers and magazines.

5. Ithiel de Sola Pool found this tendency toward opposite effects so frequently in writings about communication technologies, he labeled them "dual effects" (Steinfield, Dutton, & Kovaric, 1989).

6. However, as we argued in Chapter 4, some segments of the mass media will still deliver large audiences because many advertisers need and will demand them. In addition, a greater variety of distribution channels increases both the opportunity to create new, potentially diverse programming and to distribute existing programming or facsimiles of already successful programs. A block-buster movie can now receive a wider circulation than ever before because it can be viewed in theaters and in at least five video "windows" (pay-per-view cable, video rental/sales, pay cable, network television, station/basic-cable syndication). The original blockbuster also typically spawns multiple sequels and a myriad of imitators. Neuman (1991, p. 129) is especially firm on this point, arguing that "the economics of mass communications do not promote diversity" and "economies of scale are more pronounced for the production and distribution of information than for most other consumer goods."

CHAPTER 6

Who's in Control?
GENDER DIFFERENCES
AND FAMILY VIEWING

Bob Thomas, a Spokane, Wash. engineering consultant develops "Stop It," a remote control override that allows his wife to "freeze the channel," giving her channel-surfing husband an electronic wipe out (Hanson, 1993).

A novelty postcard shows a small girl in the presence of her mother praying "and when I grow up Lord, please send me a man who will love me, respect me, and occasionally let me use the t.v. remote control."

In Chicago, a county clerk performs a marriage ceremony that includes a vow that "the wife would get the remote control for the TV at least half of the time" (O'Malley & Collin, 1993, p. 14).

On a *Primetime Live* segment focusing on gender conflicts over the RCD, comedian Jerry Seinfeld claims that men use the RCD more than women because men are hunters and there's nothing left to hunt, except a better program on television (Sawyer, 1991).

According to columnist Judy Markey, men have a free hand with the RCD because they're the spouse whose hand is free. "The reason we [women] don't take over the household zapping is that it's very hard to hold a remote control when you are still folding laundry at 10:15 P.M." (Markey, 1991, p. 26).

Howard Markman, head of the University of Denver's Center for Marital Studies, calls RCD grazing "one of two major marital issues of the '90s." The second issue is the limited time busy couples have together (Valeriano, 1993, p. B–1).

In a McDonalds television commercial, a woman strikes a deal with her male companion. If he'll give her the remote, she will give him her bag of french fries. After struggling with the decision, he concedes the RCD, only to see her gloating with the empowering clicker in one hand and a second bag of fries in the other.

Gender conflicts over RCDs are frequent fodder for humor columnists and in casual conversations. Concerns about the RCD-dominant male are routinely expressed in women's magazines (Viorst, 1992; Kornheiser, 1993) and subjected to sound bite analysis in the press (Arrington, 1992; Elder, 1986; Valeriano, 1993).[1] The collection of news items and observations from pop culture offered above easily could be replicated several times over. In the battle of the sexes, the RCD is seen as one more tool of male oppression and a source of anguish for the embattled female. The popular image is that *he controls* and *she complains*.

In this chapter, we discuss the issue of RCD dominance in group viewing situations and the gender differences expressed in that dominance. We want to report what is known about the different ways that men and women use the RCD and how families differ in their control of the clicker. Although we offer a theoretical explanation, we try to restrain ourselves from recurrent speculation as to why men use RCDs more than women, if indeed they do. The popular press offers many engaging anthropological, psychological, psychoanalytic, biological, and commonsense explanations for the different RCD profiles of women and men.[2] We work inductively by first reviewing what is known about gender differences and RCD use in group viewing based on a striking number of studies (see Table 6.1) and then we provide theoretical explanations of these results. In most studies of RCD use, gender differences in use and/or control of the RCD has been a variable of interest to researchers, although only rarely the main focus of study (Perse & Ferguson, 1993a).

RESEARCH ON GENDER DIFFERENCES

Industry Research

Gender differences in RCD use have emerged either directly or indirectly in a number of industry reports. Some of these proprietary studies, using Nielsen data, have shown clear differences in channel changing during different dayparts or for different genres of programming. Data from a McCann-Erickson advertising agency study, reported by McSherry (1985), showed that between 1978 and 1983, as RCD penetration increased from 16% to 24% of U.S. households, the percentage of the audience changing channels increased 32% in prime time, but only 19% in daytime. Although daytime programming has more commercial clutter, which promoted a higher level of overall channel changing (see Chapter 3), flipping grew more rapidly during prime time. One explanation for this greater growth rate is the greater proportion of males in the prime time audience compared to daytime. Similarly, Marton (1989) reported that 16% of the mixed-gender prime time audience zap commercials, but during male-dominated weekend sports that figure jumps to 23%, a 44% increase in zapping. Finally, analyses of Arbitron and Nielsen data by the Network Television Association (Mandese, 1992b) found the least zapping during daytime and the most during weekend sports: only 3.3% of the predominantly female daytime viewers switched during nonprogram material, compared to 5% of the predominantly male weekend sports viewers, a 52% difference.[3]

Men also seem more likely to control the clicker and use it for a wider variety of activities. A 1988 survey sponsored by J. Walter Thompson (Orsini, 1991) found that 43% of males compared to 29% of females took primary control of the RCD in mixed-gender viewing situations. Similar gender contrasts in RCD use were reported in the *Channels'* study of grazing (*How Americans Watch TV*, 1989). Gender differences in the responses to six items were analyzed: RCD use, grazing, zapping, orienting search, enjoyment of flipping, and multiple-program viewing. For all items, males engaged in more RCD activity than females. Seventy percent of males and 65.7% of females reported that they used the remote control frequently. Fifty-one percent of males and 46% of females replied "yes" when asked if they changed channels during programs. Slightly over 14% of males but only 6.6% of females said they changed the channel when a commercial appeared, while 47% of males and 34.2% of females reported using the RCD for an orienting search at least half of the time that they sat down to watch television. About 17% of males and about 11% of females said they enjoyed watching television more when they were flipping channels, while 41.9% of males and 33.7% of females said they could follow two or more programs at the same time. To summarize, males and females report using the RCD at about the same degree of frequency, but males clearly expressed more enjoyment in grazing and greater preference for specific RCD activities, including grazing, multiple-program viewing, zapping, and orienting searches.

Finally, *Consumer Reports* ("Remote Controls," 1992) surveyed its readers on their use of RCDs, finding men much more active users and controllers of the device. Men were twice as likely as women to take charge of the remote, while 38% of women complained that men "hog" the remote compared to 15% of men complaining about women's control. Eighty-five percent of men and 60% of women claim to " 'channel surf': flicking, clicking and zapping between channels instead of sticking with one program" (p. 797). Two-thirds of the women complained about their male companion's grazing, while only 43% of males complained about their mate's RCD excesses.

The conclusions to be drawn from these few industry–consumer studies are straightforward: males use the RCD more than females to alter the nature of viewing through grazing, multiple-program viewing and advertising avoidance.[4] Males are more likely to control the device when viewing with the other gender. However, in some households, women do control the RCD and use it to alter viewing. Despite male dominance, the majority of women perceive that they use the RCD frequently.

Academic Research

Industry research paints a consistent picture of male dominance in RCD use. Although females do use the RCD, in group viewing situations males are more likely to be in control. Academic research presents a more complex representation of RCD use. When gender differences emerge, males are usually the more RCD-active gender. However, age, viewing situation, and the population sampled are intervening factors that modify the representation of gender differences in RCD uses and gratifications.

As we noted in Chapter 2, the method that is used determines what is measured. Surveys measure perceptions of behavior, while observational and electronic recording methods examine actual behavior. RCD behaviors may be different from respondent perceptions of those behaviors. Thus, our review of this research will be organized by method, reviewing survey and studies of self-perception first, then observational/behavior studies.

Survey Research

Gender differences in RCD uses and gratifications have been analyzed in eight self-report studies. With two exceptions (Wenner & Dennehy, 1993; Walker, 1991), these studies found males reporting higher levels of most RCD activities. However, gender differences in levels of gratifications derived from these activities were not consistently observed. When gratification differences were obtained, males tended to have higher scores.

Five studies of adults (Greene, 1988; Heeter, 1988b; Perse & Ferguson, 1993a; Umphrey & Albarran, 1993; Walker, Bellamy, & Traudt, 1993) and one study of undergraduates (Walker & Bellamy, 1991a)[5] reported that males have higher levels of most RCD activities (channel changing, grazing, multiple-program viewing, zipping, zapping) and some RCD gratifications. The results of these studies are shown in Table 6.1.

In her chapter on gender differences in *Cableviewing*, Heeter (1988b) summarized the results of 10 studies: adults (7 surveys), tenth-graders (2 surveys), and seventh-graders (1 survey). The adult males had significantly higher scores in (1) frequency of orienting search, (2) changing channels during both routinely and nonroutinely viewed programs, (3) checking all of the channels, (4) checking channels out of sequence (e.g., jumping from channel 2 to channel 33), (5) changing channels between and during programs, (6) zapping, and (7) multiple-program viewing. Men also had lower scores on the frequency of viewing an entire program without changing channels. Women had higher scores on the annoyance item: "How often does someone else change channels when you wish they wouldn't?" Finally, men had significantly higher scores on only one of five motivations for changing channels: to see what else is on. This pattern of results was consistent across the seven adult studies with one exception: a survey of the very specialized audience of The Playboy Channel.

Gender differences among tenth-graders and fifth-graders were much less pronounced. Of the 17 channel-changing items assessed in two studies of tenth-graders, only four produced significant gender differences: tenth-grade males were more likely to check channels out of sequence and change channels during a program (in both studies), while females were more likely to check channels in sequence. In the one survey of fifth-graders, two out of eight channel-changing items produced significant differences: males were slightly more likely to zap and view multiple programs than females. Thus, Heeter's extensive survey research on channel changing points to an interaction between gender and age. Younger viewers are less likely to exhibit the strong gender differences evident in the parents' responses.

Greene (1988) also summarized the results of multiple surveys of over 4,000 adult respondents. More males than females used the RCD the previous night (54.8% to 50.7%), zapped during at least half the commercial interruptions (10.6% to 6.1%), zapped at least some of the commercial interruptions (18.2% to 13.7%), and zipped over VCR-recorded commercials (1.2% to .5%). As noted in the industry studies reviewed earlier,

TABLE 6.1. RCD Activity by Gender: Summary of Survey Research

Study	Method	Sample	RCD variables	Results
Heeter, 1988b	1 door-to-door, 4 phone and 5 written surveys	3168 adults in 7 surveys; 407 5th-graders; 1492 10th-graders	Orienting search; grazing during programs; grazing during breaks between programs; zapping	Adult males report higher levels of each RCD activity in most studies; few gender differences were found among 5th- and 10th-graders
Greene, 1988	Multiple surveys	Over 4,000 respondents	Zapping; zipping	Males report higher levels of zipping and zapping
Walker, 1991	Phone survey	209 adults	Total RCD use; grazing; multiple-program viewing; zapping	No significant differences between males and females
Walker & Bellamy, 1991a	Written survey	455 students	RCD use; grazing; multiple-program viewing; 7 RCD gratifications	Males significantly higher in RCD use, grazing, & multiple-program viewing; gender predictor of 3 RCD gratifications: annoying others, getting more from TV, accessing news; males receive greater gratification.
Perse & Ferguson, 1993a	Written survey; phone survey	566 adults; 615 adults	Channel changing; RCD motivations; television content	Males had higher levels of channel changing and most RCD gratifications; males and females under 30 produce fewer differences
Walker et al., 1993	Phone survey	315 adults	RCD use; grazing; multiple-program viewing; 7 RCD gratifications	Males significantly higher in RCD use, grazing, and multiple-program viewing; females more likely to use RCDs for selective avoidance

(cont.)

TABLE 6.1 *(cont.)*

Study	Method	Sample	RCD variables	Results
Wenner & Dennehy, 1993	Written survey	219 under-graduate students	RCD dominance, entry scanning; commercial avoidance; muting; multiple-program viewing; grazing; total RCD activity;	Gender not a significant predictor of any RCD activity
Umphrey & Albarran, 1993	Phone survey	1241 adults: 34% white; 28% African-American; 37% Hispanic	10 RCD motiva-tion items	6 out of 30 gender comparisons were significant

males were only slightly more likely to use the RCD, but much more likely to use it for RCD activities that interrupt the normal flow of programming: zapping and zipping.

Our surveys of undergraduates (Walker & Bellamy, 1991a) and Pittsburgh adults (Walker et al., 1993) both found significant gender differences in RCD use and a few differences in RCD gratifications. In both studies, the variable median was used to split the sample into high and low users for three RCD activities (total RCD use, grazing, and multiple-program viewing). For the undergraduates, 10% to 13% more males than females were in the high RCD use groups for each of the three RCD activities. The differences among the adults were even greater, with 18% to 21% more males than females in the higher use groups for the three RCD variables. Among the undergraduates, males had higher scores for three RCD gratifications: using the RCD to get more from television, to assess news, and to annoy others. For the adults, there was only one significant gender difference among the seven RCD gratifications: females were more likely to find the RCD useful in selectively avoiding unpleasant stimuli.

Umphrey and Albarran (1993) also considered gender differences in RCD gratification scores, finding few contrasts in gratifications obtained from RCD use. For three ethnic groups (white, African-American, Hispanic), males and females were compared on 10 gratification items. Among the 30 comparisons, only 6 produced significant differences. Compared with white females, white males received more RCD gratification from commercial avoidance, checking out other channels, and the reduction of boredom. Among African-Americans, males received more RCD gratification from watching fewer commercials, while females received more from being able to catch the weather anytime. Among Hispanics, only one gender difference was noted: males received more gratification because RCDs make it possible for them to watch more news.

In the only study specifically focusing on gender and RCD use, Perse and Ferguson (1993a) in two surveys found that males 30 or over had higher levels of channel changing than females of the same age.[6] There was no significant difference in channel changing between males and females under 30. In addition, males 30 or older received more gratification from RCD use than their female cohorts. Among respondents under 30, fewer gender differences in gratifications were noted.

In their East Coast study of 566 adults, Perse and Ferguson (1993a) found that males had significantly higher gratification scores on seven out of nine stimulation items (avoiding commercials, multiple-program viewing, checking what else is on, seeing if something better is on, for variety, seeing what's on other channels, and to see what I'm missing) and females had higher scores on one out of four content items (using the RCD to watch a particular program). Significant gender–age interactions were found for two items (avoiding commercials and multiple-program viewing), indicating that these gender differences were restricted to viewers 30 or older.

In their study of 615 midwestern adults, four out of five stimulation items (multiple-program viewing, avoiding commercials, annoying others, and being curious about other programs) produced significantly higher scores for males. Males also had higher gratification scores for two out of four content items (accessing news and substituting for a print listing). Significant gender–age interactions occurred only twice. Males and females, 30 or older, differed in their use of the RCD to access news and as a substitute for listings, while those under 30 did not.

Finally, two studies in San Francisco reported no significant differences in RCD activities for males and females. Wenner and Dennehy's (1993) survey of 219 undergraduates found gender was not a significant predictor of any of seven types of RCD activity (RCD dominance, entry scanning, commercial avoidance, muting, multiple-program viewing, grazing, total RCD activity) even though it was entered first in their hierarchical regression analyses. Walker (1991) also found no significant gender differences in grazing, multiple-program viewing, zapping, and total RCD use among 209 San Francisco adults surveyed.

Although the results are not as consistent as popular press reports and industry studies would suggest, the pattern emerging from these self-report

studies is one of greater RCD activity (channel changing, multiple-program viewing, grazing, commercial avoidance) and, to a limited extent,
higher levels of gratification among males. In particular, gratifications that
involve seeking new program stimulation (e.g., checking out other channels, getting more variety) and avoiding boredom appear to be greater for
males than females. However, age and geographic location appear to
modify gender differences. Younger males and females do not differ as
much in their degree of RCD activity and the gratifications obtained from
it. In addition, two studies of respondents of different ages in San Francisco
found no gender differences (whereas studies from other parts of the
country did).

Observational and Electronic-Recording Research

Survey research cannot directly measure RCD behavior, only perceptions
of that behavior. People's perceptions of their own behavior can be
influenced by their understanding of what is typical for members of their
gender. If the popular press reports a consistent image of male dominance
of RCDs, and most respondents see their behaviors as typical for their
gender, then it would not be surprising that males would report higher
levels of RCD use than females. However, the actual behavior might be
quite different. In addition, as we noted in Chapter 2, remembering a
mundane behavior, like RCD use, is difficult. Thus, self-report perceptions
of behavior can be inaccurate for a variety of reasons. Consequently, direct
behavioral observations are an important way to confirm or refute the
results of survey research.

Three studies observing RCD behavior have reported gender comparisons (see Table 6.2). In two of these studies (Bryant & Rockwell, 1993;
Cornwell et al., 1993), both using small samples, there was little difference
between the genders. In the only observational study with a substantial
sample size (Eastman & Newton, 1995), men were much more likely to
be high RCD users.

Bryant and Rockwell (1993) used an electronic recording device to
measure the channel changing of 40 males and 40 females during a half
hour of individual viewing. There was no significant difference between
the genders; the 40 males changed channels 102 times and the 40 females
109 times. Cornwell et al.'s analysis of videotaped home viewing also found
slightly more RCD use by nine females (one use every 5.2 minutes or an
average of 11.5 times per hour) compared to six males (one use every 5.7
minutes or an average of 10.5 times per hour).

The third observational study used student observers and produced

TABLE 6.2. RCD Activity by Gender: Summary of Observational and
Electronic-Recording Research

Study	Method	Sample	RCD variables	Results
Bryant & Rockwell, 1993	Electronic recording of behavior	40 males; 40 females	RCD Channel changing	No significant difference
Cornwell et al. 1993	Observation of taped behavior	6 females; 9 males	RCD use, including channel changing, muting, turning set on/off	Males, M = 10.5 and females, M = 11.5 changes per hour
Eastman & Newton, 1995	Observation of in-home behavior	44 group and 115 individual viewing sessions	RCD use, including punching, arrowing, jumping, scanning, inserting, muting	Men 2.76 times more likely to be in the high RCD use group; males do more punching, jumping, and scanning

different results. Eastman and Newton's (1995) study of 253 adults and children over 469 hours of viewing found clear gender differences in RCD use. After dividing their sample into approximately equal groups of low, medium, and high RCD activity, they found 47% of the males but only 17% of the females were in the high activity group. Men performed three specific RCD behaviors more frequently: punching (keying in a specific number), jumping (using the previous channel button), and scanning (moving up or down with the arrow buttons slowly enough to look at each channel). However, there were no gender differences in arrowing (moving up or down with the arrow buttons to get to a specific channel), inserting (using the picture-in-picture function), and muting. Significantly, the male-dominant activities of punching, jumping, and scanning can all be used to watch multiple programs or graze from channel to channel: viewing styles associated with restless viewers. The gender-neutral activities of arrowing and muting are more useful in selecting a specific channel or controlling sound once the program is selected: activities consistent with a more traditional single-program viewing style.

Although all three of these studies have some limitations (see Chapter 2 for a more complete discussion), Cornwell et al.'s (1993) study suffers from a very small and potentially unrepresentative sample, located in a university community (Boulder, Colo.). As they note, the unexpected higher level of RCD use by females may have been the result of the intense

RCD activity of one female who viewed alone. Bryant and Rockwell's experimental study has both a limited sample and an atypical viewing situation. One's RCD use may be very different in a waiting room where the situation is public (even if there is no other viewer in the room), than in one's home where viewing is routine. Of the three observational and electronic-recording studies, Eastman and Newton (1995) have the largest and most representative sample size and the advantage of in-home observations. Their findings seem to confirm the results of survey research which finds men using the RCD more frequently and engaging in RCD activities that disrupt the typical flow of programming: grazing and multiple-program viewing.

THEORETICAL EXPLANATIONS
OF GENDER DIFFERENCES

Although there is abundant recent interest in how women use and interpret television programming (Brown, 1990; Press, 1991; Spigel & Mann, 1992), gender typically has been included as only one of several demographic variables of interest in RCD studies. Because gender differences have been of secondary interest, authors typically have provided little theoretical explanation for the differences, relying on results reported in the popular media or previous research to justify the inclusion of this variable. One important exception was Perse and Ferguson's (1993a) study of gender differences in RCD use. Using their analysis of gender differences in channel changing and RCD use gratifications, they evaluated three competing feminist explanations of gender differences: "liberal" explanations, "radical" explanations, and "socialist" explanations.

The liberal feminist tradition assumes that gender differences are primarily the result of socialization. These differences can, and do, change as the society changes. If gender roles have changed as a result of the women's movement that started in the late 1960s, then women who have been socialized in this more recent period should have less gender stereotypical behavior, including their viewing behaviors. Perse and Ferguson argue that gender differences should be more pronounced for older viewers (30 or older) than for younger viewers socialized in an era of decreasing gender differences (Hyde, 1990).

Radical feminist explanations, which are rooted in physiological and psychological gender theories, find that women are more gifted at verbal information processing and men at visual information processing. Citing Meyers-Levy's (1989) work on gender differences in information processing, they noted that "males do not comprehensively process all valuable information, relying instead on highly available and salient heuristic cues" (pp. 173–174). Females are more likely to evaluate most of the information available in a situation before proceeding. Thus, males are more naturally prone toward grazing because of their greater visual capacity and desire to gather the breadth of what is available. Women are more prone to single-program loyalty because they are more oriented toward gathering detailed information on plot and character.

Finally, socialist feminist explanations argue that gender differences in most behaviors are a reflection of the different levels of social power exerted by males and females. Since males are in the most powerful positions to develop television content and that content reflects some of their own interests, most programming, especially that of newer cable channels, reflects a male point of view. Also, since males typically control the selection of television technology in the family, the cable industry must provide content appealing to males, if it is to attract subscribers. Within the family, males are more likely to watch television at full attention (Morley, 1986), thus making it possible to graze. Women are likely to be occupied with other chores (note Markey's comment at the start of this chapter) and are less likely to view with RCD in hand. In short, men use the remote because it helps them access cable programming that has more appeal to them; they tend to control most group situations; and they are more likely to have a free hand available to click the clicker. Each of these are manifestations of the privileged position that they hold with respect to technology in the culture.[7]

Perse and Ferguson (1993a) found some support for the liberal and the radical feminist explanations of gender differences in RCD uses and gratifications. The lessening of gender differences in RCD use for younger viewers seemed to support the liberal position. Radical feminist explanations were sustained by the tendency for men to be motivated by stimulation-seeking RCD gratifications (avoiding commercials, multiple-program viewing, and seeing what else is on) and for women to use RCDs to help them watch particular programs. The socialist feminist explanation was not generally supported. Gender differences were not greater in group viewing situations than in individual viewing situations and were not related to who usually controls the remote. However, males were more likely to receive gratification from using the RCD to annoy others: a finding consistent with earlier research (Walker & Bellamy, 1991a).

Reviewing the larger body of gender research discussed in this chapter, it appears that men do engage in more stimulation-seeking RCD uses and gratifications (multiple-program viewing, grazing, checking out other channels, and avoiding boredom or unwanted commercials). This pattern of results is consistent with the male information-processing style identified by Meyers-Levy (1989) and linked to the radical feminist tradition by Perse and Ferguson: males prefer breadth over depth in information gathering, while females pay closer attention to details and have higher levels of involvement.

The liberal feminist explanation is also supported by the decrease in gender differences in RCD use among younger viewers noted in other studies (see Chapter 5). Explanations based on differences in socialization are also supported by the lack of significant gender differences in two studies conducted in San Francisco, where progressive attitudes toward gender roles are more likely to be part of the socializing process.

Although Perse and Ferguson's surveys did not strongly support the socialist feminist explanation, some studies have found males more likely to dominate the RCD (Copeland, 1989; Copeland & Schweitzer, 1993; "Remote Controls," 1992) and to use it to control the viewing of others (Walker & Bellamy, 1991a; Weaver et al., in press). We will turn our attention to the gender-based power struggle fought in the context of family viewing.

CONTROLLING WHAT OTHERS WATCH

Viewing Alone

Webster and Wakshlag's (1983) theory of program choice outlines the role of groups in the process of program selection. Group viewing brings group pressures to bear on the selection process, which may modify the initial selection and any subsequent changes. Actions of group members will help define the group, drawing in new members and/or driving away other members. Because of its annoyance potential, RCD grazing is stereotypically associated with viewing in isolation. Grazers flipping rapidly from channel to channel are a source of irritation to other viewers and are likely to drive their companions to other sets or other activities. Although a few RCD users actually find gratification in annoying or controlling the viewing of others (Walker & Bellamy, 1991a; Walker et al., 1993; Weaver et al., 1994; Wenner & Dennehy, 1993), such activities are likely to be short-lived, if memorable because of the emotions they provoke.

Thus, RCD use is likely to be greater when viewing alone than when viewing in groups. Three studies provide support for this contention. Wenner and Dennehy's (1993) survey of undergraduates found consistent positive relationships between an estimate of the percentage of time spent viewing alone and RCD activities, including RCD dominance, multiple-program viewing, grazing, and total RCD activity. Percentage of time spent viewing alone was a significant predictor in their hierarchical regressions, even though it was entered after demographic, psychological, and media-affinity blocks of variables. However, percentage of time viewing alone was not related to using an RCD for entry scanning (orienting searches), commercial avoidance, or muting. In their observational study, Eastman and Newton (1995) compared all RCD actions in group (n = 44) and individual (n = 115) viewing situations and found significantly fewer actions during group viewing. In addition, group viewing reduced the amount of channel changing during programs or commercials. However, of the specific RCD behaviors analyzed, only arrowing up and down to adjacent channels was significantly less frequent in group viewing situations. Eastman and Newton noted that "with companions—families, spouses, or friend—most RCD holders change channels only at the hourly and half-hourly breaks, if at all, and leave the channel alone during most commercials" (1995, p. 14). Finally, in their electronic assessment of cable viewing, Greenberg, Heeter, and Sipes (1988) reported that frequency of viewing alone was a weakly significant ($p < .08$) predictor of total channel changes and viewing in strings (segments of 5 minutes or less).

As expected, group pressures appear to reduce the levels of RCD activity in general, and grazing or multiple-program viewing behaviors in particular. Grazing and multiple-program viewing require individual control of the RCD. They maximize the gratifications of the viewers in control, but distress other group members. Wenner and Dennehy's (1993) findings are particularly relevant here. Grazing and multiple-program viewing are positively related to percentage of time viewing alone, while commercial avoidance, entry scanning, and muting are not. Grazing and multiple-program viewing are self-absorbing activities, directly benefiting the grazer. Commercial avoidance, muting (often used during commercials), and entry scanning (RCD activities that benefit all group members) were not related to viewing alone. Greenberg et al. (1988) also found viewing alone related to viewing in short stretches: a characteristic associated with grazing and multiple-program viewing. Similarly, Eastman and Newton (1995) found group viewing tends to work against grazing and commercial zapping by restricting channel changing to program breaks. These findings consistently support the image of grazing and multiple-program viewing as isolated activities.

This isolated viewing is also likely to increase because viewers have more receivers at their disposal and viewing options are more specialized. According to a recent report by Statistical Research, Inc., for the Committee on Nationwide Television Audience Measurement ("Trends in

Multiple TV Sets," 1994), the number of single-set households has decreased significantly, from 43% percent to 32% between 1985 and 1994. But even more telling is the increase in the number of households with three television sets from 13% to 19% (46% increase) and with four or more television sets from 7% to 14% (100% increase) during this period. This increase in the number of predominantly RCD-equipped receivers (Klopfenstein, 1993) per household coupled with the development of specialized cable networks with more original and higher-quality programming, makes individualized viewing an even more attractive option in the 1990s. Moreover, if the cost of RCD-equipped receivers continues to decline and the number and specialization of basic cable and pay-per-view networks increase as part of the much publicized 500-channel television universe (Peppers & Rogers, 1994), the trend toward individualized viewing could accelerate dramatically.

Viewing in Groups

Who Controls the Remote?

Although individual viewing may be increasing, television is still the primary medium of in-home entertainment and the focus of evening activities for many families. Research on the degree and means of parental control of viewing is well established in television (Blood, 1961; Lull, 1978; Lull, 1982; Smith, 1961) and VCR scholarship (Krendl, Clark, Dawson, & Troiano, 1993; Lin & Atkin, 1988; Lindlof, Shatzer, & Wilkerson, 1988; Kim, Baran, & Massey, 1988; Morgan, Alexander, Shanahan, & Harris, 1990). Parental control and family discussion are seen as important factors, reducing the negative consequences of television upon children. Since the RCD is now the principle tool of viewing control, its management within the family has captured the interest of both quantitative (Copeland, 1989; Copeland & Schweitzer, 1993) and qualitative (Krendl, Troiano, Dawson, & Clark, 1993; Morley, 1986) researchers (see Table 6.3). Their studies generally have reinforced the popular image of the RCD-dominant father.

Using in-depth family interviews of 18 working-class, London families with VCRs, Morley (1986) found a universal pattern of male RCD dominance, reporting that "none of the women in any of the families use the automatic control [RCD] regularly" (p. 148). Controlling family viewing was seen by some as a symbol of family power. As one man stated, "We discuss what we all want to watch and the biggest wins. That's me. I'm the biggest" (p. 148). Males also gave more undivided attention to the medium, while females frequently combined viewing with housework or

TABLE 6.3. RCD Dominance by Gender

Study	Method	Sample	RCD variables	Results
Morley, 1986	In depth, group interviews	18 working-class, London families	Control of RCD	All families reported that the father controlled the RCD
Copeland, 1989	Phone survey	218 adults with RCDs	Control of RCD and family communication patterns	Male adult con-trolled the RCD in 35% of households, female adult in 26%, and children in 19%
Krendl et al., 1993	In-home observation	3 families	Control of RCD, use of RCD to scan channels	Fathers more likely to control when couple views, fathers more likely to scan channels
Copeland & Schweitzer, 1993	Written survey	133 students	Control of RCD and family communication patterns	Males dominant in 79.7% of households

conversation. Despite the clear evidence of male RCD dominance, Morley cautions that his results are based on family interviews, which are subject to group pressures, rather than observations of actual behavior. It is also clear that his findings are based on a sample of families that is limited in both number and variety. Likewise, in another qualitative study in which three families were observed, Krendl, Troiano, Dawson, and Clark (1993) reported that once children had gone to bed, fathers controlled the RCD more often than mothers. Fathers were also more likely to use the RCD to scan the available program options, while mothers were more likely to consult program guides.

In a phone survey of 218 adults, Copeland (1989) also found evidence of paternal dominance of RCDs, although not to the same degree as in qualitative studies. Adult males were the persons who generally hold or control the remote in 35% of sample homes, adult females in 26%, and children in 19% (in most of the other homes in the sample the responses were taking turns and whoever was the first one to get to the remote). In homes without children, males dominated the RCD in 30% of homes, females in 19% of homes. In a second survey of 133 undergraduates, Copeland found even stronger evidence of male, especially paternal, dominance of the RCD. When asked, "Who usually dominates (holds) the remote control when your family watches television together?" the students indicated father 60.1%, son(s) 19.6%, mother 8.7%, and daughter(s) 6.5% of the time.

The results of both qualitative and quantitative studies point to a consistent pattern of RCD dominance by fathers, reinforcing the general pattern of male affinity for RCDs. Adult male control of the RCD, and by extension program selection (Copeland, 1989), is consistent with the socialist feminist explanation of gender differences discussed earlier in this chapter. More socially powerful males display their dominance over both program production (by dominating positions of power in the television industry) and program selection (by dominating the major agent of viewing control, the RCD).

Family Communication and RCD Dominance

Despite the tendency toward male dominance of RCDs, families do differ in how they control the clicker. In addition to measuring RCD dominance, researchers (Copeland, 1989; Copeland & Schweitzer, 1993) have explored the link between family communication patterns and RCD use. Using the Family Communication Pattern scales (McLeod & Chaffee, 1972), Copeland (1989) found that in families that attempt to reduce or control conflict ("socio-oriented" families), women are more likely to control the RCD. He speculates that in these families "mothers may take on the role of mediator between conflicting program preferences of man and children" (p. 13).

In a subsequent study using the McMaster Family Assessment Device (Epstein, Baldwin, & Bishop, 1983) to measure family functioning, including patterns of transactions among members, Copeland and Schweitzer (1993) found more emotional and direct communication styles in families in which daughters dominated the RCD than in families in which males (fathers or sons) dominated the RCD. In addition, homes in which the mother dominated the RCD had more emotional and direct communication styles than those in which sons dominated. Finally, households in which daughters dominated also had greater perceived ability to solve problems than homes in which either the father or sons dominate. Although this body of research is limited, its findings are consistent: families where males dominated the RCD appear to have less ability to openly discuss and solve family issues. Thus, male dominance of the RCD may be a symptom of wider communication problems within the family.

CONCLUSION

Based on the industry, academic survey, and academic observational–electronic-recording research that we reviewed, the following conclusions can be drawn concerning the relationships between RCD activity and gender differences in individual and group viewing situations:

1. Although not universally observed, in most studies, males use the RCD more than females.
2. Younger females closely resemble their male counterparts in many RCD activities. Thus, during individual viewing situations in which males do not dominate the RCD, gender differences may decrease over time.
3. Male RCD use is more likely to involve grazing, multiple-program viewing, and commercial avoidance: activities that are associated with the restless viewer profile (Chapter 2) and that alter the traditional nature of program viewing.
4. Gender differences in the levels of gratification derived from RCD use are not as consistently reported as differences in overall RCD use or specific RCD behaviors. When differences do exist, males generally have high gratification scores. Male gratifications are especially higher for gratifications related to exploring what else is available on television, getting more out of television, and avoiding boredom.
5. Gender differences were not observed in all geographic locations. In particular, two studies conducted in San Francisco and one in a university community produced no significant gender differences.
6. RCD activity increases in individual viewing situations, particularly self-absorbing activities such as grazing and multiple-program viewing. As the number of receivers per household and variety of distribution channels increases, the frequency of these RCD activities is likely to increase.
7. During family viewing, fathers are more likely to control the RCD.
8. In families with more open communication practices (higher socio-orientation, greater perceived problem-solving ability, more emotional and direct communication styles), the RCD is more likely to be controlled by a female.

In the last decade, the RCD has become a significant source of new gratifications, especially for male viewers. It has raised new concerns about male dominance of television viewing and gender differences in television viewing styles. As we look to a future that will offer more programming choice and new interactive forms of television viewing, these issues will increase in salience because greater choice will place more responsibility in the hand that holds the remote.

NOTES

1. Both of the authors are guilty of giving such analyses on several occasions.

2. For example, here is a "pop" analysis from the pages of *TV Guide* (Arrington, 1992, p. 12):

   > Men are hunter/gatherers, chasing quarry. Women are more responsible for stable local cultivation. Men are random, chaotic. Women tend to be linear or spiral-like. Men are polygamous: sports—sexy video—news bite—cartoon—sexy beer commercial—sports. . . . Women nurture a single program, faithfully following the plot of a good episode or movie.

3. Heeter and Baldwin (1988) noted a similar tendency toward increased zapping during sports programming.

4. In their profile of zappers, Heeter and Greenberg (1988b) also found that males were twice as likely as females to be zappers.

5. Gender differences in RCD use (total RCD use, grazing, multiple-program viewing) that are derived from our three surveys (Walker, 1991; Walker & Bellamy, 1991a; Walker et al., 1993) and reported in this chapter are based on new cross-tabulations calculated from the original data.

6. In one survey, channel changing was operationalized as frequency ("never" to "very often") of changing; while in the other, Guttman scalograms were used to identify when the changing occurred (between programs, during commercials, and during programs).

7. Male dominance of technology also appears to be related to the scarcity of that technology. When computers are scarce gender differences are greater than when the technology is more abundant (Maccoby & Jacklin, 1974).

CHAPTER 7

A Two-Way Window to the Future?

TELEVISION'S THIRD GENERATION

The RCD has forever changed the relationship between the viewer and television. Its rapid diffusion and acceptance, combined with the diffusion of other television technologies in a time of political economic change, are altering industry structures and conduct. The restlessness of second-generation viewers is manifest in the RCD activities (grazing, multiple-program viewing, zapping, zipping) used by substantial numbers of people in order to design television content that satisfies individual gratifications not received from traditional television.

With strong evidence that younger viewers are more likely to engage in RCD activities, it is probable that RCD use will become increasingly common both in terms of the total number of people who use the device and in the amount of RCD activity. It is unlikely that RCD use will decline as the population ages because (1) RCDs are nearly universal in U.S. households; (2) newer models place even more receiver functions in the hand of the users, making televisions increasingly difficult (if not impossible) to use without them; (3) the television industry, in adapting its product to the present generation of grazers, has contributed irrevocably to the change in its relationship to the viewer/user.

RCDs also have become an essential tool for increasing selective avoidance on the part of viewers. As programming and advertising has become more specialized, audiences have encountered more undesirable material. In television's first generation, programming rarely offended because it seldom challenged prevailing beliefs. Channel changing focused on program selection, not selective avoidance of distasteful programs or program segments. The second generation of television provides enough content diversity to offend nearly everyone at one time or another, making the RCD a defense mechanism and selective avoidance a consequential gratification.

RCDs have trained a generation of viewers to watch television with a controller in their hand. For these viewers, mostly younger and likely to continue the viewing habits developed in youth, the step toward a more interactive form of television is a natural one. Restless viewing is a sign of their dissatisfaction and their willingness to change the current situation. In addition, younger viewers are more comfortable controlling video images and sounds by the use of video game controls in the entertainment–play realm and computer mouses in the information–work realm. Thus, they may be more inclined to make RCD-controlled interactive television a component of their viewing repertoire.

RCDs allow these viewers to easily interrupt the narrative flow of any program by substituting another. Nonetheless, gratifying programs generally are not interrupted and advertisers maintain control over the delivery of their messages. Industry studies show that the most successful programs are not grazed from as frequently (Sanoff & Kyle, 1987). Arresting programs can arrest the grazer. However, when specific programs are not especially gratifying, viewing can continue with higher levels of gratification, because the viewer can graze among several program sources of the same type (e.g., several football, basketball, or baseball games) or different types (e.g., grazing, multiple-program viewing, or zapping to news or music videos during commercial breaks). Thus, the RCD makes it harder for weaker programs to maintain their audience, but enhances the value of stronger programs that are "zap proof." Of course, those are the programs that networks will want to promote and expand. In short, the RCD, in conjunction with cable and VCRs, leads to more program specialization, but also enhances the value of successful hit programs, making them the center of entertainment publicity and critical to network success.

In this book, we have focused considerable attention on the reaction of the television programming and advertising industries to the rise of the second-generation audience. This is because these components of the television industry are most aware of the impact of the restless audience and have been most active in attempting to limit or disempower the restless viewer. While the strategies employed by the industry are critical to an understanding of both present audience activity and projections of future activity, the most important factors in how the industry is coping with the second-generation viewer are the new structures that are evolving in the television industry.

The proliferation of new programming and advertising conduits and the means for viewer/user control of them, along with the historic fascination with and faith in technology that has afflicted the government regulatory apparatus with "a free market amnesia about antitrust" (Bagdikian, 1992, p. 15; Davis & Davidson, 1993) has led to an ongoing restructuring of the communications industries. A generation ago, Rogers and Shoemaker (1971, p. 341) argued that "the power elite in a social system screen out potentially restructuring innovations while allowing the introduction of innovations which mainly affect the functioning of the system." Others (Mosco, 1979; Winston, 1986) have echoed such arguments in their analyses of how truly innovative technologies are suppressed or limited in their application by existing entities. However, such analyses were written at a time when industrial and regulatory systems were relatively static, and when vested interests typically were able to dictate the terms of technological diffusion. But the RCD's rapid diffusion, and with it the television user's greater control over content, transpired as a new mode of regulation took hold—one that encouraged existing media industries to actively employ new technologies and enter new businesses. The result has been industrial change that would not have been possible earlier.

The primary thrusts of these changes have been consolidation and convergence, which translate into a severe decrease or, in many cases, elimination of boundaries between companies and business segments. Increasingly, the once relatively distinct lines between television and telecommunications are disappearing, as are the lines between once distinct segments within industries such as programming and advertising, broadcasting and cable, and production, distribution, and exhibition. Many claim that the unleashed synergies will lead to more consumer choice, convenience, and even a better way of life.

DEFINING THE THIRD GENERATION

The promise of synergy is central to two concepts that are receiving much attention in the television industry—interactivity and the information superhighway. Increasingly the two are seen as ways to provide a myriad of new services, or improvements on existing ones, with the added bonuses of (1) creating new profit centers for media companies, and (2) being instruments for coping with or even controlling the whims of the RCD-armed viewer/user.

Interactivity and the information superhighway promise to provide the viewer/user with virtually unlimited viewing options, as well as new, more user-friendly means to shop, bank, and communicate with others. In contrast to the *first-generation viewer*, who had limited choice and extremely limited control of television; and unlike the *second-generation viewer/user*, who has a degree of control that is recognized by the content provider over a relatively limited, although increasing, range of television offerings; the *third-generation user* will have vast control over content, time, and presentational mode. In the third generation, according to many industry and governmental supporters of the new television, the industry will have to conform to the desires of the television user—a complete reversal of the first generation and a major change from the transitional second generation.

THE 500-CHANNEL NATION

The convergence of the television industry and the information super-highway is a key concern for and harbinger of the future of television. Many of the predictions relate to the cornucopia of channels that will become available to television users. In fact, there has been so much industry and popular press discussion of the multichannel future, that the 500-channels scenario has become a cliché (Waters, with Beachy, 1993). MIT's Andrew Lippman, commenting on the heralded benefits of the 500-channel nation, predicted that the large number of channels will lead to video-on-demand (VOD) systems, whereby the televisual experience "will be changed into an experience more like walking into Barnes & Noble instead of picking up a TV Guide" (Knopf, 1992, p. 14). Employing a similar analogy, veteran television industry observer Les Brown compared the television of the future to a "shopping mall" (Maddox, 1993, p. 1). On a more pragmatic level, current industry entities believe the proliferation of channels will allow for an extension and expansion of existing operations. For example, ABC's Bob Iger predicted that "you'll see multiple networks—more than one ABC, like an ABC 1, 2, and 3" (Moca, 1994, p. 2). Cox Cable executive Ajit Davi predicted that the 500 channels would consist of the following "zones" (Maddox, 1993, p. 23):

1. 100-channel grazing zone—basically the mix of broadcast and cable channels presently available.[1]
2. 200-channel quality zone—two extra channels for each of the services in the grazing zone that would include repeat telecasts scheduled for the convenience of the viewer.
3. 50-channel event zone with pay-per-view sports and specials.
4. 250-channel video store that would provide near-VOD access to motion pictures.

If this scenario is correct, even though the quantity and convenience of television will increase to a great degree, the actual content will be no more diverse than it is today, and the audience will be required to contribute more of the cost.

The impact of the impending 500- (or more) channel environment on the industry is so pronounced that Discovery Channel executive John Hendricks called digital compression—the technology that makes the environment possible—one of the three "revolutions" in the television industry (Walley, 1993a, p. 2). According to Hendricks, the other two revolutions were the advent of broadcast television and the advent of Home Box Office and other cable services (Walley, 1993a). This sentiment is shared by such other industry figures as Time Warner's Gerald Levin, who sees the new environment as a change in "the very nature of television" (Powell, with Underwood, Nayyar, & Fleming, 1993, p. 40). Similarly, Bell Atlantic's Ray Smith claimed that the cable industry, in conjunction with telephone/telecommunications companies like his own, will move "from a broadcasting paradigm to appointment cast, meaning they will connect with the digital servers that will be available regionally and nationally" (Halonen, 1994b, p. 74).

THIRD GENERATION RCDS

The RCD will play a critical role in the new television environment because with so many channels to choose from, the user will need a convenient means to control television output. The "smart" remotes of the near future will be programmed to screen out objectionable programs and access only that content specified by the user (Heeter, Yoon, & Sampson, 1993). "Intelligent" (i.e., programmable to control a variety of devices or to delete undesirable channels when grazing) RCDs are already available. In addition to their programmability, some of these devices can read television listings, select and record programs, and delete commercials

(Kaplan, 1992). The RCDs of the future will be linked to new converter boxes that have been referred to as the "gatekeepers—or tollbooths—for the information highway" (Brandt, with Grover, Hawkins, & Ziegler, 1993). Franklin (1992) predicts the advent of Interactive Television Operating Systems (ITVOS) that will allow the user to "conveniently capture, index and watch specific programming independently of the transmission schedule" (Franklin, 1992, p. 14). The controls for such systems will become common features on the RCDs of the future. In fact, RCDs are seen by many industry observers as the essential navigational tools that will both entice and allow individuals to make use of the myriad video services that will be available. Much time and money is being spent on the development of more intuitive, ergonomically pleasing, and user-friendly RCDs (Quinlan, 1995).

As we look to that age when RCDs will be universal, except for handheld receivers, we also see devices that, while increasingly complex, are simpler to operate. RCDs will augment their current selection function with a variety of new roles. Smart remotes will work with the next generation of receivers, allowing viewers to monitor the multitude of new channels (Heeter et al., 1993). At the start of an evening's diversion, viewers may be greeted with listings of current and future programs that meet their specific viewing interests based on personal programming criteria. Used in conjunction with a newer generation of video recording devices, programming that meets their criteria will have been stored on recordable, randomly accessible disks. After reviewing what has been stored, viewers will assign the sequence of play for that evening and begin watching their personalized prime time. Or, if the viewers choose to watch in "real time," they will be alerted to desirable programming (based on their criteria) on other channels.

Although accessing an increasing array of functions, RCDs will be easier to operate. Most current RCD functions are activated by pushing particular buttons to achieve a specific result. Although some design improvements have been made (e.g., buttons shaped like numbers), most RCD buttons are difficult to locate. The next generation of RCDs, already available on high-end video products (e.g., RCA's Digital Satellite System), will function on a point-and-click basis. Just as mouse-based systems have simplified computer operations, the new RCDs or "air mouses" will simplify RCD use. Viewers will no longer have to look or feel for similarly shaped buttons on crowed RCD displays. They will point and click on selected functions from a window menu that leads to still more choices. The increased complexity of third-generation RCDs will seem much simpler, because the hodgepodge of buttons that confront today's users will be replaced by a series of graphically enhanced options. Thus, just as in the second generation of television, evolving RCD technology will compliment and enhance the value of the increasing variety of distribution systems available in the third generation of the medium. The development of a navigation system or a "favored" clicker is considered a major goal in the consumer electronics industry (Walley, 1995).

The television industry must consider how the new systems will be employed by the television user. It must devise new ways to measure and package the audience for sale to advertisers. Video dial-tone systems seem to offer one way to measure the audiences for these new services. In such systems, the once distinct telephone industry will become fully integrated with the television industry (Maddox, 1994a). Among the primary implications of this merger is that (1) there could be "as many channels as . . . phone numbers" (Knopf, 1992, p. 14) and (2) future television ratings reports will become more like telephone bills with itemized breakdowns of how much use of what type of content took place in the last billing cycle (Haugsted, 1992). Such a direct linkage of consumer payment and programming would almost certainly exclude many people from making use of many of the channels. However, author Michael Crichton (1993, pp. 57–58) argues that as this linkage "becomes more explicit, consumers will naturally want better information." Since the result might be a better product, he believes that the end of mass media and the exclusion of many members of the mass audience is beneficial.

INTERACTIVE TELEVISION

To many observers, the 500-channel television universe of the future will be driven by interactivity. According to some observers, the advent of interactive television "will make a profound change in the way we live" (Brandt et al., 1993, p. 101). Although definitions of interactive television vary, it is expected to constitute "an unprecedented mix of technology" which encompasses cable, television, telephone, and computer technology and was expected to generate a $1.64 billion business by 1996 (Parisi, 1992, pp. 101–102).

One of the most common ways of defining interactive television is to contrast it with existing television technologies and services. For example, the editor of *Digital Media* magazine stated that RCDs and home shopping channels are "fake interactive" because they do not give users the "complete viewer control" of the coming systems in which people will "use programmed electronic selectors," in the form of an RCD, to access an almost limitless array of content on "video telephony" systems (Kantrowitz, with Ramo, 1993, pp. 43–44).

Similarly, former FCC Chairperson Al Sikes referred to current services as having only a "mirror capability" and of being "utilitarian." For him, *real* interactivity is "personalization" or the "ability to customize information and entertainment as [consumers] want it" (Walley, 1994b, p. IM–6). "Personalization" is an increasingly common term in discussions of interactive television. According to Clawson (1993), "personalized television" is the new "buzzword" for systems that allow the viewer to change camera angles and otherwise alter the content of television (p. 21).

Some scholars have drawn a close connection between interactivity and interpersonal communication. Rogers (1986, p. 4) offers a rigorous definition of interactivity as "the capability of new communication systems, usually containing a computer as one component, to 'talk back' to the user, almost like an individual participating in a conversation." From this perspective, interactivity is optimal in face-to-face communication in which participants use messages sent by others to shape the messages they send. Heeter (1989) argues that the interactivity of a technology can be assessed on at least six dimensions: complexity of choice available to the user, amount of user effort needed, responsiveness to the user, degree of monitoring of information access by the user, degree to which the user can add information, and facilitation of interpersonal communication.

These communication-centered characterizations of interactivity are more descriptive of the interactivity possible in telephone and videophone conversations, computer-aided communication, and teleconferencing, than of the possibilities touted by the first generation of interactive television. For the most part, interactive television, according to its promoters, allows the television user to shop, play games, and order movies and other programming on demand. In essence, it allows the viewer to "evolve from being a mini-programmer [as in the use of VCRs and RCDs] into a mini-director" (Reith, 1991, p. 34) with control over almost every facet of the televisual experience. Absent from the discussion of interactive television is its potential for interpersonal communication. Viewers will choose from a wider range of possibilities offered by program providers, but most viewers will not interact directly with those providers. Viewers may play along with a game show contestant or manage alongside a baseball manager, but they will not talk to the contestant or manager while they play or manage.

Thus, rather than approaching true interactivity, interactive television is seen as a key means of regaining control of the restless viewer. The president of the proposed "Interactive Network" claims that his network will "stop flipping and zapping" with its mix of action, games, and contests (Donlon, 1993, p. 2D). Another industry executive claims that the combination of place-based media (which he calls television in nontraditional settings) and interactive television "transforms the damage of viewer empowerment into the opportunity of the '90s" (Reith, 1991, p. 34). But interactive services are considered a potential godsend to a shaken television industry for reasons besides their touted ability to attract and hold user attention. Since "interactivity will be a billable commodity," it will create important new revenue streams for television entities (Barlow, 1994, p. 128).

Industry Plans for an Interactive Multichannel Future

There is no doubt that the television industry is interested in interactive services. Almost every company in the existing broadcast, cable, telephone, and computer industries has plans to participate in the interactive future. Because the plans and alliances are shifting so quickly, the following review will no doubt be somewhat outdated by the time of publication. However, it is indicative of the range and scope of current plans.

Among the major deals in progress is the Interactive Network, a joint venture of NBC; Telecommunications, Inc. (TCI); A. C. Nielsen; and Gannett. It will use FM and television side bands to provide an over-the-air mix of programming in which the audience can, for instance, play along with game shows and, if they choose to pay extra, even compete. NBC executives believe that interactive applications will become an increasing part of its business, similar to the emphasis that rival ABC placed on cable in the early 1980s ("Building NBC's," 1993; Walley, 1993b). The interest of traditional broadcast entities in interactivity and the information superhighway obviously extends beyond NBC. One of the major lobbying activities of the National Association of Broadcasters is to ensure information superhighway access for all broadcasters on the grounds that the broadcast industry is far too important to society "to be shunted aside" ("Broadcasters Want," 1994). In addition, the impetus for the ongoing economic consolidation of electronic media industries is regarded by most observers as a positioning strategy, allowing for a move into the new television environment (Jensen, 1994b; Mermigas, 1993, 1994a).

The 1992 FCC decision to allow telephone companies to enter the video dial-tone business by leasing to third parties was a major impetus to the development of new services (Maddox, 1994a). Soon after this decision, AT&T gave video providers access to its existing system of delivering multiple video signals to supplement or substitute for the as yet unbuilt fiber optic networks (Maddox, 1992). AT&T also joined Time Warner, Matsushita, and Electronic Arts as investors in 3DO, a company that is to develop a "multiplayer" for use with compact discs, video games, and interactive television (Brandt et al., 1993).

Most of the other major telephone and media companies are also developing new systems. GTE, for example, instituted a test of a 500-channel interactive service in Cerritos, Calif. It offered several levels of service, from a 30-channel pay-per-view service to a "full" interactive video service that provides instant access to movies as well as a "Main Street" component that allows users to shop, pay bills, play games, and so forth (Lippman, 1993). Time Warner is testing its Full Service Network (FSN) in Orlando, Fla. According to Time Warner executive Walter Isaacson, "The model of the American couch potato is as such a myth. If you give people control, they love to take control" (Murrie, 1994, p. 26). US West is testing an advanced network with fiber optics in Omaha, Neb. (Powell et al., 1993; "What's to Come," 1993, p. 29). US West's full-service networks will offer data, VOD, educational, and telecommuting services ("What's to Come," 1993). US West, AT&T, and TCI were partners in a viewer-controlled cable television test in Denver, Colo. (Maddox, 1994c). AT&T and Viacom plan to test a similar system in Castro Valley, Calif. (Maddox, 1994c). Although the announced merger of Bell Atlantic and TCI did not occur, Bell Atlantic has been particularly aggressive in seeking new opportunities in interactive digital communications. It has announced plans to construct full interactive networks in the top 20 markets in its service area (the mid-Atlantic region from Pennsylvania to Virginia) by 1998 ("What's to Come," 1993), and to aggressively enter into equity arrangements with program distributors in order to "influence in some ways what might be appropriate new interactive, creative content" (Halonen, 1994b, p. 46). The Media Company (Pacific Telesis, Bell Atlantic, NYNEX, and Creative Artists Agency) and Americast (Disney, Ameritech, Bell South, SBC Communications, and GTE) consortia are other examples of the attempt of major telecommunications and entertainment firms to continue to be major players in the evolving television industry (Lafayette, 1995; Tyrer, 1995).

In addition to these activities, many other software and hardware suppliers are hoping to become participants in the interactive television business. ACTV and Cablevision are introducing an interactive television service that emphasizes sports programming, with the hope that sports will be the software (programming) that drives the interactive business in much the same way that televised sports spurred the diffusion of broadcast television in the 1950s (Pols, 1994; "Sports Fans," 1994). The success of the Videoway system in Canada (with 350,000 subscribers) encouraged that company to enter the U.S. market (Helyar, 1994).

In the hardware–distribution system segment of the business, a variety of companies are working on projects. Apple and IBM, for example, are working with Scientific-Atlanta to produce receiving devices that are "part computer, part telephone, and part TV and radio tuner" ("Apple and IBM," 1994). A series of other alliances are working on similar receiving systems, including Intel, Microsoft, and General Instrument; Time Warner, Scientific Atlanta, and Toshiba; Silicon Graphics and Time Warner; Hewlett-Packard and TV Answer; and United Video, Scientific Atlanta, Zenith, General Instrument, and Kaleida Labs (Brandt et al., 1993).

On a more exotic level, the founders of Microsoft and McCaw Cellular combined efforts to propose the Teledesic worldwide system of satellite delivery. The system will operate through 840 relatively low-powered satellites that will theoretically reach every person on the globe ("Gates, McCaw," 1994). Although such a system will not be as exclusionary as the information superhighway, it is unlikely to have the full interactive capabilities of the other systems. On a much simpler level, the Panasonic REAL system for interactive television is being marketed as a video game in order to get it into U.S. homes (Goldman, 1993).

Governmental Intervention

The U.S. government has been quick to embrace interactivity and the information superhighway as vital to the economy and to the public. In a speech outlining the Clinton Administration's policy toward the information superhighway, Vice President Al Gore said that the information superhighway "will connect and empower the citizens of this country through broadband interactive communication" (Gore, 1994). The Clinton administration proposed a new deregulatory classification for broadband, digital services to enable cable and phone service providers to compete with one another and combine their efforts to provide access to the information superhighway (Halonen, 1994a). The 1996 telecommunications bill further reduces the traditional barriers between the broadcast, cable, and telephone industries, and is likely to spur many more joint television ventures (Halonen, 1996).

Although government regulators are on record as opposing high concentration of ownership and as favoring universal access (Gore, 1994; Halonen, 1994b; Maddox, 1994b), the economics of the industry seem to suggest that only a limited number of companies will eventually survive as information superhighway providers. This posture has even been adopted by influential industry officials. TCI's John Malone, for example, has suggested that the government should stop "squabbling about transient monopolies" and get out of the way of progress (Donlan, 1992, p. 10); furthermore, he predicted that only two to three "branded communication bubbles" will eventually control the worldwide television business (Halonen, 1994c, p. 31). So far, the government has not used its antitrust powers to stymie the many deals taking place, because it is fascinated, or even mesmerized, by the potential of the new television technology (Noam, 1993). The result has been a large increase in technological development and in economic consolidation. Although the present administration may have substituted a policy based on a "faith" in technology "as the engine of the economy and the protector of the consumer" (Davis & Davidson, 1993), the result seems nearly indistinguishable from faith in a "free market."

Prospects for Interactive Television

As is the case of every new technology, the interactive multichannel television of the future is regarded optimistically by many as a cure for the ailments of the present system. For the user, the new systems supposedly will offer many specialized channels of programming for entertainment and information as well as a variety of other services to make life easier. For the program and service providers, the system will arrest if not eliminate the problems of the restless audience. Despite the typically rosy scenarios being promulgated and acted upon by many, there is a growing body of evidence that interactive applications are going to have a difficult time attracting users.

While some surveys have found that many people want interactive television (Clawson, 1993; Donlon, 1993; Kaplan, 1992), there is a substantial amount of contradictory evidence. In a survey conducted by *Advertising Age*, 80.4% of the respondents were not aware of the concept of interactivity. Not surprisingly, 65.9% had no interest at all in subscribing to such a service. When the respondents were asked which of the various interactive television services they would be interested in, only movies and television on demand interested a majority, 55.4% (Fawcett, 1993). In another survey, Odyssey Ventures divided the respondents into six attitude groups finding that only the "new enthusiasts" desired and were able to afford interactive television ("Proceed Cautiously," 1994).

Of course, survey data asking opinions about what consumers might do is probably not as important as data from actual tests of interactive multichannel systems. At this point, it is difficult to regard the data from GTE's Cerritos, Calif., test as a positive indicator of consumer acceptance of interactive television. In fact, the results have been characterized as "poor" to "a bomb" (Lippman, 1993; Maddox, 1994c, p. IM-2). Although GTE denies that the system has been a failure, one executive says that one of the things the company has learned is that interactivity is not a mass market service, and that "user-friendly is not enough. It had better damn well look like TV" (Lippman, 1993). Time Warner's FSN test in Orlando, Fla., with its mix of content on demand and interactive shopping also has been categorized as a failure (Meyer, 1995).

Many industry observers concur that the audience is seeking a more convenient way of using the services to which they already have access (Maddox, 1994c). Bogart has stated that the major portion of the audience is likely to use the information superhighway for access to conventional television and motion picture programming ("Media, Democracy," 1993).

Several scholars have argued that there is little consumer demand for interactive services. According to Becker, "there is no evidence the audience wants to talk to the TV" (Lippman, 1993). Noll observed that "virtually every service that has been suggested for the superhighway [i.e., teletext, videophone, the Qube interactive television system] has been tested and has consistently bombed" ("Data Highway," 1993; Maddox, 1993, p. 31).

Even industry figures are starting to adopt a similar posture, although with more optimism for the future. A Sony executive, for example, argued that most television viewers "don't want to interact with anything but the refrigerator" (Powell et al., 1993, p. 41). One analyst concluded that "what is addictive about TV is the mindless, passive, relaxing nature of the beast" (Graham, 1994). Although the widespread use of the RCD would appear to contradict this notion, there is a general consensus developing in the industry that traditional content forms will have to be a major component of future systems if such systems are to succeed (Beacham, 1993; Graham, 1994).

Technological and cost reasons are often given to explain the failure of the early systems or are seen as problems to overcome before the information superhighway will become a major part of the media mix for most consumers. The complete wiring of the nation for such services has been estimated to be about 20 years away ("Data Highway," 1993), with even industry officials conceding that interactive services will not have a significant base of potential customers for a minimum of three to five years (Maddox, 1994c). An industry panel concluded that the need to upgrade or replace television receivers and/or personal computers in order to access interactive multimedia services is what is holding such services back ("Panel: Interactive," 1993). Of course, as discussed above, availability of service does not necessarily mean the customer will want to use it. In a nation in which up to 80% of VCR owners do not know how to program their machines (Zoglin, 1992) and only about 20% of people have used pay per view (Graham, 1994), the market for interactive services does not look that strong, unless the interface between user and conduit becomes as transparent as the RCD of today.

The question of whether or not the consumer will (or can) pay for the new services is highly salient in the industry. With a $30 per month "brick wall" (i.e., price resistance when service exceeds this amount) generally recognized in the cable industry (Beacham, 1993), there is serious doubt about how much households can allocate to all of the new services. As might be expected, and as detailed in Chapter 3, advertisers see substantial opportunity in the information superhighway. According to one executive from Bozell, Jacobs, Kenyon, and Eckhardt, the probability that the consumer will not be willing (or able) to pay the bill for the new services means that "advertising is still going to have to carry the day" (King, 1994). Others have argued that the well-educated, technologically savvy, and affluent users of the information superhighway will have great appeal to advertisers and will ensure cheaper access for everyone ("Flamers on," 1994). Although the forms of advertising are certain to change (Nelson, 1994), there is little doubt that advertising subsidy will be critical to the new systems.

The prognosis for the multimedia, multichannel, interactive future is unclear. It remains an open question whether it will become the replacement for all existing forms of mass media or simply "a solution in search of a problem, doing what other things do already, only slightly less well" (Max, 1994, p. 70). What is known is that major communications businesses in this country have two incentives: a government "green light" to pursue various economic arrangements, and a need to contain a restless audience by continuing the technological push for new services until market pull takes over (Rodriguez & Robina, 1993).

Interactive Niches

Qualifying interactive television's government–industry push is the reality that certain viewing gratifications, probably the most salient ones, are not related to interactivity. There is little evidence that comedy or drama can profit much from interactivity because the element of surprise (plot twists or punch lines) is a major component of the enjoyment. Beyond an initial novelty effect, few viewers want to pick their own ending because that means they know what is going to happen. The entertainment value comes from having the plot resolved by its creators in a way that the audience finds satisfactory. Similarly, viewers do not want to select characters or camera angles; they want talented experts to do so in ways that viewers will find satisfying. Comedy is much the same. We may use the RCD to select a particular comic that we like via pay per view, but we want the comic to put on a show for us, not to be programmed by us.

Despite these reservations, some entertainment niches may exist for interactive television. Because games and sports are naturally interactive (viewers answer questions or predict coaching strategy), the audience often is playing along already. The success of video games tells us that there is an audience for this kind of interactivity, if it is delivered in a convenient way and at a low enough cost. Indeed, the marketing plans of the Interactive Network emphasize viewer participation in ongoing television game shows and sporting events. The real issue is the relative advantage (Rogers, 1986) of interactive television games compared to current and developing video game technology. A second issue affecting the success of interactive television is the traditional use of television by families for group activity. Despite the increase in the number of receivers per household, the continued success of some domestic, family-oriented situation comedies ("Season-to-Date Ratings," 1994) shows that television, at least network television, is still in many respects a family medium.

Interactivity, and grazing as well, is essentially a self-absorbing personal activity that disrupts family viewing. In family viewing, the important interactions are the interfamily interactions (discussion of the program or other matters), not television-to-family or family-to-television interactions. Even group interactive games are not likely to be successful family activities because of the different skill levels of family members. The better players may want to compete, but weaker players are likely to withdraw from the game.

Although the future of interactive entertainment programming may be restricted to niche markets, interactivity is especially useful in selecting information. The computer allows the storage of vast quantities of information, and future RCDs in conjunction with television–computer hybrid monitors will make it easy to select that information. As explained by Shaw (1995), "on-screen menus and directions will be the point of entry for interactive television programming" (p. 14). The basic window structure that allows the selection and retrieval of information through a series of menus is universal in popular computer software. Students and adults have learned this system for selecting information in schools and through in-home computers.

Computer on-line information services see the potential for teletext services delivered on cable. The Prodigy information service is developing a television version to be delivered by cable systems (Mannes, 1994; "Media General Agrees," 1994; Shapiro, 1993). In addition, both Prodigy and America Online are developing closer ties with broadcast and cable networks ("America Online Strengthens Position," 1994; "Capital Cities/ABC," 1994; "CNBC and Prodigy Link Up," 1994; "MTV Teams Up," 1994). These information services could be desirable stopping points for zappers in search of brief current news, weather, or sports summaries during commercial breaks. However, the future of such commercially branded services is in question because of the recent popularity of direct connection to the Internet and the World Wide Web. This is leading both cable and telephone companies to develop their own access services for television (Sandberg & Ziegler, 1996).

The downside for any interactive information service is that television, at least in the United States, is not an information–work medium. It is an entertainment–play medium. Indeed, one theorist (Stephenson, 1967) has argued that all media are used predominantly for play. Viewers frequently turn to television for diversion (Kubey & Csikszentmilhalyi, 1990) and only rarely for solutions to their problems. Even when information is presented, it has strong entertainment elements.

Information services may eventually develop a small niche by providing services that viewers can quickly access during commercial or program breaks (or when a brief sports, weather, or news summary is desired), but this service will have to be very inexpensive. This is because viewers can already get some of the same information, although not with the same degree of control, by flipping to sports, news, and weather channels. Many of these channels provide data summaries (sports scores, weather forecasts, market reports) as overlays to their main programming.

Although RCD-accessed interactive television is not likely to become a true mass medium, it is likely to provide economically viable niche services. Entertainment services that deliver desirable programming that is less conveniently available (e.g., pay-per-view movies, special events, restricted content) are the best bet for growth. Information services that deliver information that is most redundant with existing sources (cable channels, newspapers, computer information services) are the poorest bets. Game- and sports-based interactive services are likely to have a niche, if they are tied to real events and the interactive technology is easy to use and cheap. But this will never be more than a small part of viewing time, because games and sports are relegated to a small part of viewing time, except for sports buffs, and even dedicated interactive fans will most likely prefer simply to watch most events. RCDs will make the growth of interactive services easier because the device makes interactivity more convenient (or even possible), but interactivity will always be a supplement to traditional program viewing. Prospects for interactive dramas and comedies are particularly grim. As noted above, television ultimately is a "tell me a story" medium, not a "let's make up a story" medium. However, even as the provider of limited appeal services, interactive multichannel television can be a highly lucrative business, especially attractive to advertisers in an era of restless viewers.

CONTEXTUALIZING AND CRITICIZING THE NEW TELEVISION

The economics and probable patterns of consumer use make it likely that the multichannel services of the future will appeal to specific niche audiences, who will use their RCDs to access and interact with a variety of television content. Such specialized services will be "at the margin" of mass communication (Neuman, 1991, p. 162). Nonetheless, direct viewer payment for such services makes it possible for them to succeed financially with a limited subscriber base. The highly desirable demographic characteristics of the probable users of such services also will attract advertisers who need new ways of reaching a roaming audience.

A major problem of such a scenario is that most of the new services, which will have limited appeal to the mass audience, will be highly desired by advertisers because of their interactive qualities (see Chapter 3). Although certain advertisers will still want to reach the mass audience that broadcast television has traditionally provided, the appeal of interactivity as a means of reaching the restless audience and the high cost of developing the new systems are likely to increase the diversion of popular programming to outlets that combine advertising with direct consumer payment.

In short, more advertisers will seek to reduce "waste" by using the highly targeted offerings of the new distribution systems and consequently will reduce their spending, or at least the rate of increase in spending, on mass appeal programming. At the same time, those excluded from the new systems will see schedules made up of cheaper fare, more repeats, and more integrative program forms such as infomercials. Broadcast television will remain a major element of program and advertising delivery for the foreseeable future, although barring governmental backlash, it will begin to lose certain popular program forms (e.g., sports) and "desirable" audiences to new services that rely on multiple revenue streams.

The combination of direct costs and niche marketing will serve to disenfranchise those who either cannot afford or who are not desired by the advertiser. The coming integration of television, computers, and telephones means that this exclusion will affect much more than simply the availability of entertainment television, much of which is likely to survive in a mass television system. There is concern that the National Science Foundation's ending of a subsidy for the Internet will make access more costly, particularly in rural areas and for small businesses (Harmon, 1994). One obvious effect of the subsidy's end and the increased corporate interest in new media is the vast and rapid growing increase in Internet commercialization. At the beginning of 1996, the Internet had approximately 170,000 commercial sites, a sixfold increase in one year. The World Wide Web component of the Internet had 20,000 commercial sites compared to 1,700 one year earlier (Sandberg & Ziegler, 1996). Public access cable channels are in danger of being eliminated because of the pressure on and desire of cable systems to add new, more profitable services (Sharpe, 1994). The restriction of access is a global concern.

The 1994 MacBride Round Table on Communications concluded that "the 'information superhighways' will inevitably bypass poorer regions"; the result is likely to be an increase in "the gap between the information rich and information poor" ("Statement," 1994). The commercialization and consequent access restrictions of what were once envisioned as liberating or empowering media technologies is, of course, a historical and continuing trend in technological diffusion (Dizard, 1989; Williams, 1983; Winston, 1986). The "new" television will not only not change this trend, it probably will exacerbate it.

Access is, or should be, a substantial public policy issue, both domestically and internationally. Among the concerns are universal access, public subsidy, economic development, user privacy, and, ultimately, the fundamental question of whether or not the development of the new multichannel interactive systems is a positive one. Unfortunately, the lure of new technology, the current vogue for privatization and deregulation, and the selling of that technology as an undeniable good are likely to keep issues of public concern marginalized. In addition, the increasing consolidation of media and telecommunications firms (across industrial lines and national boundaries) mitigates against the promulgation and enforcement of public policy guidelines, due to the difficulty of reaching agreement on any issue beyond the reliance on market mechanism as the answer to most every problem.

Many observers have written of the wonders of the new media technologies (Gates et al., 1995; Gilder, 1992; O'Neill, 1993; Toffler, 1980), while others have adopted the more neutral position that these technologies probably will not have all that great an impact (e.g., Neuman, 1991). Still, there is no way to avoid the reality that the rise of the new television is not only a break from the past, but a harbinger of even greater power for the providers of our basic electronic communications services. The RCD has been a primary instrument of this change, as its use has created a changed television audience with which the industry is compelled to cope. As access and use become increasingly predicated on the ability to pay or on the desirability of an audience member to an advertiser, the argument that the new systems will contribute to increased social division, cultural domination, and alienation (Crain, 1993; Lynes, 1993; Mosco, 1982; Postman, 1992; Schiller, 1991) seems more compelling.

CONCLUSION

Maddox (1972, p. 23) wrote that "communications is a liberating technology in need of liberation." Although she was writing at a time when the oligopoly of the Big Three completely dominated the television industry, her words remain relevant in this time of vast technological and regulatory change. This change has produced an ever increasing amount of television product for the audience and enabled that audience to exercise a degree of control that could only be imagined 20 years ago.

The structure of the television industry two decades ago was rigid, virtually immune from competition, and empowered to assert considerable influence on the parameters of its regulation. The system of today is no less empowered and is becoming even more consolidated in order to counter the power of the audience to shape its media menu. The same forces that have empowered the users of television have also increased the power of the television industry to commodify the audience. In their book on computer-mediated communication, Chesebro and Bonsall (1989) called "the elimination of information discrimination" the social goal of the most importance (p. 236). Unfortunately, the fullest expression of the benefits of television and computer technology is likely to be reserved for a limited audience. As Neuman (1991, p. 42) argued, "the net result is that although the new media make possible new forms of political and cultural communication, in the main they are not likely to be used that way."

However, the RCD has made available to many viewers/users of television a level of control that does temper some of the excesses of increased audience commodification. Regardless of the ultimate shape of the third generation of television, the RCD will continue to play a major role in the audience's selection and monitoring of content. As the number of channels increase, the RCD will become indispensable for most viewers in managing the television environment. This fact alone means that the television and advertising industries will have to work harder to attract an audience. The RCD has undermined the "fundamental conservatism" of an advertising-supported medium that has been said to "limit experimentation" (Neuman, 1991, p. 172). Because dissatisfaction with existing content is a major factor in RCD use, an increased amount of experimentation with program forms is probable for those who have access. While the economic structure of the media industries mitigates against innovation, the RCD has impacted these industries to the degree that a level of limited innovation probably will be encouraged, at least until the industries feel confident that they have reexerted control over the audience. Only by more adequately satisfying viewer/user gratifications will they decrease the use of RCDs.

Even if the media industries are better able to satisfy audience gratifications and temper the use of RCDs, the audience members who are gratified with the "simple" enjoyment of grazing activity (i.e., RCD use as play) will continue to use their RCDs to subvert the provided content. The increase in available channels, even if only previews and samples of PPV/VOD services, will just increase the level of this activity. In addition, the grazers, who are attracted to stimulus-based viewing rather than following the narrative conventions of television, now have the tool to seek their own forms of gratification. For the viewers who primarily seek play or stimulus gratification, the restructuring of the television industry means very little, as the RCD arguably has allowed them to build up some limited immunity to industry excess. Unfortunately, the size of this audience probably is too small to counteract the marketing and commodification of the television audience that will likely find its greatest level of expression in the third generation of television.

Ultimately, the third generation will be less about interactivity and the information superhighway, and more about the further segregation of the audience into salable commodities. For one group, the wireless mouse RCD will provide an exciting entrée to a quantitative increase in programming and services, although probably not as many as the industry and government presently predict. For those who can pay and those who are "desirable commodities," the third generation of television will, indeed, take on many of the characteristics of a two-way window.

For the other, much larger group, the RCD will allow for the grazing of a much less expansive terrain than the one available to the smaller group; a wasteland like the one Minow (1991) described in 1961, although likely to be even vaster. This audience will continue to have value for television entities, if for no other reason than its sheer size, but the television choices widely available to it not only will remain conventional, but are likely to be less than what is now available in the second generation of television. The continuing development of pay per view and video on demand, the tiering of cable systems, and the diversion of much desirable sports product to pay channels are all evidence of this trend.

The first generation of television was a relatively long era of stable network dominance. The second generation is a transitory era and, for the television industry, an experimental one. It is a time when the RCD has been instrumental in the renegotiation of the relationship between the viewers/users of television and the industry. However, as with other challenges, the industry has been able to define the relational terms. They have modified programming and advertising in order to arrest, or at least neutralize, the restless RCD-armed viewers. Although the television industry has not recaptured the glory days of the first generation, it has used the euphoria over new technologies and a "free market," technologically mesmerized government to push for a historic restructuring and consolidation of the industry. In a commercial milieu and in the absence of countervailing forces, these new technologies will further segregate and divide the television audience. For less privileged viewers/users of television, the window offered in the third generation will be narrower, more distorted, and relentlessly one way.

NOTE

1. Once again, the ubiquity of the grazing phenomenon in industry planning is such that the concept is now commonly used by media analysts and practitioners.

References

Abernethy, A., & Rotfield, H. (1991, January 7). Zipping through TV ads is old tradition—but viewers are getting better at it. *Marketing News*, pp. 6, 14.

Ainslie, P. (1985, February 28). Commercial zapping: TV tapers strike back. *Rolling Stone*, pp. 68–69.

Ainslie, P. (1988, September). Confronting a nation of grazers. *Channels*, pp. 54–57.

Ainslie, P. (1989). The new TV viewer. In *How Americans watch TV: A nation of grazers* (pp. 9–20). New York: C. C. Publishing.

Akhavan-Majid, R., & Wolf, G. (1991). American mass media and the myth of libertarianism: Toward an "elite power group" theory. *Critical Studies in Mass Communication, 8*, 139–151.

Alexander, A., Owers, J., & Carveth, R. (Eds.). (1993). *Media economics: Theory and practice.* Hillsdale, NJ: Erlbaum.

Alfstad, S. (1991, September 9). Don't shrug off zapping. *Advertising Age*, p. 20.

Allen, C. (1993). *Local TV journalism and the audience: What consultants are telling the producer about the RCD.* Paper presented at the Annual Meeting of the Broadcast Education Association, Las Vegas, NV.

Allman, W. F. (1989, May 1). Science 1, advertisers 0. *U.S. News and World Report*, pp. 60–61.

America Online strengthens position in cable market. (1994, May 19). *America Online Personal Information Service*.

Apple and IBM strike another deal. (1994, May 23). *Prodigy Interactive Personal Service*.

Arens, W. F., & Bovée, C. L. (1994). *Contemporary advertising* (5th ed.). Burr Ridge, IL: Irwin.

Note. All online references are available from the authors.

Arrington, C. (1992, August 15). The zapper: All about the remote control. *TV Guide*, pp. 8–13.

A telecom act primer. (1996, February 5). *Electronic Media*, p. 54.

Aversa, J. (1994, April 6). FCC acts to ease cable TV frustration. *The Pittsburgh Post-Gazette*, p. A-10.

Bagdikian, B. H. (1992). *The media monopoly* (4th ed.). Boston: Beacon Press.

Bain, J. S. (1968). *Industrial organization* (2nd ed.). New York: Wiley.

Barlow, J. P. (1994, March). The economy ideas: A framework for rethinking patents and copyrights in the digital age. *Wired*, pp. 84–90, 126–128.

Barnouw, E. (1978). *The sponsor: Notes on a modern potentate*. New York: Oxford.

Barwise, P., & Ehrenberg, A. (1988). *Television and its audience*. Newbury Park, CA: Sage.

Beacham, F. (1993, October 25). A new kind of sticker shock. *Advertising Age*, p. 20.

Bechtel, R. B., Achelpohl, C., & Akers, R. (1972). Correlates between observed behavior and questionnaire response on television viewing. In E. A. Rubenstein, G. A. Comstock, & J. P. Murray (Eds.), *Television and social behavior* (Vol. 4, pp. 274–344). Washington, DC: U.S. Government Printing Office.

Bellamy, R. V., Jr. (1988). Constraints on a broadcast innovation: Zenith's Phonevision system, 1931–1972. *Journal of Communication, 38*(3), 8–20.

Bellamy, R. V., Jr. (1992). Emerging images of product differentiation: Network television promotion in a time of industry change. *Feedback, 33*(3), 22–26.

Bellamy, R. V., Jr. (1993). Remote control devices and the political economy of a changing television industry. In J. R. Walker & R. V. Bellamy, Jr. (Eds.), *The remote control in the new age of television* (pp. 211–219). Westport, CT: Praeger.

Bellamy, R. V., Jr., McDonald, D. G., & Walker, J. R. (1990). The spin-off as television program form and strategy. *Journal of Broadcasting and Electronic Media, 34*(3), 283–297.

Bellamy, R. V., Jr., & Walker, J. R. (1995). Foul tip or strike three? The evolving marketing partnership of Major League Baseball and the television industry. *NINE: A Journal of Baseball History and Social Policy Perspectives, 3*(2), 261–275.

Benjamin, L. (1993). At the touch of a button: A brief history of remote control devices. In J. R. Walker & R. V. Bellamy, Jr. (Eds.), *The remote control in the new age of television* (pp. 15–22). Westport, CT: Praeger.

Berelson, B. (1949). What "missing the newspaper" means. In P. F. Lazarsfeld & F. N. Stanton (Eds.), *Communications research 1948–1949* (pp. 111–129). New York: Harper.

Bianco, R. (1991, July 23). ABC shoots for appeal. *Pittsburgh Press*, p. C-10.

Blankenhorn, D. (1994, January 31). New VCR device zaps commercials for viewers. *Electronic Media*, p. 18.

Blood, R. O. (1961). Social class and family control of television viewing. *Merrill-Palmer Quarterly of Behavior and Development, 7*, 205–222.

Bollier, D. (1989). What grazing means for TV programmers and advertisers: A glimpse at the future. In *How Americans watch TV: A nation of grazers* (pp. 41–52). New York: C. C. Publishing.

Bower, R. T. (1985). *The changing television audience in America.* New York: Columbia University Press.

Brandt, R., with Grover, R., Hawkins, C., & Ziegler, B. (1993, June 7). Boob tube no more. *Business Week*, pp. 101–102.

Broadcasters want role in planning. (1994, February 2). *Prodigy Interactive Personal Service.*

Bronson, G. (1984, November 12). Why TV zappers worry ad industry. *U.S. News and World Report*, pp. 66–67.

Brown, M. E. (Ed.). (1990). *Television and women's culture: The politics of the popular.* Newbury Park, CA: Sage.

Bryant, J. (1986). The road most traveled: Yet another cultivation critique. *Journal of Broadcasting and Electronic Media, 30,* 231–235.

Bryant, J., & Rockwell, S. C. (1993). Remote control devices in television program selection: Experimental evidence. In J. R. Walker & R. V. Bellamy, Jr. (Eds.), *The remote control in the new age of television* (pp. 73–85). Westport, CT: Praeger.

Building NBC's future. (1993, September 27). *Advertising Age*, p. 32.

Burger, J. M., & Cooper, H. M. (1979) The desirability of control. *Motivation and Emotion, 3*(4), 381–393.

Buyer's guide to universal remotes. (1993, May 31). Advertising supplement to HFD.

Cable homes' affluence grows more than non-cable homes. (1994, May 9). *Electronic Media*, p. 28.

Cable Communications Act, Pub. L. No. 98-549, 98 Stat. 2779 (1984).

Cable networks say peoplemeter ratings of children are not same as those from diaries. (1988, November 14). *Broadcasting*, pp. 81–83.

Cable subscribers by system size. (1994, August 8). *Electronic Media*, p. 28.

Cable Television Consumer Protection and Competition Act of 1992. Pub. L. No. 102-385, 106 Stat. 1460 (1992).

Cable television report and order. 36 FCC2d 143 (1972).

Cantril, H. (1947). *The invasion from Mars: A study in the psychology of panic.* Princeton, NJ: Princeton University Press.

Capital Cities/ABC, Inc. and America Online, Inc. announce alliance. (1994, July 6). *America Online Personal Information Service.*

Carter, B. (1991, July 8). TV industry unfazed by rise in "zapping." *New York Times,* pp. D1, D6.

Carveth, R., Owers, J., & Alexander, A. (1993). The global integration of media industries. In A. Alexander, J. Owers, & R. Carveth (Eds.), *Media economics: Theory and practice* (pp. 331–354). Hillsdale, NJ: Erlbaum.

Castro, J. (1993). Feeling a little jumpy. In *Time Magazine Compact Almanac 1993* [CD-ROM]. Washington, DC: Compact Publishing. (Original article in *Time* [1991, July 8], pp. 42–44)

Caves, R. (1964). *American industry: Structure, conduct, performance.* Englewood Cliffs, NJ: Prentice-Hall.

CBS and NBC using other media to woo new viewers. (1990, June 11). *Broadcasting*, pp. 80–81.

CBS, USA to share show. (1991, August 5). *Electronic Media*, p. 1.

Cheers and jeers. (1991, August 24). *TV Guide*, p. 22.

Chesebro, J. W., & Bonsall, D. G. (1989). *Computer-mediated communication: Human relationships in a computerized world.* Tuscaloosa, AL: University of Alabama Press.

Clawson, P. (1993, August 23). Study: Consumers want interactive TV. *Electronic Media*, pp. 3, 21.

Coates, J. (1994a, January 16). From on-line hangout to data superhighway. *The Chicago Tribune*, pp. C1, C-6.

Coates, J. (1994b, February 13). If you can't beat 'em modem. *The Chicago Tribune Magazine*, pp. 10–12, 14–15.

Cohen, A. A. (1981). People without media: Attitudes and behavior during a general media strike. *Journal of Broadcasting, 25,* 171–180.

Cohen, B. C. (1963). *The press and foreign policy.* Princeton, NJ: Princeton University Press.

Cole, B., & Oettinger, M. (1978). *Reluctant regulators: The FCC and the broadcast audience.* Reading, MA: Addison-Wesley.

Copeland, G. (1989, November). *The impact of remote control tuners on family viewing.* Paper presented at the annual meeting of Speech Communication Association, San Francisco, CA.

Copeland, G. A., & Schweitzer, K. (1993). Domination of the remote control during family viewing. In J. R. Walker & R. V. Bellamy, Jr. (Eds.), *The remote control in the new age of television* (pp. 155–168). Westport, CT: Praeger.

Cornwell, N. C., Everett, S., Everett, S. E., Moriarty, S., Russomanno, J. A., Tracey, M., & Trager, R. (1993). Measuring RCD use: Method matters. In J. R. Walker & R. V. Bellamy, Jr. (Eds.), *The remote control in the new age of television* (pp. 43–55). Westport, CT: Praeger.

Cowles, S. B., & Klein, R. A. (1991). Network television promotion. In S. T. Eastman & R. A. Klein (Eds.), *Promotion and marketing for broadcasting and cable* (2nd ed., pp. 168–185). Prospect Heights, IL: Waveland.

CNBC and Prodigy link up to link on-air and online. (1994, July 25). *Prodigy Interactive Personal Service.*

Crain, R. (1993, October 18). "Superhighway" or dialogue dead-end? *Advertising Age*, p. 28.

Crichton, M. (1993, September/October). The mediasaurus: Today's mass media is tomorrow's fossil fuel. *Wired*, pp. 56–59.

Cronin, J. J., & Menelly, N. E. (1992). Discrimination vs. avoidance: "Zipping" of television commercials. *Journal of Advertising, 21*(2), 1–7.

Curran, J. (1990). The new revisionism in mass communication research: A reappraisal. *European Journal of Communication, 5*(2–3), 135–164.

Data highway full of potholes, experts say. (1993, October 15). *Prodigy Interactive Personal Service.*

Davis, B., & Davidson, J. (1993, October 28). Clinton team is split about antitrust policy as big mergers wait. *The Wall Street Journal*, p. A1.

Davis, D. M., & Walker, J. R. (1990). Countering the new media: The resurgence of share maintenance in primetime network television. *Journal of Broadcasting and Electronic Media, 34*, 487–493.

de Bock, H. (1980). Gratification frustration during a newspaper strike and a TV blackout. *Journalism Quarterly, 57*, 61–66, 78.

Demographic estimates of new Nielsen TV universe. (1994, August 22). *Electronic Media*, p. 20.

Dempsey, J. (1992, February 17). Basic nets fear for tiers. *Variety*, pp. 33, 38.

Dizard, W. P., Jr. (1989). *The coming information age* (3rd ed.). New York: Longman.

Dolan, R. J. (Ed.). (1991). *Strategic marketing management*. Boston: Harvard Business School.

Domestic communication satellite facilities. 35 FCC2d 844 (1972).

Dominick, J. R., & Pearce, M. C. (1976). Trends in network prime-time programming, 1953–1974. *Journal of Communication, 26*, 70–80.

Donlan, B. (1993, July 19). A tube that listens when you talk back. *USA Today*, pp. 1D–2D.

Donlan, T. G. (1992, March 16). A man to watch: TCI's chairman points the way to change. *Barron's*, p. 10.

Donnelly, W. J. (1986). *The confetti generation: How the new communications technology is fragmenting America*. New York: Henry Holt.

Duncan, T. (1993, October 11). To fathom integrated marketing, dive! *Advertising Age*, p. 18.

Eastman, S. T. (Ed.). (1993). *Broadcast/cable programming: Strategies and practices* (4th ed.). Belmont, CA: Wadsworth.

Eastman, S. T., & Klein, R. (Eds.) (1991). *Promotion and marketing for broadcasting and cable* (2nd ed.). Prospect Heights, IL: Waveland.

Eastman, S. T., Neal-Lunsford, J., & Riggs, K. E. (1995). Coping with grazing: Prime-time strategies for accelerated program transitions. *Journal of Broadcasting and Electronic Media, 39*, 92–108.

Eastman, S. T., & Neal-Lunsford, J. (1993). The RCD's impact on television programming and promotion. In J. R. Walker & R. V. Bellamy, Jr. (Eds.), *The remote control in the new age of television* (pp. 189–209). Westport, CT: Praeger.

Eastman, S. T., & Newton, G. D. (1995). Delineating grazing: Observations of remote control use. *Journal of Communication, 45*(1), 77–95.

Elder, J. (1986, November 17). Who gets to switch channels? *New York Times*, p. B-10.

Epstein, N. B., Baldwin, L. M., & Bishop, D. S. (1983). The McMaster family assessment device. *Journal of Marital and Family Therapy, 9*, 171–180.

Ettema, J. S. (1989). Interactive electronic text in the United States: Can videotext ever go home again? In J. L. Salvaggio & J. Bryant (Eds.), *Media use in the information age: Emerging patterns of adoption and consumer use* (pp. 105–123). Hillsdale, NJ: Erlbaum.

Eysenck, S. B. G., Eysenck, H. J., & Barrett, P. (1985). A revised version of the psychoticism scale. *Personality and Individual Differences*, 6, 21–29.

Faber, R. J., O'Guinn, T. C., & Meyer, T. F. (1987). Television portrayals of Hispanics: A comparison of ethnic perceptions. *International Journal of Intercultural Relations*, 11, 155–169.

Fawcett, A. W. (1993, October 11). Interactive TV's toughest question. *Advertising Age*, pp. 39–40.

Ferguson, D. A. (1992). Channel repertoire in the presence of remote control devices, VCRs and cable television. *Journal of Broadcasting and Electronic Media*, 36(1), 83–91.

Ferguson, D. A. (1994). Measurement of mundane TV behaviors: Remote control device flipping. *Journal of Broadcasting and Electronic Media*, 38, 35–47.

Ferguson, D. A., & Perse, E. M. (1994, April). *Viewing television without the remote: A deprivation study*. Paper presented at the annual meeting of the Broadcast Education Association, Las Vegas, NV.

Flamers on the Internet. (1994, May 2). *Prodigy Interactive Personal Service*.

Fountas, A. (1985, January). Commercial audiences: Measuring what we're buying. *Media and Marketing Decisions*, pp. 75–76.

Franklin, N. (1992, June 1). Managing your TV household. *Electronic Media*, p. 14.

Gable, D. (1994, July 29). Sounding a death knell for theme music? *USA Today*, p. 3D.

Gates, B., with Myhrvold, N., & Rinearson, P. (1995). *The road ahead*. New York: Viking.

Gates, McCaw join in $9B project. (1994, March 21). *Prodigy Interactive Personal Service*.

Gerbner, G. (1993). "Miracles" of communication technology: Powerful audiences, diverse choice and other fairy tales. In J. Wasko, V. Mosco, & M. Pendakur (Eds.), *Illuminating the blind spots: Essays honoring Dallas W. Smythe* (pp. 367–377). Norwood, NJ: Ablex.

Gerbner, G., & Gross, L. (1976). Living with television: The violence profile. *Journal of Communication*, 26(2), 173–199.

Gerbner, G., Gross, L., Morgan, M., & Signorielli, M. (1994). Growing up with television: The cultivation perspective. In J. Byant & D. Zillmann (Eds.), *Media effects: Advances in theory and research* (pp. 17–41). Hillsdale, NJ: Erlbaum.

Gerson, W. (1966). Mass media socialization behavior: Negro-White differences. *Social Forces*, 45, 40–50.

Gilder, G. (1992). *Life after television*. New York: Norton.

Gill, P. (1993, May 31). Remote controls becoming more widespread. *Buyers' Guide to Universal Remotes* [a supplement to HFD], pp. 4–8.

Goldenson, L. H., with Wolf, M. J. (1991). *Beating the odds*. New York: Charles Scribner's Sons.

Goldman, K. (1993, October 23). Half-minute video explosions pitch technology to MTV teens. *Prodigy Interactive Personal Service*.

Goldman, K. (1994a, April 30). Some place-based TV suppliers regaining resistant audience. *Prodigy Interactive Personal Service*.

Goldman, K. (1994b, August 1). Sponsors of Goodwill Games go global. *Prodigy Interactive Personal Service*.

Goldman, K. (1994c, July 28). Stay tuned for no commercials in between television shows. *Prodigy Interactive Personal Service*.

Gomery, D. (1989). Media economics: Terms of analysis. *Critical Studies in Mass Communication*, 6, 43–60.

Gomery, D. (1993a). The centrality of media economics. *Journal of Communication*, 43(3), 190–98.

Gomery, D. (1993b). Who owns the media? In A. Alexander, J. Owers, & R. Carveth (Eds.), *Media economics: Theory and practice* (pp. 47–70). Hillsdale, NJ: Erlbaum.

Gore, A. (1994, January 11). Address on the national information infrastructure. University of California at Los Angeles. (Available from *CRTNet*, Department of Communication, Pennsylvania State University, University Park, PA. E-mail: CRTNET@PSUVM.EDU)

Graham, E. (1994, September 9). Report on TV: The new TV era is going to be confusing. *Prodigy Interactive Personal Service*.

Graham, J. (1990, October 18). Networks encourage channel changes. *USA Today*, p. 3D.

Graham, J. (1994a, July 20). Whither the theme song? *Prodigy Interactive Personal Service*.

Graham, J. (1994b, July 25). Cocky CBS says it's not for sale. *Prodigy Interactive Personal Service*.

Granger, R. (1991, June 24). Promotions, controversy highlight BPME meeting. *Electronic Media*, pp. 3, 39.

Greenberg, B. S., & Dervin, B. (1972). *Uses of mass communication by the urban poor*. New York: Praeger.

Greenberg, B. S., & Heeter, C. (1988). Conclusions and a research agenda. In C. Heeter & B. S. Greenberg (Eds.), *Cableviewing* (pp. 289–305). Norwood, NJ: Ablex.

Greenberg, B. S., Heeter, C., & Sipes, S. (1988). Viewing context and style with electronic assessment of viewing behavior. In C. Heeter & B. S. Greenberg (Eds.), *Cableviewing* (pp. 123–139). Norwood, NJ: Ablex.

Greenberg, B. S., & Lin, C. A. (1988). *Patterns of teletext use in the UK*. London: John Libbey.

Greene, W. F. (1988). Maybe the valley of the shadow isn't so dark after all. *Journal of Advertising Research*, 28(5), 11–15.

Grimm, M. (1993, July 19). Garden variety. *BrandWeek*, pp. 20–25.

Halonen, D. (1992a, February 3). Senate OKs crackdown on cable TV. *Electronic Media*, pp. 1, 31.

Halonen, D. (1992b, September 14). TV stations eyeing lessons from radio. *Electronic Media*, pp. 3, 49.

Halonen, D. (1993, July 5). Shopping stations get must carry. *Electronic Media*, pp. 1, 23.

Halonen, D. (1994a, January 17). Clinton TV plan revealed. *Electronic Media*, pp. 1, 111.

Halonen, D. (1994b, January 24). Twelve to watch in '94: Ray Smith. *Electronic Media*, pp. 46, 73.

Halonen, D. (1994c, January 31). Malone: Few will rule superhighway. *Electronic Media*, pp. 31–32.

Halonen, D. (1994d, March 21). Q&A with the NAB chief. *Electronic Media*, pp. 4, 50.

Halonen, D. (1994e, August 1). Suit puts ABC deal on record. *Electronic Media*, pp. 1, 31.

Halonen, D. (1996). Historic rewrite finally passes. *Electronic Media*, pp. 1, 54.

Halonen, D., & Mermigas, D. (1993, April 5). FCC guts fin-syn rules. *Electronic Media*, pp. 1, 31.

Hanson, C. (1993, December 19). How to wrest control of your set. *The Chicago Tribune*, sec. 6, p. 8.

Harmon, A. (1994, September 11). Grown-up Internet is on its own. *The Pittsburgh Post-Gazette*, p. A-8.

Hart, M. (1993, January 24). WPWR makes a bid for action-oriented series. *Chicago Tribune TV Week*, p. 5.

Haugsted, L. (1992, June 22). L.A. ops armed with micro-marketing reports. *Multichannel News*, p. 24.

Heeter, C. (1988a). The choice process model. In C. Heeter & B. S. Greenberg (Eds.), *Cableviewing* (pp. 11–32). Norwood, NJ: Ablex.

Heeter, C. (1988b). Gender differences in viewing styles. In C. Heeter & B. S. Greenberg (Eds.), *Cableviewing* (pp. 151–166). Norwood, NJ: Ablex.

Heeter, C. (1988c). New fall season viewing. In C. Heeter & B. S. Greenberg (Eds.), *Cableviewing* (pp. 74–88). Norwood, NJ: Ablex.

Heeter, C. (1989). Implications of new interactive technologies for conceptualizing communication. In J. L. Salvaggio & J. Bryant (Eds.), *Media use in the information age: Emerging patterns of adoption and consumer use* (pp. 217–235). Hillsdale, NJ: Erlbaum.

Heeter, C., & Baldwin, T. F. (1988). Channel type and viewing style. In C. Heeter & B. S. Greenberg (Eds.), *Cableviewing* (pp. 167–176). Norwood, NJ: Ablex.

Heeter, C., D'Alessio, D., Greenberg, B. S., & McVoy, D. S. (1988). Cableviewing behaviors: An electronic assessment. In C. Heeter & B. S. Greenberg (Eds.), *Cableviewing* (pp. 51–63). Norwood, NJ: Ablex.

Heeter, C., & Greenberg, B. S. (1988a). A theoretical overview of the program choice model. In C. Heeter & B. S. Greenberg (Eds.), *Cableviewing* (pp. 33–50). Norwood, NJ: Ablex.

Heeter, C., & Greenberg, B. S. (1988b). Profiling the zappers. In C. Heeter & B. S. Greenberg (Eds.), *Cableviewing* (pp. 67–73). Norwood, NJ: Ablex.

Heeter, C., Yoon, K., & Sampson, J. (1993). Future zap: Next generation smart remotes. In J. R. Walker & R. V. Bellamy, Jr. (Eds.), *The remote control in the new age of television* (pp. 87–99). Westport, CT: Praeger.

Helyar, J. (1994, September 9). Report on TV: Technology, demand change view of sports. *Prodigy Interactive Personal Service*.

Hobson, D. (1978). ABC's quarter-million-dollar man performs heroics too. In J. S. Harris (Ed.), *TV Guide: The first 25 years* (pp. 256–259). New York: Simon & Schuster.

Horwitz, R. B. (1989). *The irony of regulatory reform*. New York: Oxford.

How American's watch TV: A nation of grazers. (1989). New York: C. C. Publishing.

How to avoid being zapped. (1984, April 30). *Broadcasting*, pp. 130, 132.

Hsia, H. J. (1989). Introduction. In J. L. Salvaggio & J. Bryant (Eds.), *Media use in the information age: Emerging patterns of adoption and consumer use* (pp. xv–xxviii). Hillsdale, NJ: Erlbaum.

Hyde, J. S. (1990). Meta-analysis and the psychology of gender differences. *Signs: Journal of Women in Culture and Society, 16*(1), 55–73.

In the spotlight: Sources of TV viewing. (1992, June 1). *Electronic Media*, p. 28.

Iyengar, S., & Kinder, D. R. (1987). *News that matters: Television and American opinion*. Chicago: University of Chicago Press.

Jensen, E. (1994a, May 24). Fox to take some affiliates from rivals, stuns industry. *Prodigy Interactive Personal Service*.

Jensen, E. (1994b, September 9). Report on TV: Networks seemed headed for extinction. *Prodigy Interactive Personal Service*.

Kantrowitz, B., with Ramo, J. C. (1993, May 31). An interactive life. *Newsweek*, pp. 42–44.

Kaplan, R. (1992, June). Video on demand. *American Demographics*, pp. 38–43.

Karlin, S. (1995, June 5). Dynamic duo of NBC promos. *Electronic Media*, pp. 1, 38.

Katz, E., Blumler, J. G., & Gurevitch, M. (1974). Utilization of mass communication by the individual. In J. G. Blumler & E. Katz (Eds.), *The uses of mass communications: Current perspectives on gratifications research* (pp. 19–32). Beverly Hills, CA: Sage.

Katz, E., & Lazarsfeld, P. F. (1955). *Personal influence: The part played by people in the flow of mass communications*. New York: Free Press.

Kaye, B. K. (1994). *Remote control devices: A naturalistic study*. Unpublished doctoral dissertation, Department of Communication, Florida State University.

Kaye, B. K., & Sapolsky, B. S. (1995). *"57 Channels and nothin' on": Electronic monitoring of television remote control device usage in the home environment*. Paper presented at the annual convention of the Association for Education in Journalism and Mass Communication, Washington, DC.

Keefe, P. (1992, September 28). Monday memo. *Broadcasting*, p. 14.

Kessler, F. (1985, January 21). In search of zap-proof commercials. *Fortune*, pp. 68–70.

Kiersh, E. (1992, February 10). Packaged goods. *AdWeek*, pp. 14–15.

Kim, W. Y., Baran, S. J., & Massey, K. K. (1988). Impact of the VCR on control of television viewing. *Journal of Broadcasting and Electronic Media, 32,* 351–358.

Kimball, P. (1959). People without papers.*Public Opinion Quarterly, 23,* 389–398.

King, T. R. (1994, September 9). Report on TV: Marketers need new ways to reach consumers. *Prodigy Interactive Personal Service.*

Klapper, J. T. (1960). *The effects of mass communication.* New York: Free Press.

Klein, P. L. (1978). Why you watch what you watch when you watch. In J. S. Harris (Ed.), *TV Guide: The first 25 years* (pp. 186–188). New York: Simon and Schuster.

Klopfenstein, B. C. (1993). From gadget to necessity: The diffusion of remote control technology. In J. R. Walker & R. V. Bellamy, Jr. (Eds.), *The remote control in the new age of television* (pp. 23–39). Westport, CT: Praeger.

Klopfenstein, B. C., & Albarran, A. B. (1991, April). *Is VCR use declining? An examination of primary and secondary research evidence.* Paper presented at the annual convention of the Broadcast Education Association, Las Vegas, NV.

Knopf, T. A. (1992). Preparing for a TV revolution. *Electronic Media,* pp. 14, 30.

Kornheiser, T. (1993, April). Control freaks. *Ladies' Home Journal,* p. 108.

Kostyra, R. (1984, March). Zapping—a modest proposal. *Media and Marketing Decisions,* pp. 94–95.

Krasnow, E. G., Longley, L. D., & Terry, H. A. (1982). *The politics of broadcast regulation* (3rd ed.). New York: St Martin's.

Krendl, K. A., Troiano, C., Dawson, R., & Clark, G. (1993). "OK, where's the remote?": Children, families, and remote control devices. In J. R. Walker & R. V. Bellamy, Jr. (Eds.), *The remote control in the new age of television* (pp. 137–153). Westport, CT: Praeger.

Krendl, K. A., Clark, G., Dawson, R., Troiano, C. (1993). Preschoolers and VCRs in the home: A multiple methods approach. *Journal of Broadcasting and Electronic Media, 37,* 293–312.

Kubey, R., & Csikszentmihalyi, M. (1990). *Television and the quality of life: How viewing shapes everyday experience.* Hillsdale, NJ: Erlbaum.

Lafayette, J. (1993, August 23). Time Warner deal marks NBC's first for retransmission. *Electronic Media,* pp. 2, 21.

Lafayette, J. (1994a, February 7). CBS affiliates seek more prime-time ads. *Electronic Media,* p. 3.

Lafayette, J. (1994b, August 1). Networks sign flurry of deals. *Electronic Media,* pp. 1, 31.

Lafayette, J. (1994c, August 8). WCCO sets 2-channel newscast. *Electronic Media,* pp. 1, 31.

Lafayette, J. (1995, February 27). Stringer heads to Media Co. *Electronic Media,* pp. 1, 55.

Lapham, L. (1994, January). Robber barons redux. *Harper's,* pp. 7–11.

Lavery, D. (1993). Remote control: Mythic reflections. In J. R. Walker & R. V. Bellamy, Jr. (Eds.), *The remote control in the new age of television* (pp. 223–234). Westport, CT: Praeger.

Lawrence, P. A. (1990). *Arousal needs and gratifications sought from theatrical movies*. Unpublished doctoral dissertation, Communication Department, University of Kentucky.

Leckey, A. (1994, June 5). Better picture for broadcast stocks. *The Chicago Tribune*, sect. 7, p. 8.

Leland, J. (1993, October 11). Battle for your brain. *Newsweek*, pp. 48–53.

Levy, M. R. (Ed.). (1989). *The VCR age: Home video and mass communication*. Newbury Park, CA: Sage.

Lewin, K. (1988, December). Getting around commercial avoidance. *Media and Marketing Decisions*, pp. 116–121.

Lieberman, D. (1991, August 24). 10 ways to keep a network running. *TV Guide* (Pittsburgh Metropolitan Edition), p. 21.

Lin, C. A., & Atkin, C. J. (1988, May). *Parental mediation and adolescent uses of television and VCRs*. Paper presented at the annual conference of the International Communication Association, New Orleans, LA.

Lindheim, R. (1992, April 6). Big 3 networks must evolve or die. *Electronic Media*, p. 18.

Lindlof, T. R., Shatzer, M. J., & Wilkinson, D. (1988). Accommodation of video and television in the American family. In J. Lull (Ed.), *World families watch television* (pp. 158–192). Newbury Park, CA: Sage.

Lippman, J. (1992a, February 3). Merchants begin to shift their ad focus to cable TV. *The Los Angeles Times*, pp. D1, D2.

Lippman, J. (1992b, February 28). Fox seeks lucrative romance with cable. *The Los Angeles Times*, p. D1.

Lippman, J. (1993, August 31). Tuning out the TV of tomorrow. *The Los Angeles Times*, p. A1.

Litman, B. R. (1979). The television networks, competition, and program diversity. *Journal of Broadcasting, 23*, 393–409.

Lublin, J. S. (1991, January 4). As VCRs advance, agencies fear TV viewers will zap more ads. *The Wall Street Journal*, p. B3.

Lull, J. T. (1978). Choosing television programs by family vote. *Communication Quarterly, 26*(4), 53–57.

Lull, J. T. (1982). How families select television programs: A mass observational study. *Journal of Broadcasting, 26*, 801–811.

Lynes, K. (1993, July/August). Channel surfing hits print. *Utne Reader*, pp. 109–110.

Maccoby, E. E., & Jacklin, C. (1974). *The psychology of sex differences*. Stanford, CA: Stanford University Press.

MacDonald, J. F. (1990). *One nation under television: The rise and decline of network TV*. New York: Pantheon.

Maddox, B. (1972). *Beyond Babel: New directions in communications*. Boston: Beacon Press.

Maddox, K. (1992, June 1). AT&T unit opens phone lines to video. *Electronic Media*, p. 29.

Maddox, K. (1993, November 9). The big picture. *Electronic Media*, pp. 1, 23, 31.

Maddox, K. (1994a, January 24). Telcos push video dial-tone plans. *Electronic Media*, pp. 3, 164.

Maddox, K. (1994b, January 24). Twelve to watch in '94: Larry Irving. *Electronic Media*, pp. 70, 113.

Maddox, K. (1994c, March 21). Setbacks on the superhighway. *Advertising Age*, pp. IM-2–IM-4, IM-14.

Mahler, R. (1991, December 30). While you wait: TV marketers hunt captive audience. *Electronic Media*, pp. 1, 4, 29.

Mahler, R. (1993, December 31). Are we really close to this? *The Los Angeles Times*, pp. F1, F32.

Mandese, J. (1992a, March 9). Video technology foils measurement. *Advertising Age*, p. 30.

Mandese, J. (1992b, July 27). How dayparts stack up on zapping. *Advertising Age*, p. 32.

Mandese, J. (1993a, July 12). NBC dials interactive. *Advertising Age*, pp. 1, 36.

Mandese, J. (1993b, September 13). New way to fund a TV show. *Advertising Age*, p. 60.

Mandese, J. (1994, February 14). Measuring the info superhighway. *Advertising Age*, p. 5.

Maney, K. (1994, February 17). Info highway needs bait to lure traffic. *USA Today*, pp. 1B–2B.

Mannes, G. (1994, July). The cable box powers up. *Popular Mechanics*, pp. 37–39.

Marin, R. (1996, February 12). Let the backlash begin! *Newsweek*, p. 77.

Markey, J. (1991, July 2). TV-zapping women: A remote possibility. *The Chicago Sun-Times*, p. 26.

Martell, H. (1994, March 28). The value of an audience data base. *Electronic Media*, p. 14.

Martinez, A. (1994, December 11). Heinz pours out new ad strategy. *The Pittsburgh Post-Gazette*, pp. B-1, B-3.

Marton, A. (1989, September). Ad makers zap back. *Channels*, pp. 30–31.

Max, D. T. (1994, September). The end of the book? *Atlantic Monthly*, pp. 61–71.

Mayer, W. G. (1994). The polls—poll trends: The rise of the new media. *Public Opinion Quarterly*, 58, 124–146.

McAllister, M. P. (1993). *Place-based advertising as economic and symbolic control.* Paper presented at the annual meeting of the Speech Communication Association, Miami Beach, FL.

McCarroll, T. (1993). Grocery cart wars. In *Time Magazine Compact Almanac 1993* [CD-ROM]. Washington, DC: Compact Publishing. (Original article in *Time* [1992, March 30], p. 49)

McChesney, R. W. (1993). *Telecommunications, mass media, and democracy: The battle for control of U.S. broadcasting, 1928–1935.* New York: Oxford.

McClellan, S. (1991, December 30). Tracking the kids: Programmers complain that Nielsen is underreporting. *Broadcasting*, p. 16.

McCombs, M. E., & Shaw, D. L. (1972). The agenda-setting function of mass media. *Public Opinion Quarterly*, 36, 176–187.

McCready, N. (1992, April 20). Preparing for the new kids market. *Electronic Media*, p. 12.

McDonald, F. (1986, September 29). Zapping the clutter. *Advertising Age*, pp. 18–20.

McGann, A. F. (1992). Comment on "Speculations on the future of advertising research." *Journal of Advertising*, 21(3), 83–85.

McGuire, W. J. (1974). Psychological motives and communication gratification. In J. G. Blumler & E. Katz (Eds.), *The uses of mass communications: Current perspectives on gratifications research* (pp. 167–196). Beverly Hills, CA: Sage.

McLeod, J. M., & Chaffee, S. H. (1972). The construction of social reality. In J. T. Tedeschi (Ed.), *The social influence process* (pp. 50–99). Beverly Hills, CA: Sage.

McQuail, D., & The Euromedia Research Group. (1990). Caging the beast: Constructing a framework for the analysis of media change in Western Europe. *European Journal of Communication*, 5(2–3), 285–311.

McSherry, J. (1985, June). The current scope of channel switching. *Media and Marketing Decisions*, pp. 144–145.

Media, democracy and the information highway. (1993). Arlington, VA: Freedom Forum.

Media empire is Whittled down. (1994, August 15). *Prodigy Interactive Personal Service*.

Media firms scramble to form TV networks. (1993, October 27). *Prodigy Interactive Personal Service*.

Media General agrees to deliver Prodigy via cable. (1994, May 26). *Prodigy Interactive Personal Service*.

Meehan, E. (1993). Commodity audience, actual audience: The blindspot debate. In J. Wasko, V. Mosco, & M. Pendakur, (Eds.), *Illuminating the blind spots: Essays honoring Dallas W. Smythe* (pp. 378–397). Norwood, NJ: Ablex.

Meehan, E., Mosco, V., & Wasko, J. (1993). Rethinking political economy: Change and continuity. *Journal of Communication*, 43(4), 105–116.

Merger mania is in fashion again. (1994, August 6). *Prodigy Interactive Personal Service*.

Mermigas, D. (1984, July 23). Opinions splinter over zap's sting. *Advertising Age*, pp. 3, 83.

Mermigas, D. (1992a, May 25). Networks, affiliates draw battle lines. *Electronic Media*, pp. 1, 24.

Mermigas, D. (1992b, June 8). Affiliates square off with CBS. *Electronic Media*, pp. 1, 24–25.

Mermigas, D. (1992c, September 28). Media analyst sees networks' future demise. *Electronic Media*, pp. 26, 31.

Mermigas, D. (1993, March 1). Changing marketplace forcing broadcast networks to evolve. *Electronic Media*, p. 23.

Mermigas, D. (1994a, February 21). Viacom gets Paramount; sets strategy. *Electronic Media*, pp. 1, 38.

Mermigas, D. (1994b, May 30). Fox sees more switches to come. *Electronic Media*, pp. 1, 30.

Mermigas, D. (1995, August 7). Colossal combos. *Electronic Media*, pp. 1, 30.

Meyer, M. (1995, May 14). Rupert's road to the internet. *Newsweek Interactive* [On-line], Prodigy Interactive Personal Service.

Meyer, T. P., Eastman, S. T., & Wimmer, R. D. (1993). Program and audience research. In S. T. Eastman (Ed.), *Broadcast/cable programming: Strategies and practices* (4th ed., pp. 41–79). Belmont, CA: Wadsworth.

Meyerowitz, J. (1985). *No sense of place: The impact of electronic media on social behavior*. New York: Oxford.

Meyers-Levy, J. (1989). Gender differences in information processing: A selectivity interpretation. In P. Cafferata & A. M. Tybout (Eds.), *Cognitive and affective responses to advertising* (pp. 219–260). Lexington, MA: Lexington Books.

Miller, T. (1989, October). Video lifestyle. *Media and Marketing Decisions*, pp. 73–74.

Millman, N. (1994a, June 5). Marketers' serenade: "Getting to know you . . . " *The Chicago Tribune*, sec. 7, p. 3.

Millman, N. (1994b, August 2). Ad ease. *The Chicago Tribune*, sec. 5, p. 2.

Minow, N. N. (1991). *How vast the wasteland now?* New York: Gannett Foundation Media Center.

Moca, D. J. (1994, January 17). Critics hear superhighway plans. *Electronic Media*, p. 2.

Molitor, F. (1992, April). *A theory for accurately measuring and forecasting ad avoidance behaviors*. Paper presented at the annual convention of the Broadcast Education Association, Las Vegas, NV.

Morgan, M., Alexander, A., Shanahan, J., & Harris, C. (1990). Adolescents, VCRs, and the family environment. *Communication Research, 17*, 83–106.

Moriarty, S. E., & Everett, S. (1994). Commercial breaks: A viewing behavior study. *Journalism Quarterly, 71*, 346–355.

Morley, D. (1986). *Family television: Cultural power and domestic leisure*. London: Comedia.

Morley, D. (1993). Active audience theory: Pendulums and pitfalls. *Journal of Communication, 43*(4), 13–19.

Mosco, V. (1979). *Broadcasting in the United States: Innovative challenge and organizational control*. Norwood, NJ: Ablex.

Mosco, V. (1982). *Pushbutton fantasies: Critical perspectives on videotex and information technology*. Norwood, NJ: Ablex.

Moshavi, S. D. (1992, December 21). Programmers, Nielsen disagree over claim peoplemeters underreport kids. *Broadcasting*, p. 10.

MTV teams up with America Online to create interactive service for MTV viewers. (1994, June 7). *America Online Personal Information Service*.

Murdoch, G., & Golding, P. (1979). Capitalism, communication, and class relations. In J. Curran, M. Gurevitch, J. Woolacott, J. Marriott, & C. Roberts (Eds.), *Mass communication and society* (pp. 12–43). Beverly Hills, CA: Sage.

Murrie, M. (1994, December). Convenience, control and choices. *Communicator*, pp. 26, 28–29.

National Broadcasting Co. et al. v. U.S. 319 U.S. 190 (1943).

NBC, ABC unveil fall slogans. (1990, August 6). *Broadcasting*, p. 36.

Nelson, T. (1994, April). The big scare. *New Media*, pp. 41–42.

Network lotto. (1990, September 18). *USA Today*, p. 3D.

Network rating/share trend data. (1992, August 31). *Electronic Media*, p. 20.

Neuman, W. R. (1991). *The future of the mass audience*. Cambridge, England: Cambridge University Press.

New life at the nets. (1994, July 28). *Prodigy Interactive Personal Service*.

Noam, E. (1993). Reconnecting communications studies with communications policy. *Journal of Communication*, *43*(3), 199–206.

Norins, H. (1990). *The Young & Rubicam traveling creative workshop*. Englewood Cliffs, NJ: Prentice-Hall.

O'Malley, & Collin (1993, February 17). INC. *The Chicago Tribune*, sec. 1, p. 14.

O'Neill, M. J. (1993). *The roar of the crowd: How television and people power are changing the world*. New York: Times Books.

Orsini, P. (1991, April 8). Zapping: A man's world. *Adweek*, p. TV-3.

Owen, B. M., & Wildman, S. S. (1992). *Video economics*. Cambridge, MA: Harvard University Press.

Pahwa, A. (1990, September 17). Boom generation more receptive to quality TV ads. *Marketing News*, pp. 8, 17.

Palmgreen, P., Wenner, L. A., Rosengren, K. E. (1985). Uses and gratifications research: The past ten years. In K. E. Rosengren, L. A. Wenner, & P. Palmgreen (Eds.), *Media gratifications research: Current perspectives* (pp. 11–37). Beverly Hills, CA: Sage.

Panel: Interactive technology ready, but viewers are not. (1993, November 9). *Prodigy Interactive Personal Service*.

Papazian, E. (1986, April). Zapping: Not just a media problem. *Media and Marketing Decisions*, pp. 103–104.

Parisi, P. (1992, August 27). Interactive TV view: $1.64 billion by 1996. *Hollywood Reporter*, pp. 1, 8.

Pearson, P. H. (1970). Relationships between global and specified measures of novelty seeking. *Journal of Consulting and Clinical psychology*, *34*(2), 199–204.

Peppers, D., & Rogers, M. (1994, April 18). Let's make a deal (If you pay attention, we'll pay your way). *America Online Service*. (Original article in *Wired* [1994, February], pp. 74, 124–126)

Perse, E. M. (1990). Audience selectivity and involvement in the newer media environment. *Communication Research*, *17*, 675–697.

Perse, E. M., & Ferguson, D. A. (1993A). Gender differences in remote control use. In J. R. Walker & R. V. Bellamy, Jr. (Eds.), *The remote control in the new age of television* (pp. 169–186). Westport, CT: Praeger.

Perse, E. M., & Ferguson, D. A. (1993B). The impact of the newer television technologies on television satisfaction. *Journalism Quarterly*, *70*, 843–853.

Perse, E. M., Ferguson, D. A., & McLeod, D. M. (1994). Cultivation in the newer media environment. *Communication Research, 21*, 79–104.

Picard, R. G. (1989). *Media economics: Concepts and issues.* Newbury Park, CA: Sage.

Polic, J. G., & Gandy, O. H., Jr. (1993). Regulatory responsibility and the emergence of the marketplace standard. In J. Wasko, V. Mosco, & M. Pendakur, (Eds.), *Illuminating the blind spots: Essays honoring Dallas W. Smythe* (pp. 222–247). Norwood, NJ: Ablex.

Pols, M. F. (1994, October 27). Cablevision plans to test "interactive" service in '95. *The Los Angeles Times*, p. D1.

Pomper, S. (1993). The big shake-out begins. In *Time Magazine Compact Almanac 1993* [CD-ROM]. Washington, DC: Compact Publishing. (Original article in *Time* [1990, July 2], p. 50)

Postman, N. (1992). *Technopoly: The surrender of culture to technology.* New York: Knopf.

Powell, B., with Underwood, A., Nayyar, S., & Fleming, C. (1993, May 31). Eyes on the future. *Newsweek*, pp. 39–41.

Press, A. L. (1991). *Women watching television: Gender, class, and generation in the American television experience.* Philadelphia: University of Pennsylvania Press.

Proceed cautiously on superhighways. (1994, March 9). *Prodigy Interactive Personal Service.*

Promotion executives compare notes on winning viewers and influencing people. (1990, June 10). *Broadcasting*, p. 39.

Promotion: The hook and the niche. (1990, June 18). *Broadcasting*, p. 39.

Quinlan, J. (1995, February 10). *Time Warner's full service network.* Presentation to the Annual International Radio-Television Society Faculty Industry Seminar, New York.

Reilly, P. M. (1994, August 2). Whittle pulls plug on medical network in doctor offices. *Prodigy Interactive Personal Service.*

Reiss, C. (1986, October 27). Fast-forward ads deliver. *Advertising Age*, pp. 3, 97.

Reith, R. (1991, December 2). 3 strategies for viewer control. *Electronic Media*, p. 34.

Remote controls: Can one do the work of many? (1992, December). *Consumer Reports*, pp. 796–799.

Rice, R. E. (1984). *The new media: Communication, research and technology.* Beverly Hills, CA: Sage.

Rodriguez, G., & Robina, S. (1993). Communications, computers and networks. *Communication Research Trends, 13*(3), 1–17.

Rogers, E. M. (1983). *Diffusion of innovations* (3rd ed.). New York: Free Press.

Rogers, E. M. (1986). *Communication technology: The new media in society.* New York: Free Press.

Rogers, E. M., with Shoemaker, F. F. (1971). *Communication of innovations.* New York: Free Press.

Rotter, J. B. (1982). *The development and applications of social learning theory: Selected papers.* New York: Praeger.

Roush, M. (1990, September 4). Networks nudge season forward. *USA Today*, pp. 1D–2D.

Rouvalis, C. (1994, November 27). TV's future will revamp advertising. *The Pittsburgh Post-Gazette*, pp. B-1, B-8.

Rubin, A. M. (1984). Ritualized and instrumental television viewing. *Journal of Communication*, 34(3), 67–77.

Rubin, A. M., & Bantz, C. R. (1987). Utility of videocassette recorders. *American Behavioral Scientist*, 30, 471–485.

Ruotolo, A. C. (1988). A typology of newspaper readers. *Journalism Quarterly*, 65, 126–130.

Sandberg, J., & Ziegler, B. (1996, January 18). Web trap: Internet's popularity threatens to swamp the on-line services. *The Wall Street Journal*, (Midwest ed.), pp. A1, A9.

Sanoff, A. P., & Kyle, C. (1987, June 10). Zapping the TV networks. *U.S. News and World Report*, pp. 56–57.

Sapolsky, B., & Forrest, E. (1989). Measuring VCR "ad-voidance." In M. R. Levy (Ed.), *The VCR age: Home video and mass communication* (pp. 148–167). Newbury Park, CA: Sage.

Sawyer, D. (Reporter). (1991, May 30). *Primetime live*. New York: ABC Television Network.

Schement, J. I., & Lievrouw, L. (Eds.). (1987). *Competing visions, complex realities: Social aspects of the information society*. Norwood, NJ: Ablex.

Scherer. F. M. (1970). *Industrial pricing: Theory and evidence*. Chicago: Rand McNally.

Schiller, H. I. (1987). Old foundations for a new (information) age. In J. I. Schement & L. Lievrouw (Eds.), *Competing visions, competing realities: Social aspects of the information society* (pp. 23–31). Norwood, NJ: Ablex.

Schiller, H. I. (1991). Not yet the post-imperialist era. *Critical Studies in Mass Communication*, 8, 13–28.

Schiller, H. I. (1993). Anticipating the next radical moment: An unexpected locale. In J. Wasko, V. Mosco, & M. Pendakur (Eds.), *Illuminating the blindspots: Essays honoring Dallas W. Smythe* (pp. 334–348). Norwood, NJ: Ablex.

Schrage, M., with Peppers, D., Rogers, M., Shapiro, R. D., & Dix, D. (1994, April 18). Advertisers, digimercials, and memgraphics: The future of advertising is the future of media. *America On-Line Service* (Original article from *Wired* [1994, February], pp. 71–74)

Schultz, D. E. (1990). *Strategic advertising campaigns* (3rd ed.). Lincolnwood, IL: NTC Business Books.

Season-to-date ratings/shares of prime-time programs for Sept. 20–April 17 (1994, April 25). *Electronic Media*, p. 32.

Selnow, G. (1989). A look at the record: Why grazing can't be ignored and what to do about it. In *How Americans watch TV: A nation of grazers* (pp. 31–40). New York: C. C. Publishing.

Shapiro, R. D. (1993, December). This is not your father's Prodigy. *Wired*, pp. 98–103.

Sharpe, A. (1994, September 9). Report on TV: Public-access stations may not be wanted. *Prodigy Interactive Personal Service.*

Shaw, R. (1995, May 15). Interactive ease. *Electronic Media,* p. 14.

Signorielli, N., & Morgan, M. (Eds.). (1989). *Cultivation analysis: New directions in media effects research.* Newbury Park, CA: Sage.

Smith, D. C. (1961). The selectors of television programs. *Journal of Broadcasting, 6,* 35–44.

Smolowe, J. (1993). Read this!!!!!!!! In *Time Magazine Compact Almanac 1993* [CD-ROM]. Washington, DC: Compact Publishing. (Original article in *Time* [1990, November 26], pp. 62–70)

Spigel, L., & Mann, D. (Eds.). (1992). *Private screenings: Television and the female consumer.* Minneapolis, MN: University of Minnesota Press.

Sports fans targeted for interactive applications. (1994, June 27). *Interactive Video News,* pp. 1, 5.

Statement of the 6th MacBride round table on communications. (1994, January 23). (Available from CRTNet, Department of Communication, Pennsylvania State University, University Park, PA. E-mail: CRTNET@PSUVM.EDU)

Stefanac, S. (1994, April). Interactive advertising. *New Media,* pp. 43–52.

Steinfield, C. W., Dutton, W. H., & Kovaric, P. (1989). A framework and agenda for research on computing in the home. In J. L. Salvaggio & J. Bryant (Eds.), *Media use in the information age: Emerging patterns of adoption and consumer use* (pp. 61–85). Hillsdale, NJ: Erlbaum.

Stephenson, W. (1967). *The play theory of mass communication.* Chicago: University of Chicago Press.

Sterling, C. H., & Kittross, J. M. (1990). *Stay tuned: A concise history of American broadcasting* (2nd ed.). Belmont, CA: Wadsworth.

Stern, J., & Stern, M. (1992). *Jane and Michael Stern's encyclopedia of pop culture.* New York: HarperCollins.

Stewart, D. W. (1992). Speculations on the future of advertising research. *Journal of Advertising, 21*(3), 1–18.

Stipp, H. (1989). New technologies and new viewers: A different perspective. In *How Americans watch TV: A nation of grazers* (pp. 24–30). New York: C. C. Publishing.

Stokes, G. (1990, January 8). Eco Eco Eco Eco. *The Village Voice,* p. 40.

Stout, P. A., & Burda, B. L. (1989). Zipped commercials: Are they effective? *Journal of Advertising, 18*(4), 23–32.

Sylvester, A. K. (1990, February). Controlling remote. *Media and Marketing Decisions,* p. 54.

Teeter, Jr., D. L., & LeDuc, D. R. (1992). *Law of mass communications* (7th ed.). Mineola, NY: Foundation Press.

Thomas, L., & Litman, B. R. (1991). Fox Broadcasting Company, Why now? *Journal of Broadcasting and Electronic Media, 35*(2), 139–157.

Toffler, A. (1980). *The third wave.* New York: William Morrow.

Trends in multiple TV sets. (1994, August 29). *Electronic Media,* p. 20.

Tsiantar, D., & Miller, A. (1989, April 17). Tuning out TV ads. *Newsweek*, pp. 42–43.

Turow, J. (1992a). *Media systems in society: Understanding industries, strategies, and power*. White Plains, NY: Longman.

Turow, J. (1992b). Reconceptualizing "mass communication." *Journal of Broadcasting and Electronic Media, 36*(1), 105–110.

Tyrer, T. (1991, July 29). Networks must adapt to survive, Iger says. *Electronic Media*, p. 8.

Tyrer, T. (1992a, February 3). Super Bowl posts 4% drop from '91. *Electronic Media*, pp. 8, 21.

Tyrer, T. (1992b, May 4). CBS-made film to debut on showtime. *Electronic Media*, pp. 3, 43.

Tyrer, T. (1992c, July 27). CBS caters to over-50 crowd. *Electronic Media*, pp. 5, 15.

Tyrer, T. (1992d, September 7). Fall hits producer-driven. *Electronic Media*, p. 22.

Tyrer, T. (1992e, December 16). Fox sets halftime attack on Super Bowl. *Electronic Media*, pp. 4, 54.

Tyrer, T. (1993, May 10). Reality check. *Electronic Media*, pp. 1, 35.

Tyrer, T. (1994, May 23). Fall lineups: Buyers, sellers all mixed up. *Electronic Media*, pp. 1, 50.

Tyrer, T. (1995, October 2). Disney telco venture gets name, CEO. *Electronic Media*, p. 3.

Umphrey, D., & Albarran, A. B. (1993). Using remote control devices: Ethnic and gender differences. *Mass Comm Review, 20*, 212–219.

Valeriano, L. L. (1993, November 24). Channel-surfers beware: There's a channel-surfer zapper afoot. *The Wall Street Journal*, p. B-1.

Vaughn, C. (1993, January 18). Quality programming still prime concern. *Electronic Media*, p. 117.

Viewers add mute button in their war against TV ads. (1992, August 28). *Marketing News*, p. 10.

Viorst, J. (1992, November). Change one thing about your husband. *Redbook*, pp. 44, 48, 56.

Walker, J. R. (1988). Inheritance effects in the new media environment. *Journal of Broadcasting and Electronic Media, 32*, 391–401.

Walker, J. R. (1990). Time out: Viewing gratifications and reactions to the 1987 NFL players' strike. *Journal of Broadcasting and Electronic Media, 34*, 335–350.

Walker, J. R. (1991). [Survey of RCD use among adults in San Francisco, CA]. Unpublished raw data.

Walker, J. R. (1992). Grazing, source shifting, and time shifting: Television viewing styles in the 1990s. *Feedback, 33*(2), 2–5.

Walker, J. R. (1993). Catchy, yes, but does it work? The impact of broadcast network promotion frequency and type on program success. *Journal of Broadcasting and Electronic Media, 37*(2), 197–207.

Walker, J. R., & Bellamy, R. V., Jr. (1991a). The gratifications of grazing: An exploratory study of remote control use. *Journalism Quarterly, 68*, 422–431.

Walker, J. R., & Bellamy, R. V., Jr. (1991b). Remote control grazing as diversionary viewing. *Feedback, 32*(1), 2–4.

Walker, J. R., & Bellamy, R. V., Jr. (1993a). The remote control device: An overlooked technology. In J. R. Walker & R. V. Bellamy, Jr. (Eds.), *The remote control in the new age of television* (pp. 3–14). Westport, CT: Praeger.

Walker, J. R., & Bellamy, R. V., Jr. (Eds.). (1993b). *The remote control in the new age of television*. Westport, CT: Praeger.

Walker, J. R., Bellamy, R. V., Jr., & Traudt, P. J. (1993). Gratifications derived from remote control devices: A survey of adult RCD use. In J. R. Walker & R. V. Bellamy, Jr. (Eds.), *The remote control in the new age of television* (pp. 103–112). Westport, CT: Praeger.

Walley, W. (1991a, January 7). Fox affiliate to simulcast on rival. *Electronic Media*, pp. 2, 31.

Walley, W. (1991b, November 11). CBS sees "Scarlet" miniseries for '93. *Electronic Media*, pp. 10, 41.

Walley, W. (1993a, March 8). Hendricks sees TV revolution. *Electronic Media*, p. 2.

Walley, W. (1993b, August 23). Interactive network to roll out. *Electronic Media*, pp. 1, 23.

Walley, W. (1993c, September 6). Murdoch maps course for global growth. *Electronic Media*, p. 4.

Walley, W. (1994a, January 24). Twelve to watch in '94: Anne Sweeney. *Electronic Media*, pp. 98, 126.

Walley, W. (1994b, March 21). Sikes pulls Hearst into interactive. *Advertising Age*, pp. IM-6, IM-14.

Walley, W. (1995, July 3). Remotely related. *Electronic Media*, pp. 13, 21.

Waters, H. F., with Beachy, L. (1993, March 1). Next year, 500 channels. *Newsweek*, pp. 75–76.

Weaver, J. B., Walker, J. R., McCord, L. L., & Bellamy, R. V., Jr. (in press). Exploring the links between personality and television remote control device use. *Personality and Individual Differences*.

Webster, J. G. (1989a). Assessing exposure to the new media. In J. L. Salvaggio & J. Bryant (Eds.), *Media use in the information age: Emerging patterns of adoption and consumer use* (pp. 3–19). Hillsdale, NJ: Erlbaum.

Webster, J. G. (1989b). Television audience behavior: Patterns of exposure in the new media environment. In J. L. Salvaggio & J. Bryant (Eds.), *Media use in the information age: Emerging patterns of adoption and consumer use* (pp. 197–216). Hillsdale, NJ: Erlbaum.

Webster, J. G., & Wakshlag, J. J. (1983). A theory of television program choice. *Communication Research, 10*, 430–446.

Weekly averages. (1996, February 12). *Electronic Media*, p. 24.

Wenner, L. A. (1985). Transaction and media gratifications research. In K. E. Rosengren, L. A. Wenner, & P. Palmgreen (Eds.), *Media gratifications research* (pp. 73–94). Beverly Hills, CA: Sage.

Wenner, L. A., & Dennehy, M. O. (1993). Is the remote control device a toy or tool? Exploring the need for activation, desire for control, and technological affinity in the dynamic of RCD use. In J. R. Walker & R. V. Bellamy, Jr. (Eds.), *The remote control in the new age of television* (pp. 113–134). Westport, CT: Praeger.

What's to come. (1993, November 8). *Electronic Media*, p. 29.

Wilkes, R. E., & Valencia, H. (1989). Hispanics and blacks in television commercials. *Journal of Advertising, 18*, 19–25.

Will, G. (1990, January 2). *Northern Virginia Daily*, p. 4.

Williams, F. (1983). *The communications revolution*. New York: New American Library.

Williams, F., Phillips, A. F., & Lum, P. (1985). Gratifications associated with new communication technologies. In K. E. Rosengren, L. A. Wenner, & P. Palmgreen (Eds.), *Media gratifications research: Current perspectives* (pp. 241–252). Beverly Hills, CA: Sage.

Williams, F., Rice, R. E., & Rogers, E. M. (1988). *Research methods and the new media*. New York: Free Press.

Windahl, S., Höjerback, I., & Hedinsson, E. (1986). Adolescents without television: A study in media deprivation. *Journal of Broadcasting and Electronic Media, 30*, 47–63.

Winston, B. (1986). *Misunderstanding media*. Cambridge, MA: Harvard University Press.

Wool, A. L. (1985, May). Zipping, zapping, flipping, whizzing. *Media and Marketing Decisions*, p. 100.

Yorke, D. A., & Kitchen, P. J. (1985). Channel flickers and video speeders. *Journal of Advertising Research, 25*(2), 21–25.

Zappers 'r' us. (1984, July 30). *Advertising Age*, p. 18.

Zillmann, D., & Bryant, J. (Eds.). (1985b). *Selective exposure to communication*. Hillsdale, NJ: Erlbaum.

Zoglin, R. (1992, November 23). Can anybody work this thing? *Time*, p. 67.

Zoglin, R. (1993a). And now for the hard sell. In *Time Magazine Compact Almanac 1993* [CD-ROM]. Washington, DC: Compact Publishing. (Original article in *Time* [1989, August 14], p. 76)

Zoglin, R. (1993b). Goodbye to the mass audience. In *Time Magazine Compact Almanac 1993* [CD-ROM]. Washington, DC: Compact Publishing. (Original article in *Time* [1990, December 19], pp. 122–123)

Zoglin, R. (1993c). It's amazing! Call now! In *Time Magazine Compact Almanac 1993* [CD-ROM]. Washington, DC: Compact Publishing. (Original article in *Time* [1991, June 17], p. 71)

Zoglin, R. (1993d). Why show live or die. In *Time Magazine Compact Almanac 1993* [CD-ROM]. Washington, DC: Compact Publishing. (Original article in *Time* [1992, June 8], pp. 81–82)

Zornow, D. (1994, July). Fox, football, and cable. *CableAvails*, p. 46.

Zuckerman, M. (1974). The sensation seeking motive. *Progress in Experimental Personality Research, 7*, 79–148.

Index